This book is
if you enj

- A totally gripping true crime story

- A first hand account of living as a child during the troubles in Northern Ireland

- Powerful plots with unexpected twists

- A real page-turner of a story

- A insight into the gritty reality of London's organised crime scene

- A story of transformation and redemption

- Behind the scenes of a real life police drama

- The positive outcome of a transformed life

WHAT PEOPLE ARE SAYING
ABOUT THE AUTHOR

'I have had the honour of working with Stephen over the past two years. To think at one point, we were on opposite sides of the legal spectrum, with me as a senior police officer, is just incredible. His insight into his life and the revelations that came from his enlightened thinking should be shared far and wide. Stephens's story is a testament to the fact that your past does not have to define your future...'

Kul Mahay Former Senior UK Police Commander - Leadership Development Specialist

'Stephen Gillen has made such an impressive transformation from violent criminal to a successful businessman and mentor empowering people across the world. His life story provides hope for each of us and in this truly gripping book, 'The Monkey Puzzle Tree' shows each of us how to overcome our difficulties and limitations from any background turning it into a positive contribution to society...'

Robin Marsh Secretary-General UK of the Universal Peace Federation

Malala Yousafzai once said, 'Let us remember: One book, one pen, one child, and one teacher can change the world.' Here is a book that is sure to change the world. Utterly Exhilarating!

Mariett Ramm Founder and Editor in Chief 'The Billionaire Chronicles'

'It matters not what someone is born, but what they grow to be...A must-read!'

Andy Loveday, Producer & Director of the 'Rise of the Foot Soldier' franchise

'...Even by my standards, 'The Monkey Puzzle Tree' was very emotional, fascinating, and exciting all at the same time. Stephen's story is an amazing true story and living proof that despite being incarcerated for over 20 years you can turn your life around. He is an inspiration to many. Well done!'

Veronica Richardson wife of Notorious Gangland figure Charlie Richardson

'Stephen Gillen's story is one of redemption - overcoming adversity to be the person each of us knows is deep inside. 'The Monkey Puzzle Tree' also uncovers a wider scandal in the UK. From his humble beginnings during the dark days of the troubles in Ulster, to his imprisonment and being branded one of the UK's most dangerous prisoners, and his meteoric rise to peacemaker and entrepreneur, the boy from a troubled early life has shown that the hammer-wielding magistrates, barristers and sections of the public who prefer to judge a book by its cover, can quite frankly, shove it...'

Jamie McDowell Journalist Sunday World Newspaper

'Amazing and inspirational! Stephen Gillen's story -from incarcerated criminal to Ambassador for Peace. A heart-stopping transformational real-life story that will have you gripped to the edge of your seat! One man's triumph, creating massive change in the world against all odds - winning hearts and minds - a must-read!'

Caroline Heward, The Harley Street Stress Expert, Ambassador for Peace

'The Monkey Puzzle Tree' is an insightful, inspiring must-read. Reading his story was pure joy...'

Kevin Leslie, Lead Actor playing Reggie Kray in 'Fall of the Krays'

'The Monkey Puzzle Tree' is a unique, extremely powerful story about overcoming unimaginable odds and hindered by an emotive past to find redemption, true happiness, and inspiring global success that is changing the world!'

Roseita Royce President of the British Film Festival & Producer of the upcoming adopted film 'The Monkey Puzzle Tree'.

'Stephen Gillen's tale is as terrifying as it is inspiring and when I was asked to adapt it for the screen there was no question that I would do it. The story of his life gives such potent meaning to that universal truth that a person's future does not have to be defined by their past. The bravery which Stephen has shown in making a conscious effort to do the right thing each day is an example we should all follow.'

Kieran Suchet Screenwriter of 'The Monkey Puzzle Tree'

'Stephen Gillen is the epitome of true resilience under adversity. The Kind of adversity that mortal men would diminish from. In 'The Monkey Puzzle Tree' he defines tragedy & how he overcomes his challenges in a way that is truly unbelievable and inspiring. A really gripping story that shows the human spirit like no other. READ IT NOW!'

Sir Marco Robinson No1 bestselling author, Award-winning Entrepreneur, Philanthropist & Filmmaker

'I must recommend this massive book! Stephen Gillen's book 'The Monkey Puzzle Tree' will keep you glued from the start with its many twists and turns. It really is a roller coaster of a ride. What a great book...!'

Linda Calvey, Author of 'The Black Widow' Gangster and Adored by the Krays

'Thanks, Stephen for guiding us through an extraordinary, and incredibly inspiring life-journey. Hard, gritty, pacey, and riveting. A remarkable transformation.'

Steve Frew Scotland's first Gymnastics Commonwealth Games Gold Medallist

'This book inspired me to write mine. Now, Stephen is a mentor and friend...'

Darren Hamilton Former British Light welterweight Champion

'I've known, Stephen since we were tearaways. I'm proud to call him my friend. His book is an amazing example of dark turning to light against all the odds. His book is a true gift to the world.'

Jack Ramdan Founder of Factory East Community Project/ Charity (in the East End nominated for the QAVS Queens Award for Voluntary Services)

಄

ACKNOWLEDGEMENTS

On this magical, at times tough and exhausting, and certainly cathartic journey of creating, reliving, and writing 'The Monkey Puzzle Tree', there are many great and unique people who deserve a heartfelt thank you. This diligent and wonderful process, compounded by a major motion picture on the work being scheduled and positioned with a screenplay being written while a business empire was being built and family, rest, and responsibilities had to be juggled, although embraced was an eminence task, to say the least.

I must thank many friends, business partners, collaborators, and most importantly my 'inner circle' who, diligently supporting me throughout all and everything I faced in the world, truly they are my greatest strength. They know who they are, but a special thank you must be given to Daphne, my partner in life and business who, forever seeing the real me and the massive global vision I have in the world, is with her unique and special talent forever behind me and working hard towards all that we are creating. To Lucia, Stevie, Sophie, Sydney, Mikie, Dustin, and the rest of the family and friends who, in their many colourful ways support and enrich my life more than they know. To Delroy my childhood friend who, for all these years, has been forever my shadow. And especially for all those who, being faced with hardship, challenges and doubts, never the less believed, supported, and stood beside me on my journey and to build and develop the wonderful things in the world we do today.

For all the heroes in the world who inspire me the most, you are, and always will be the finest. A Special dedication to the Howie family, Gerard, Margret, Tom, Jack & Tony – forever in my thoughts and gratitude for a chance at life

ABOUT THE AUTHOR

Born in England, Stephen Gillen spent his first nine years in Belfast in the height of 'The Troubles'. After coming back to England and then London he progressed through an unsettled childhood and care system until going to prison for the first time at fourteen. He then progressed to serious crime and for the next twenty years was involved in organized crime ending up with a seventeen-year sentence as a Category A prisoner in the UK's most Secure prisons and Units. After having overcome many challenges in his life, including addiction, Stephen then transformed his life becoming an Award-Winning International Public Speaker, a successful Entrepreneur in many industries, Humanitarian and in 2020 was nominated by the Universal Peace Federation for the 'Sunhak' International Peace Prize for his work. Stephen today is very focused on helping people to build new innovative businesses empowering society, his humanitarian and Peace work, and his goal of improving hundreds of millions of lives worldwide.

In his globally awaited book, 'The Monkey Puzzle Tree', based on the true story of his life and inspired by true events, Stephen has written a literary masterpiece that not only takes the reader through early civil unrest in Northern Ireland, London, and Organised Crime and life in Britain's most secure prisons as a High-Security Prisoner, but a unique and inspiring story of transformation, his redemption and how he forged a new life of success in the highest business, media and political circles in the world.

CALL TO ACTION

To book Stephen for Speaking Events, interviews or Company training: stephen@stephengillen.com

For merchandise and further free content and information, go to Stephen's personal website at www.stephengillen.com

For exclusive coaching services, contact his PA at hello@stephengillen.com

To work with Stephen Gillen & his team for Business Development, to upscale, Global or National PR, Profile Development, Branding, Marketing and or Filmmaking and other Media Services email: stephen@stephengillen.com

For collaboration or to offer services or donate to humanitarian work Hello@stephengillen.com

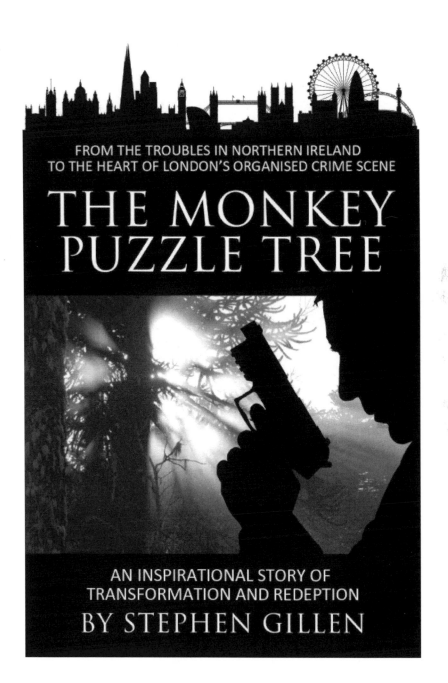

FROM THE TROUBLES IN NORTHERN IRELAND
TO THE HEART OF LONDON'S ORGANISED CRIME SCENE

THE MONKEY PUZZLE TREE

AN INSPIRATIONAL STORY OF
TRANSFORMATION AND REDEPTION

BY STEPHEN GILLEN

Published by
Filament Publishing Ltd
16, Croydon Road, Beddington,
Croydon, Surrey CR0 4PA
+44(0)20 8688 2598
info@filamentpublishing.com

The Monkey Puzzle Tree by Stephen Gillen
ISBN 978-1-913623-15-9
© 2020 Stephen Gillen

Printed by 4Edge

Table of Contents

Table of Contents (continued)

Foreword

As one of the UK's top celebrity psychologists, and ex academic, having taught lectured and examined in various areas of social, developmental and experimental psychology in a British University also in the Hong Kong Polytechnic, Stephen Gillen has written the most compelling mind absorbing autobiography I have ever known.

With compassion, clarity and humility , its authenticity is rich in detail, Stephen shows the reader who might have experienced a feeling of entrapment and loss of focus in life, with a blurred future and uncertainty, how they can now find the ultimate solution to personal psychological and commercial success guaranteed.

This rich new book breathes new life into the readers mindset, going where no other book has gone before, packed with not only Stephens life experience as a young boy like myself growing up in the Northern Ireland bloodbath of what is now dubbed "the troubles", as he and I also not knowing each other personally at the time, but who had an identical experience of daily bombs bullets death and bloodshed in our streets, trauma after trauma, where this political entropy for Stephen influenced the growth of his personal threatened identity and the struggle for human survival. As I read this book, I rediscovered my own identity, my human weaknesses , my own sense of entrapment and the monkey puzzle I experienced as I began to rediscover my future life goals and how they could be realized.

Now inspired by the entrepreneurial spirit and human power motives Stephen shares with you in this autobiography. Stephen Gillen I can personally testify, is a much sought after International

Foreword continued

business coach , creating his business empire form scratch imbued with power motivation drive and ambition intertwined with humanity and humility in his zest to be an international peacemaker and advocate.

As an academic health psychologist practitioner, I was deeply moved by how Stephen has experienced in his childhood, traumas, family dysfunction the plethora of human struggles to overcome separation anxiety from his parents, the sense of loss and acute loneliness, isolation and emotional distress before he found himself in the dark world of inner city crime. It was the norm, the reality of coping with the transition from early to late adolescence and young adulthood in the east end of London in Bethnal Green. In this world classic you will discover how to become empowered to achieve your goals and dreams, to understand how Stephen utilized the human capacity and inner drive to change his mental processing of information all around him and maximize his human efficacy on the world stage.

Psychologically the world is currently at a standstill amid the entropy of the coronavirus that has shaken the world to its roots socially politically and economically. The Monkey Puzzle provides you the reader with a blueprint of how you can become part of the race to help us rewire human minds across the globe enabling a fallen and broken world to rise in power to maintain its economic success and equilibrium. For those of you who have experienced some degree of mental illness , family dysfunction, low self worth and self esteem,should it have been chronic anxiety, trauma, acute and chronic depression, suicide attempts or self-

Foreword continued

harm, the author has been there and survived and so can you. The book is a psychological masterpiece of human functioning and it is beautifully straightforward, refreshing to read deeply honest to the very core of Stephens personal identity, and consistently profound. Stephen Gillen not only gives you the reality of his huge success on the world stage, but also gives us a compelling insight into the dark shadows of the criminal underworld, anxiety stress and depression. He pulls no punches, but consistently and winsomely points us to how you can become massively successful just like him.

The time you invest in reading this book will leave an imprint firmly inside your mind that will remain for ever. It will challenge your every thought sequence rethink every basic drive and motive and will also change the way you think about mental health illness and issues.

Arthur Cassidy Ph,D C.Psychol. AFBPsS

Introduction

2nd June May 2020

As I sit here to recount this story of my life I am wondering how I will be able to do it and stay alive and I wonder if someone had told me at my birth what awaited me in this life would I have had the courage to continue. What I have to talk about is galloping through hell on horseback. Brutal, violent content. About deaths and people who have done and do unspeakable things. Some of these people are still unspeakable and still live unspeakable lives. Many are dead. Some hold grudges. Some still think that I hold grudges.

Even now, some of it I find it hard to speak of, I think it should not see the light of the day. Other parts of it, I question, do not serve humanity. Yet other parts I am without doubt are crucial towards helping humanities progress. To the problems as human beings we have and still do carry with us. We will see parts of us scattered in all of it. especially in the emotion, in the pain. In the struggle, in the challenges. In the identification of having to constantly overcome unsurmountable odds and climb unscalable mountains.

This is ultimately a story of overcoming the impossible. Of becoming something I was never meant to be. But, ultimately, it is a story of transformational inspiration. A true story of travelling through great darkness to get to the light, of finding my way back to myself.

Today I am human. These days I am not the person I used to be.

I'm writing this book for many reasons. One so that there may be a record of the truth, and I may serve as a testament not only to tell other people how to change their lives and what to do, but what not to do. Also, I suppose a part of it is so that I may go into the past and unravel it in a way that finally makes sense to me. So that I can pick over the bones of history, of extremes and lay to rest a lot of ghosts of the past. I believe the ghosts, of the power of a person's past in their history remain forever. The demons that we have in silence. We can only really find ways to rise above them and keep them in check.

But I also believe that they are there to remind us not to go back. Also, that if it is possible to understand them on a deeper, knowledgeable level, that we may find the courage to change and that we may pass on what we have found to other generations to empower them with new knowledge. A new, better, quicker, easier way forward. That they may not make the same mistakes in their pursuit to find the best of themselves.

I am sure, unfortunately, that this earth and the human beings in it have a defined purpose. That when the past is created, it takes a momentous effort to unmake it. That this purpose, this horrendous push, and pull, is ultimately that we may learn and grow, that we may stretch ourselves. Not return to bad choices and outcomes and through that, we would forge a journey and become something.

I know now in the middle of this, that like us all - I was blessed and cursed. The curse was that I would always have a part of the human condition which was unstable. Which could do unspeakable things. Which was not normal. Which on the other side of great anger, hatred, destruction, loneliness, and rejection in the rich tapestry that was my character, was the opposite to my immense kindness, forgiveness, love, bravery, honour and hope. The human condition is that we are bound by the paradox of these traits, that we must find ways to understand them, that we are, in many ways, destined to wade through darkness until we reach the light.

Chapter One
Living Through The Troubles

My name is Stephen Gillen…
I have cheated death a hundred times. I have been in the company of princes, kings and queens, and I have touched the stars. But I've also been to the very darkest depth of the human soul. Where darkness and death, cruelty, pain and torture lie, and I have been consistently for many years. It can be said that there are many things that can trigger a man's demons. I'm no different. I suppose for me, it was a sense of always feeling different. Of being abandoned in this world and being filled with fear of what was coming next. I've seen death and destruction and suspicion around me, wondering how I would survive this and what skills I would need to make a life for myself. I was brought up in Belfast in the early 70s in the centre of the troubles where a civil war raged between the Republicans and the loyalists and British forces.

It was a constant battle, but I had in fact been born in England in 1971. Then as a young child, some months old, I had been taken back to Belfast by my mother, which was the place of her birth. I had been left there with aunts and uncles. While she returned to England to forge a life for herself. Apart from this my life in Ireland as a child was magical. You could navigate six streets in areas and be close to the Morne mountains, or the rich wild greenery of the forest by the Antrim road. The people there were the salt of the earth. They loved nothing better than good food, a great laugh and banter, a good session of drink. They were also very tough, hard, loved to fight and did not shy away from confrontation. Then there was the war. The divide. Everywhere the brightly painted paramilitary murals demanded attention. The green of the Tricolour, clenched fists and balaclava figures on gable walls. Two streets later the red, white and blue of the union jack, kerb stones painted to match and slogans like 'No Surrender'. I lived with four people in the house. I had my mother, my surrogate mother, Madge.

She and her brothers were my surrogate family. There were three brothers, Jack, Gerard and Tom. They were bricklayers. They were decent, God-fearing people. Every Sunday like clockwork I would make the journey up to the Antrim road and church. They were well known in the community for helping, for their kindness, for their honesty. Also, for their bricklaying and building skills and for their wonderful way of living. The community was very tight knit there in those days, introverted and insular. Everyone seemed to know everyone. My uncles were the go-to people if the neighbours wanted an extension or good quality bricklaying work.

Times were very hard. There was no money, no luxuries. People neither had nor cared for anything extravagant. People were simpler, humbler, more focused on day to day survival, and more grateful. Madge was a strong steely woman with a loving and engaging manner that converted every one. She was wise with a giving and kind nature that changed people. She was the boss between the brothers, but let them think they were in charge. Together they made space in their lives to help this young baby who had come from England. Looking back I now understand the many sacrifices they made to give me an upbringing.

I felt I was cocooned in the house in Belfast. It was a place of calm safety and normality that little three-bedroom house. It had a little kitchen extension which my uncles had built before I was born and I remember the colours being drab but comforting.

The front room was where everyone congregated, round the coal fire that was prepared early every morning, burning bright all day and late into the evening.

My uncle Thomas was a quiet and soft man. He smoked Embassy constantly and went nowhere apart from down to his boxing club to watch the boxing which he loved. He would usually be found by that fire smoking his Embassy red as he had once been caught in a bombing and suffered terribly with his nerves. My Uncle Jack was a tall and silvered haired man. He was always busy and talkative. He had been in the navy and had travelled the world. He had fantastic stories and smoked the strong Players cigarettes. Gerard was my father figure. He was central amongst the brothers and seemed to be the guiding dominant hand in most affairs. I can see now that they had agreed, defined roles in my life there growing up. Madge would be my mother, and Gerard my father. Together, between them, they guided my life and managed all my affairs.

Outside the door was a raging inferno of death, civil war, paramilitaries, suspicion, finger pointing and cruelty. Everywhere were the check-points. You would walk through and bags, people, faces and demeanours would be scanned, checked and searched. I pointed once at the group of soldiers who weaved in and out of house doorways.

'Look guns, soldiers!'.

Gerard smacked me round the head quick and hard.'Shhhh don't point, Stephen. Never point. They may think you're holding something and fire!'.

Even as a child, I became aware straight away, as far back as I can remember, that there was suspicion everywhere. That you always had to be careful of bombs going off, of the riots. That there were police checkpoints everywhere and hidden malice. That the authorities were not to be relied on, or trusted, or talked to. That you couldn't trust, and had to be careful what you said, whom you spoke to. It was the strangest thing, but coded with the caution and worry of the times I could usually tell the difference between a catholic or a protestant at a hundred paces. It was in the look on the face, in the eyes. The way they stood and moved. The way they spoke, even the clothes they wore.

The soldiers would arrive in armoured cars at any time and jump out with rifles and machine guns. They would weave in and out of doorways. They would move all in their path and they would bring attitude and wrath and fear with them. There would be snipers. There would be helicopters, there would be cold stares, and there would be frightened and cautious movements. Some of them would be nice to us kids. They would throw a smile or even give sweets. But I would always be cautious.

'Hey mister, why you here?"

"…Go back to your home'.

'What's the gun for mister?'

Silence.

People talked in hushed tones. People always worried about what they would say, and who was listening. My strongest memory at 5 years old was - I had this bright little yellow Tonka truck and just outside the door and over to the left of the street was a little hill that used to go down to the next junction. I wasn't allowed too far at that age, but one of my greatest joys was riding it down the hill. At 5 years old, I knew nothing about the environment I was in, the people, the horrors, or the deeds that were a part of daily life. I just knew you had to be careful, forever watchful. Not trust no one outside my family home and keep my mouth shut. You have no real understanding that there is any difference. In the mind of a child it is not strange that you would have to watch traveling from one street to the next. That one street would be friends, and the other deadly enemies - it just was.

It's only when you become older that you realise and know more about other cultures and the world beyond your own environment, that you realise that there is something very terrible, very unique that you have grown up with.

The pain the war caused was terrible. The people had to be brutal. Over a thousand years of religious war had kept this beautiful island in continuous bloody turmoil. Brother turned against brother. Community turned against community. Family turned against family. It was a civil war.

It was two opposites of hell that made no sense. There were always conflicts, riots and dangerous hair-trigger movements. They would just appear, usually at night but they could come in the day as well. They would always be accompanied by gunshots and bottles and fire and roads being cordoned off, shouting, smashing of windows and stones being thrown. My real mother in England, the person at this point I had not met or had any knowledge of, had grown up in this land of suspicion and caution, with the paramilitaries like everyone, be they republicans or loyalist. Through the long years I would long for her. It would be a long time till I would meet her.

At this time, I didn't really understand in any sense that I had another mother. I had been left there as a small child that didn't have any understanding of the world. I can't even remember been left there. I was months old when it had happened, so the only mother I knew was Madge. I was very happy with her. She was my reality. My daily rituals were built by this wonderful kind soul. She had a kind, knowing oval face with dark greying wavy hair that would always be hidden by a blue patterned silk headscarf tied at the chin. She was my world and like clock-work I would be washed down twice a day with the imperial leather soap in the sink or the little yellow plastic basin under the bathroom sink. She was my sweetness in this world, my protection. Together with her three brothers made sense of a confusing and brutal environment. Together they created a wonderful safe haven inside that house that kept the horrors outside contained and a million miles away. They were solid figures in my life. There was a calm security as long as I stayed close. There was love, above all that there was protection, there was wise instruction and principles, and there was consistency.

The back garden, which was about eight meters up and six meters across, had a little slim concrete path which had two short steps up to the next level. To the left was a little bit of grass and at the back two little coal bunkers which we used to use for the coal fire in the front room. Just at the back of the bunker was the monkey puzzle tree.

I would always go out there. It was my main place where I used to always play because I wasn't really allowed out in them days because of the trouble. I would more often than not stand at the front room window and watch the other kids of the street play. They would laugh and, shout, push and pull each other, play on their bikes and I would just watch. I would yearn to be part of it, to be involved and to play also.

My world was the back garden.

My thoughts were of cowboys and Indians and great military conquests. Behind the monkey puzzle tree was the Nochers family garden. They were a big family, four boys and one girl and would always be climbing up on their shed roof throwing things and fighting. One of those boys, David would be shot dead later on as he went to buy breakfast for his children. My family knew the mother well, so did I, but they were different to me. They also seemed to have a freedom I didn't. More often than not I was ignored.

The monkey puzzle tree stood proud, unmoving and alone.

My uncle used to tell me a wonderful fantasy as a child. How curved streets had giants buried under them, how you couldn't go out at night because of banshees, and how certain places were dangerous because of giant praying mantis. They were ridiculous yarns – and I loved them.

I asked him one day, in the back garden in Belfast, 'What is that spikey tree?'.

'The what?'.

"Tell me about that, the tree that's always there?".

'That's a monkey puzzle!'

'A Monkey Puzzle?'.

"Never speak in front of a monkey puzzle tree. Be careful of what you are thinking when you are close to it, especially what you say! They can live to be a thousand years old. As old as some of the mountains in these parts. They have a secret language. But they are truly magical. It is said that Monkey Puzzle Trees hold all the secrets of the land… but beware, for they are so loyal, so silent that whoever they hear speak loses the gift of speech and can never speak again!'

I looked at the spikey arms of the tree, its armoured tallness, and I looked at how alone it was and how strong it looked. I felt it could never be moved, climbed even. Resilient. It looked lucky and independent in this place of suspicion and spirits. I was always in awe of it. I felt frightened of it in some little way as well. My mind as a child, worried constantly, 'was it listening, could it read my thoughts?'.

In the days my thoughts were about cowboys and Indians and the brown plastic fort I constantly played with. About my cars, plastic soldiers, generals and armies. Making camps and hiding in dug outs. Building things and going with the other children and being mysterious and running away free when I wasn't cocooned. Playing toy guns and on my bike. I would hear the excitement and riots, and gunshots in the night and I would want to be with the big boys. I would want to be doing what they were doing, to be part of their excitement and I had no fear

Then I remember. The deafening noise was the first thing. The shouting, the crashing, loud swearing. The shattering of glass, of armoured police and army vehicles accelerating. Gun fire peppered the night somewhere close, the deafening barrage of rhythmic volleys quickening, stopping then erupting again. Then there was the fire lighting the night sky like burning rainbows as petrol bombs arched. I could see a coach, on its side as a road block, flames ravished it, crackling, sending embers into the darkness. I can feel the heat of the flames and see their glow dancing in the night. My heart was beating in my chest. I was 7, and I wiped the sweat and dirt of my hands onto my trousers searching for comfort. I was out alone. I was lost, the riot had emerged from nowhere and I was cornered.

I ran. I felt the fear of danger course through me and being in the darkness lost. Bodies ran in all directions as there was the crack of rubber bullets. These impressions have stayed with me throughout my life from this time. Locked away, I have been unable to speak of them in clarity. It has at times haunted me. It has held me in depression. It has made me question things, and It has spurred me into action in the worst most dangerous of circumstances.

The day light had dissipated fast but the dark evening coldness had come in quicker. I knew my aunty Madge and everyone would be worrying now. Everyone was throwing stones at the police and armoured vans. The army pigs (green armoured vehicles with riot mesh & hatches) crashed into the burning bus. The barricade started to swing open. People scattered. The gunfire elevated. My eyes widened in panic, and I ran. I was unaware of the people that ran and dispersed behind me, beside me. But I could feel them. I thought only of a place to hide, to get away from the noise and the gun fire. My face was in the damp earth, in a front garden under a hedge. My breathing rattled in my ear. Through the gaps in the bottom of the hedge I tried to be invisible.

Stiffening with fear and cold I watched.

The armoured vans roared up the street. There was an eerie silence then full out gun fire again. The main crowd had been directed to the next street, but the battle continued. I had been there a while rooted to the spot and afraid to move. Then the Republicans started shooting from the flats. It was a strategy to draw the security forces in. Gun fire was traded.

Then I saw him. There were two at first, but the other one took up a crouched firing position and with his SLR and fired. They both had on jeans, faces covered. The one who drew closer to me zig zagged, rifle in hand in a dark duffel coat that was buttoned against the night. I was sure for a moment his eyes met mine, that he was aware of me. A child cowering in the hedgerow. But he raised the rifle as if to take a shot up the road where the wreckage of the bus was. That part of the street was desolate now.

Then it happened. I watched it all. The shot he took to the chest flung him backwards. The wind was squeezed from his lungs. I watched terrified as he hit the ground in front of me and winced. He gasped for breath and spluttering coughed blood. I could see the blood run from the side of his mouth as he rolled in pain. The gunfire continued close by.

I wanted to say something but could not talk. He was mumbling to himself. I couldn't understand it.
Then, 'Mother, god mother. Help me'.

The tears were rolling down my cold cheeks. I was frozen in terror but could not move. I tightened the grip of my little fingers in the earth and felt the dampness of the mud. I was sure he saw me now as I managed to say, 'Sorry'. I'm sorry. Are you ok', stretch out my hand through the gap in the bottom of the hedge to try and comfort him.

He didn't answer. I watched him. I felt his pain. It was over 20 minutes; his movements were slowing as he was dying. He still called for his mother, his family.

I travelled this time with him in terror and pain and I felt it deep inside me like a stain I couldn't remove.

Two of his comrades appeared from the darkness. One pointed his rifle. Together they pulled him back, hopefully to safety. I saw his legs drag along the pavement lifelessly and I saw the black doc martin boots he wore. They did not see me cower in the darkness or that I had tightly closed my eyes.

Across the road, on the fourth-floor balcony of the high flats the man with the binoculars watched the balaclaved figure twisting on the floor from the gun shot wound and winced. He stood, eyes focusing through the highly intensified lenses and he could not express the feeling he was experiencing. A figure clan in jeans, a jacket and a black balaclava, gasping, twisting. A pavement being stained by running blood.

The chaos was about him. It stained the night he thought in the vantage point he had chosen. Hammering his ears. In the drilling sound of the bullets and the running crowds and the bricks and the bottles, but he was transfixed with the boy who was dying in front of him. He paused, as he saw a small hand appear from under the hedge row, the private exchange as the dying boy turned toward it and his lips moved.

They pulled him back now, his comrades, the boy who bled, out of the line of fire towards cover. The gun shot had slowed the movement of his struggles. The man with the binoculars studied the garden and the bottom of the hedge where the hand had appeared. He saw the young boy crawl back. Saw him, face stamped with terror and a redness of tears on his face, climb the gardens to the side of him and get to safety at the end of the road. From his high and hidden vantage point, the man who was known in Belfast as 'the gardener' watched as the boy turned toward his line of sight one more time. The sharp black hair, the small frame, the jeans and coloured jumper, he saw it all, imprinted the memory and the picture in his mind before he lowered the binoculars. On his right hand he had only three fingers. A wound that had come years after his birth his ring and little finger were missing.

Icy Fear still gripped me. I could smell the earth and undergrowth as I crawled through the garden in an attempt to save myself. Although it was cold, my little body was sweating inside my ripped and dirty jeans, top and heavy jumper. I still felt the fear of the boy who reached for his mother while he died. My insides screamed that I must find a way out of here but to use the road was death. The next garden had a small brick wall. I vaulted across it quickly feeling exposed and rushed to the next hedge.

My feeling was the shooting was further away now, fainter. But the road remained empty and looked more dangerous than ever.

I listened intently, trying to trace movement for the lost sounds of gunfire.
What should I do?

My mind was filled with my front room at home. The fired burned healthily, and my uncle Tom sat deep in the chair watching the news. Jack squinted on the couch beside him smoking a Player, Gerard read his big double sized paper and my aunt Madge washed the dishes preparing for dinner.
I forged a way through the next garden.

I was at the corner of the road and my eyes peered suspiciously down and along three stretches of street. The small tenement houses were barred and quiet. Not a soul. Lights were on. There was an ominous feeling hanging in the air.
Everyone will be worried about me I realised.

The pain and horror of what I had witnessed of the boy dying before me lingered, couldn't be moved from my mind. I thought of him. The gun, the hidden face in the mask. The impact. A figured that pleaded. Why did they go? I had to move.

Sprinting across the open stretch of road. My target the slim concrete alley that separated the backs of the tenement houses.

'What are you up to wee man?' She stood there a young but towering figure face hidden by a hood and scarf. The dog she controlled pulled hard on its leash and snarled and barked. A strong, healthy Alsatian type that was big for its size.

'Stop', she bellowed and pulled on the lead.

I pulled back.

'She's ok'. She gave a tight smile and her eyes narrowed. 'As long as you're not a Brit'?

There was waning light in the ally, cover. She pulled me quickly by the hand.

'Quick', She forced a quick break forward down the concrete. 'I know you. You're the Gillen boy, aren't ye?'

Silence.

'Margret? Gerard, Serpenton parade?

'Yes', my voice cracked in a battered voice that stretched into a whisper.

'No worries wee man. I'll get you home. You got some ballacks to be out and about here tonight!'

Her hand had tightened in a vice like grip around mine. In the cold air I watched the breath of the dog. It pulled us into a back garden. There was a tin bath, and the enclosed walls of the garden illuminated the back-door kitchen window. It opened in a burst and people passed us carrying a box.

'Don't mind them', we were through the tiny kitchen and into a small front room. The aged curtains were drawn and a dim light burned in the corner. There were three of them. Two with rifles and one with a revolver. They wore green jackets, jeans and balaclavas. One stroked the barrel of the guy stretched across his knee. The one near the window pointed his rifle. The one with the short had his finger on the trigger guard.

Everyone looked.

'Jesus', they sighed. 'What the fuck. You not see its brutal here tonight'.

The room was dirty, littered with old furniture, tins and bottles. A safe house. The TV squawked. I realised it was tuned into the security forces frequency as I heard the crackle of walkie talkies.

'I found the wee man'. We stood there me, her and the panting dog. 'I know the family he's from up the road. I'm going to take him back.'

'Well go on then. Fecks sake'.

The dog was made to heel, told to quieten down. I was pulled quickly behind her again, fast in the cold evening air. Marching quickly, no talk, brisk strides. Up the alley and over the road. I kept turning behind me, as if someone chased us. The air remained menacing as we marched, and in my mind was the boy.

Six months later…

The morning ritual had started at 7am. In a cold bathroom as the coal fire was being built I had stood tall in the yellow basin and been washed down briskly by the flannel. I had dressed in my school uniform and Margret had fixed my black and white tie. I was fed as the house struggled to wake, and I was escorted out the door by my uncle I was with, Gerard. We went down the path and up the road. Around the corner at the top of Serperton parade and up the steep street hill to the Antrim Road. The boy still stayed in my thoughts. The visions of the night would creep back unannounced and spoil my moments, steal my joy. Streets were on either side of us as we climbed still upwards near where the church was. I would never be the same after the boy. The gunshots still rang in my ears to remind me of the imminent danger. I had become sullener since that evening. More aware of the world.

A place of fun and pranks had restructured into lurking dangers and moving shadows.

Gerard carried a paper rolled up in his hand. It swung as we walked. We had walked the same route clock-work since as far back as I could remember. School was on my mind now. The Christian brothers and the nuns that ran it. The school, Park Lodge was a two-story building by itself on the Antrim Road. It was for infants and primary and held about 150 children. I had been through infants there and I struggled now through primary. We pulled close to the school now. I buttoned my little blazer, tided my grey short trousers. My satchel was at my shoulder, and I felt dread.

It was the usual feeling I always felt drawing near to the school. Even before I had arrived I saw my teacher. The Christian brother in charge of our class. A large man he towered above all of us. His black flowing robes would dance when he moved and always he seemed to glower at us through round spectacles. The nuns were not much better, sometimes even worse. Brutally strict, it was a brave soul who forgot his homework. Being disrespectful was suicidal. They would line the class up for one misdemeanour and punish us all with the strap. They made us learn. They had a class full of high achievers in the making because of it. I was no different. I liked school but feared the punishments. I was a bright child with a clear intellect and enquiring inquisitiveness. I excelled in most things, and was a great reader and interested in history. Nearly there. My hands recoiled and their muscle memory remembered the painful stinging of the leather strap. My uncle Gerard had always escorted me here.

At break time we would kick the ball in the fenced playground and the time would stretch out there until I yearned to get home. On a good day just further down along was Cave Hill, and there were mountain goats there which would climb the rocky grey side of the sheer rockface by the two caves in the mountain. We would watch them and their aerobatics and then on the way back down the hill through the woods play soldiers.

I was at the front entrance. Kids rushed in past me. I see again the smile of my uncle Gerard. He raised the clenched fist and pointed the rolled paper towards me. Nodded. I gave a small smile. He was gone and I watched him walk back the way we come. I steadied myself to settle in class. I was a changed boy. There was different feeling in my stomach, unrecognisable notions in my head. I walked slowly in. I was unaware that my little reality was soon to be changed beyond anything I could have imagined…

ֆ

Chapter 2
Across the Sea, A New Life

I stood then looking at the dock, the great ship, the depth and green blue vastness of the swelling and moving water, and I had never known so much loneliness, so much anxiety. Fear was close by. I couldn't get a solid shape to it, but it was in the unknown, the going into alien places where I had never been before. I was buttoned against the early grey of the morning in my heaviest coat. I had just turned nine. I tightened my small grip on the little blue suitcase that rested on my jeans. I saw the men of the ferry work with the massive ropes that anchored the ship, and inside I winced as I tried to steel myself for what was to come.

Beside me, Gerard with sparse thinning grey hair stood with bowed shoulders. He had always looked strong to me, a champion who would always win through. I saw a difference in him now. He fixed a face against the world, but I knew inside he screamed. He gazed more these days, as if he was there but was not there. As if things had become less important and interesting. He looked across the docks his eyes every now and then taking a sideways glance to check on me. It was my feelings he felt. My worry and anxiousness, and it pained him.

I was a happy child, joyous against the sharp edges of life. Always curious to engage the next adventure. I was now a changed boy. The numbness of how I now navigated myself had been thrown, rewired. I looked across the far water, out into the great ocean that stretched out as far as my eyes could see, and my thoughts were thrown back to the crying. It was the news.

The words I thought could not be real.

We had stood in the little green main bathroom downstairs in the house. We had held each other adult and child and we had cried hard. Madge had died. She had been in hospital with what I now know was aggressive cancer. She had been in hospital for six weeks as she fought to the end. I had missed her. I had continuously called for her, for her warmth and the comfort she gave me. They had kept me away. They had mourned from my sight and wrung their hands in worry and concluded that it was no place for a little child. That they could hardly bear it themselves. That if, and it looked certain an end was here, a wonderful woman who was a sister and a matriarch and a mother should be remembered the way she was last seen.

The seagulls were up. Floating they hung in the air and I watched them glide. It had been decided that the Irish troubles were becoming too dangerous with an escalation in activities, especially riots and bombings. The sectarian cauldron was boiling over into all-out war as the tit for tat killing fields were being primed for completed annihilation. The seagull dipped, dived, used its wings to navigate a circular sweep. It had been further discussed and decided that the little house in Belfast was broken without Madge's influence. That although it was not spoken of or voiced clearly, it felt like the beginning of the end for the brothers. That the pain they held would translate into a lengthy and dark mourning.

It was best the little bundle which was brought from England as a baby and was now a child should go back across the Irish sea. He had searched for weeks to try an locate my mother. He had searched every avenue he could but sadly couldn't find her. I was to go to Foster parent who had been recommended by our extended family. I know now with heavy hearts the decisions they made were out of necessity not choice.

People lined up to board the ferry. We were in the line. Gerard looked at me again to check. He pulled a large black suitcase. I imagined what he thought. That he felt the worst he ever had. That the future looked bleak. That he was sorry, but it was for the best, that I needed a woman's hand. That behind me everything I had known was crumbling and deteriorating. That there was nothing left there that I would recognise. He tried a smile. He would miss me terribly, the warmth of my innocence, the responsibility that focused him and helped his health and purpose. He would miss the moments of family love shared.

Also, he would worry. He would sit in the chair by the fire with his brother smoking a cigarette making the best of it while people killed each other outside the door. He would think of the decisions they had made, and he would consider if they had been right. He would put a brave face on, he would get up earlier and do extra work and build the fire. He would think of his sister Margret and he would imagine the child in England.

He had already had one mild heart attack. He would take care of himself. He would pay more attention to these things because with his sister gone, he felt responsible for the other two They checked the passports and the faces and scrutinised the baggage.

'Go through,' they said. Waved through we were on the steel bridge up to the deck of the ship. We had travelled through the night from Belfast by coach to Larne. We would cross the Irish sea to Stranraer in Scotland. We would be on the mainland of the United Kingdom and we would again take the awaiting coach through the night to Victoria Station in London. The wind picked up. I glanced round. Way beyond the smooth hills at the back of the docks were winding roads that stretched like the branches of a tree. Belfast and the little house in Serpenton Parade had to be somewhere over to the left behind that.

'Come on son. Let's get settled. We can get a cup of tea'. He didn't turn. I was somewhere else. Everything was changing too fast; I had no control. I had left everything. No toys. No need for toys, or soldiers, or the fort, or the bike. Only the need for the case. Only the pushing into a place I didn't know into the embrace of people I had not met. I had a strange picture of my aunt Madge in front of me. It was the back of her. I saw the headscarf, the silhouette, the movement that she had, but she walked away from me and I pointed, and I called her name. I moved to get close to her but the figure, the back of her continued to move away from me.

'Stephen. Stephen'. We were on the deck, our luggage tight beside us. He grasped my little shoulders and shook me again, 'Stephen, can you hear me?'

'God son, you day dreaming. You ok?'

We were moving I heard the ships horn bellow as it prepared to carve its path. I looked down as the water swelled, rippled and was pushed by the movement of the great ship. One hand grasped tightly the smooth iron railing, the other sought comfort and held my Uncle's hand. I could see far in the distance to makings of a new land, a strange place of the unknowing. My nervousness played with my fear with a slight excitement.

The ship moved beneath our feet. I looked at him deep into his eyes for the first time that morning. 'I am, Uncle Gerard', I whispered. 'I'm fine'.

Back in the port of Larne, as the rain lashed through the blowing wind, the man with three fingers looked far out into the mighty ocean. There was a ball of strange feelings rising and falling inside him. A central anger taunted him in the pit of his stomach, a turning, searing sensation like the twist of a long knife. He had left his home in the Divis flats part of West Belfast early, when the night strangled the light and the dampness of the morning was positioning itself. With the strong feelings driving him he had trailed the desolate and dirty streets and then drove to the port in his tweed jacket with his matching cap pulled tight at his ears.

A well-known figure in Northern Ireland, it was important for him to travel to his destination unseen, un-tracked, and invisible. The sea swelled in front of him. A ginormous, untameable soup that twirled and turned with the fierceness of the rain. He had arrived in good time to see the boy. A young, slip of a thing with a small suitcase and a stumbling air of fear and uncertainty. The man known as the Gardener had held far back, hood covering his features as he sipped a coffee and he had studied hard the small boy with his suitcase as he walked unsteadily and held tight to his uncles' hand.

He had done the checks. He knew the boy, and his uncle, his family. He had confirmed he had the right target.

As the small boy who held a hand tightly and his uncle had gone to the ticket office, he took a sandwich, sat in the waiting room with the other departing passengers and boarded the ferry. From his clandestine vantage point, he had watched closely.

He took a last look out into the vastness of the rough and troubled waters of the Irish sea. With the wind hitting him from the east and the lashing rain attacking at the phone box he rang the number given to him on a piece of white paper.

In a calm steady, sure voice, he said, 'Yes, it's him alright. I saw him, had a good look. It's definitely him...'

9 years later...

'   Gillen, hurry up!' The prison officer growled. A big barrelled man with a strong black beard. Ex Naval and proud of the blue uniform he wore.

I was strong and lithe and the anger I felt inside me burned bright and could be focused easily. I had been incarcerated for nine months already from an 18 months sentence handed down by the court in Bow road for affray charges. The fight had broken out outside a club and people had fought and bottles and knives had been used and there had been blood and a person had been stabbed twice. It had been a fight for survival which had spilled out onto the street and the bouncers also had to fight their way out of trouble. Everyone had scattered, ran. Four people had been arrested. I had been one of them. Screws were my favourite target. I cut my eyes at him. They personified all I felt threatened by, didn't trust, fought against. I passed him on the landing of the prison, a stale long warehouse shape landscape with drab colours with the crashing of gates and keys and parked the annoyance I felt.

I carried my slop-out bucket of urine into the of recesses. I was at the corner of the wing and the stale smell of old urine and faeces filled my nostrils. God, I hated this place. But they would not break me, could not break me. I emptied the contents of the bucket in the sluice and as I rinsed it with water, looked out the barred recess window. It was a bright clear day. I looked down the sheer cliff face below us out into the sea. I could feel the power of the sea and my heart sank.

I was on an island. I would end up on others, but this was the first. I saw the big naval destroyers out from their base just along the sea line. I knew how I ended up here, but I always hoped for escape. As soon as I had arrived at the reception wing in a special guarded escort from Dover Borstal for being uncontrollable, I had been hatching a plan. This sentence of youth custody had begun a pattern, a violent battle of wills. The authorities, well versed in solutions to characters like me, were throwing everything at it. It was mental, emotional, physical even spiritual torture. But both sides were only warming up.

I paused there a moment as I felt the beauty of the day on my pale face through the window. A glimmer of hope, of freedom was dangerous to a man's mind in here.

I considered my dilemmas...

Portland borstal was seen as the end of the road. Opened in 1848 as an adult prison for convicts of the day to use their hard labour in the construction of the breakwaters of Portland Harbour. Before that, it had a prison for the Napoleonic period. It stood at the highest point of Portland, on Portland Bill. There was one road on and off the island. In bad weather, the sea would rise, and it was un-crossable. It had high menacing grey walls that were first level of security. Inside, there was a high fence tipped by coiled, razor wire and 24-hour cameras and security. This was the starters, as for inside the prison behind the fence was a no-man's land with a grass moat.

It had been chosen especially for me. I was already classed as a highly disruptive prisoner, had been moved from Hunter Comb in Henley-on-Thames, to Dover situated on the white cliffs, and now to Portland. I was trouble and a nuisance. A serious problem like the others I congregated with, and they were turning the screw.

The screw was still on the landing, twisting his neck to track my progress. There was hatred and confidence in his eyes. I swung my bucket as I strolled with purpose past him again on my way back to the cell. I could swipe that smug look from his face, give him a good hard uppercut to the belly that protruded in the blue jumper. I replayed it in my mind. I smiled.

His eyes followed me, daring me.

'Move yourself, Gillen!' He couldn't resist it. 'Get in your cell', he shouted. 'You know it's one trip here. On the double!'

They had jumped me, not two weeks previously, six heavy bodies that twisted my arms to submission and punched, kicked and dragged me along the segregation floor to a strip cell where the struggles had continued and they had burnt my leg as they held it against a roasting water pipe. They had laughed. They had

had a great time restraining the flash Londoner, and they had reminded me I was in Portland now. Once in them gates no one left for another prison. That this was the last stop and they had broken in bits much bigger and tougher than me. It was one trip here, on the double. I would do as I was told, or I would get more of the same.

I passed him on the landing, felt the coarse breath of his hatred, and in my mind, I smashed his head across the iron banisters of the landing.

'No worries, governor', their penchant for quick reactive violence here had made me restructure my strategies. I would play the long game. Show one face and hide the others. However I would plot and scheme and I would position myself for escape and to get even. The cell door slammed behind me. I was again alone with the torture of my thoughts, with my personal silence.

Incarceration is a serious thing for a person's mind. It can teach, it can punish, it can torture and make unstable, or it can even free a person. It all depends on a person's core, the strength of their beliefs. The resilience that runs through them like the words in a stick of Brighton rock. Its conditions will test and stretch the strongest and bravest of men. It demands the constant summoning of things that people never knew they possessed. I considered my cell. The little wooden table and cupboard, the chair. A blue metal single bed was bolted to the floor. The walls painted depressing blues showed the old brickwork. The sun had dipped, and half the cell was in shadow.

This space was my sanctuary. Ten foot by eight foot it was my world here. I would always make myself ready for the unseen, the unplanned for. I would be up early in the morning before they opened the door and I would already have trained. Hundreds of press-ups, dips on the makeshift chair, squats, stretches. The sweat would pour along my eyes and across my face and body, my natural body chemicals would kick in and, in that moment, I would be free. I would punish myself with training and sometimes as the sun rose and weakened, I would sit there with the sweat on my body and my mind and thoughts would be the clearest they had ever been.

The prison held around 800 inmates, mostly Welsh and from the surrounding areas. There were quarries over the back just outside the prison and very rarely they would take us there so we could use the rugby field beside it. The prison was split into halls which were called houses. They were all named after Admirals, Nelson, Benbow, Raleigh. Security was tight. The regime beyond strict. The grudge matches appeared on the sports field. Often, I would have a weapon close by, a small knife taped down my long sport socks, just in case. I yearned for freedom. The streets of the city, east London. Bethnal green road would be busy now. Market traders and a hub of fast activity. There was pie and mash and liquor at Kelly's. Piellicci's would be serving breakfast. In Brick Lane the 24-hour bagel shop would have cheeses and salt beef and apple strudel. The area all the way up to Shoreditch and Hoxton and back down to Bow and Limehouse would be preparing for an evening's drinking, dancing and partying.

The seagulls squawked hard as they flew past the window. I jumped up on the chair, looked clear of the central square walkway of the prison and searched for the freedom of the sky. I was an alien in this place. I had one friend, a small black-haired, clued-up Londoner called Jeff from Islington in North London. We had bonded straight away in this outpost of a place. In solidarity. In brotherhood. In protection. For our sanity. There had been a few fights already. One in the TV room with a person who from fear, had started the fracas by jumping up and smashing his own head on the association wall. We had also had to venture into the main shower one evening, through the naked bodies, the steam, with a blade and a cosh in a sock to confront people who thought we could be threatened.

It was two against eight but our quick appearance and the no nonsense actions we gave them averted further violence. The screws were the governors there. I was sure most would have been through the services and the navy together and felt wholly confident in the saturation of their numbers. They were a strange breed. They called Jeff and I Ronnie and Reggie, and were treated as an exotic pain in the arse that had to be constantly watched.

The night had come in strongly. I looked out into the dip of the grass moat. I saw the high fence and cutting razor wire on top of it. Behind it the tall wall was dark and impregnable. They had really done their homework here. A seagull flew in from above and settled on the pale green fence post. There was a colony of the bastards here. The size of them, pure scavengers. They were twice the size of any other I had ever seen

My eyes trailed the prison defences. I looked for the measurements a person could deal with. The problems. What could not be done. The weaknesses and the possibilities. I looked at the barred iron square that held my window. One corner of it over the years had become weak, I had seen it immediately on my first inspection of the cell and I had pushed and leveraged its weakness for weeks now.

The prison and its sounds were finally settling into its evening, night-time patterns. I prepared for the long night ahead…I thought I would take my chance and go for it.

We had gone deep into the Irish sea. We had put the cases safe, had a tea and a sandwich and the bad weather had swept in. We sat inside the ship on the top level and the metal walls and ferry windows were crashing against spraying water. It was ok. It was normal in this water that weather like this could suddenly appear out of nowhere. I was reassured. I always believed everything my Uncle Gerard told me.

'How you feeling, Stephen'. He had forced the words out slowly, low as if it hurt him to speak.

I felt his day was hard. I could see the tiredness round his eyes. The haggard energy that draped around him. There was strength in his eyes now, brightness.
'Everything's going to be alright, Stephen. Ok son'.

I watched the red metal floor of the ship sway and heave. I kicked my little legs under my seat, fiddled with my hand in my lap. 'yes'.
He told me of England. It was better, a good life. The Doherty's, the family I was going to were grand people. Alice would be my new mother, she was a fine woman. I was not to worry and I would have great friends and the schools were ok.

He stopped a moment. I watched his furrowed brow search for the next sentence. The ship went right, left. The floor rolled in an uncertain sea. I stopped swinging my legs under the chair.
'I know it's hard, he continued,' his hands, together in front of him tightened.
I sat there and England although drawing closer seemed an unreal picture to me in my imagination. A place I could not put a picture or shape too in my mind.
'I so wish it were different, Stephen. I wish your aunt Madge was still here.' His face had turned then, slightly betraying his still raw feelings. 'It is better this way. We've decided... You need a woman's hand... I can't give you that.'

The water splashed violently outside against the windows of the boat. My uncle Gerard was saying something else in a soft tone it continued, a further description of the difference of a better England...

My focus had strayed. My mind was taken against my will and there was a mixture of sadness and panic in my stomach. I was remembering. I was in the back garden again. It would be not three years past. I had a little green plastic soldier in my hand. I had been in the mud and earth and stones of the back garden playing with it. I had been angry about not being allowed out into the front road where it was busy with children I knew playing. The monkey puzzle tree had covered my back with the shadow of a midday sun and aunt Madge in her head scarf scowled through the back-kitchen window at me as she washed dishes.

I felt the rebellion inside me and I watched the Nocher kids play on the tin roof of their shed. I thought I was too protected. I was big. The other children ran wild. I saw them do it. I had stamped my feet. I had closed my face to Madge and my Uncles, and I had run and thrown one of my plastic soldiers in the open hearth of the fire. I had stood there a moment as it burned to reinforce my point. My uncle Tom, perched in the arm chair next to the chimney breast, had looked had me with soft confused eyes. I had run again out into the garden in anger.

Madge still watched behind the window from the kitchen sink. One of the Nochers at the back starting smashing the tin corrugated iron of his roof with a stick. The green soldier was clasped in my hand. It had cast dark green, legs rooted in a standing firing position from the shoulder. I was still troubled by frustrating anger. Margret was there. She had come out from the kitchen by the side door. She dried her hands on a checked tea towel and there was love and mischief in her eyes. She smiled knowingly. My anger slid, my love rose...

'Please get ready to embark. All passengers with cars go down to be ready to embark!' the bark and vibration of the ships speaker cut my thoughts. My memories were stolen back and my mind recoiled. My little hand rested in Gerard's and people moved. The ship turned, still unsteady. We joined the activity stuck waiting with our cases in a slowly moving queue to the lower decks. There was an uncertain future ahead of me that was sure. The trust was with my Uncle Gerard. I clung to his hand tightly. There was dread in my chest. It had found a place there and removing it was difficult. I had memories of the little house back behind us. The people and places I had left behind. England. Faceless people who were not my blood and who were strange to me and who I must settle and make a life with. I tried hard to imagine her, this Alice Doherty, her love, her smile. There was nothing to anchor to. No photograph, no letters, no phone calls. My trust was with Gerard.

My hope was that this new surrogate mother was a great figure. In my mind she was like my aunt Madge. Hopefully she would be all I could wish for and more? Would I be safe? Would I be looked after? Would I have a great crack? Would I have great new toys, better solders? Would the garden be grand and big with greenery and would I run wild with the other children?
In my heart the burning was the wish to find my own mother, my own father.

We had navigated the lower levels of the ship and then we stood on the hard concrete of the dock with our cases. We were in Scotland, the Cairn Ryan port of Stranraer. It was a day of predicted lashing rain. The wind was picking up. Grey clouds gathered. Rain threatened. We walked, half directed by one of the stewards, towards where the coach would soon depart. It was a long journey, many hours, slow and cost effective. It would hit the motorways towards London and the roads would stretch into the late evening.

We would arrive at Watford gap services and everyone would get a stop to eat and use the toilet, stretch their weary legs that were stiff and full of pins and needles.

We were at the holding room now, the wind blowing and tearing at our jackets. We sat. A drab faceless room for commuters with no energy and no personality. Gerard guided me to a chair, a comforting hand on my shoulders. I saw his features. He smiled. I trusted the smile as we settled ourselves on the wooden seats to wait. The grey skies outside reminded me of the darkening concern inside me. I had been brave since it had been explained to me. I was to leave Ireland, all I knew. I was to go to England, to a strange land, to strange people.

The wind steadied its self and clashed into another reconfiguration. I settled deep into the depth and safety of my blue padded jacket collar, and the uncertainty spread through me…

…I walked the tight length of the reception holding cell. It was less used and a different feel and energy to ones on the main prison wing. The red floor shined by the orderly squeaked as I paced. A wooden bench and pale blue wall with a grey white celling. I could hear the keys, pulled on a key chain to open a cell door further along to the right. I listened. My heart was full of excitement, of the unknown, of embracing a new-found freedom.
Freedom.

I went to a small lightly barred window at the end of the room. The side windows were screwed and wouldn't open. I could see the sun of a fair day. I could sense a soft breeze out there, and I could feel it massage my face already as I walked away from this place. I waited for the reception officer to bring the rattle of his keys towards my direction. That would be freedom to me. The spark of it, the start of claiming my life back. One of them whistled out there. They signed a prisoner out, completed the paperwork, issued his discharge grant and travel warrant.

The orderly whistled, another scrubbed the corridor with the industrial cleaner. It was a good job I confirmed to myself, reception orderly in a prison. Specially picked by security as a good two-shoes, no trouble, and not a risk to security. Trusted. I paced. I felt elation at finally having completed this sentence, this test, this torture. Within the hour I would leave this place, three hours later I would be in London. My smile travelled along my face and through my body. My body was chiselled from relentless training, from an unnatural but stable thirteen months away from drink, or parties or late nights wandering. I was ready for the streets. I was ready to execute my dreams of wealth, the status of remaining forever with friends. I would keep my liberty. No one would ever take it again. I would be clever. I would stay away from crime, and gangs and police and trouble. I would leave these walls where pain, loss, depression dwelt. I would learn the needed lessons, and I would make a life that lasted.

Standing at the window. Squinting into the brightness of the sun. Blue bright rays transmitted downwards infused with a calming lightness of a soft wind. I could feel it. More crashing doors.

Jesus, I considered… and my mind thought of the nearly falling out cell window back on the house block. How I swerved that was beyond me. I considered the desperation of this place. That it had impelled me to fight and scratch. To dream, to dig, to push and pull at people, places and brickwork to end the torture of my mind and escape.

It had been a miscalculation.

I sat on the wooden bench a moment. The memory filled me. The silence of the night as the prison had slept and a changing wind whistled. I had looked out at the green of the moat and I had seen a bit to climb. I had makeshift spikes made out of pieces of metal worked into a pair of boots to scale the fence. I had fashioned a rope from shredded sheets tied around my waist. I would have the green wool sheets to cushion the piercing razor wire, and I had plotted the section I would climb, next to the side of the gatehouse that would help me scale the wall. I had pushed and leveraged the barred window. It was the way out for escape, I had realised. I had braced it, dug with a piece of metal. With my ears as my guide, a long and sharp piece of metal from the bedframe and a length of wood as my tools, I pushed and scratched the wall and the concrete that fixed the frame of the bars.

It is a strange landscape, the inside of a prison at night. Darkness hung, lingered. Silence floated timidly. Always, in the distance, or close, splitting the peace, jingling keys. The padded feet of the night guard as he checked the landings the other side of the door and his check-in key turning somewhere on the wing every hour. The changing wind was a cover. I had fixed my eyes on my route of escape in front of me. Sweat rolled down my eyes. I was on the second floor. I knew that if I was successful the whole window would drop with a thud below into the quietness. I listened for alarms from outside the window and the other side of the light green metal cell door. I dug. I scratched. I pushed and braced. I hissed and swore and ruined my hands trying to get the window out. I had felt so close, but it would not move as I had hoped and expected…

The reception orderly hit the outside of my cell with the spinning plate of industrial cleaner. My mind jolted to the realisation of imminent freedom.

'Thank Fuck,' I reasoned. I remembered the worry of that night. I had made paper Mache from toilet roll. The window frame although solid was hanging off on one corner. I had plugged the hole. I had dressed-up my nights work. I had put toothpaste along it as if laying filler in an office refurbishment, and I had even sprinkled dust and dirt on it to add age. I had not slept a wink for two nights for fear of capture, and then had been shrewd and got a move from the cell to another part of the wing.

'Gillen...' He stood there blocking the light, the key in the cell door, they were fixed to a belt on his waist. He weighed me up, glanced quickly at the blue file in his hand.
'Stephen Anthony Gillen?'
'Yes.'
'This way'.
I followed, across the shining red tiles, with closed green metal cell doors with peepholes either side. The whistling had stopped. The humming of the floor cleaner. White crashing closing gates.
...It would soon be over. I was happy the escape had failed. I had got away with it and the bad ending it would bring.
'Sign here,' he pointed to the line on the other side of the counter. There were three of them now. 'And here...here.'
'Your address?'
'No fixed abode.'

My stored property was presented from the see-through plastic bag it had waited in. A good quality watch, few coins. A little worn address book. Keys. There were some trainers, a few pieces of clothes...no much to show for a life. Apart from jewellery a friend kept diligently for me, I had nothing. He counted the money out in front of me on the hatch.
'one hundred and seven pounds...and thirty pence. Sign here... Travel warrant'.

It was in a white envelope. Two weeks social security money.
The screw looked at me knowingly. He reckoned I would be back.
Along the way we had come, faster across the same route.
My body felt lighter. Excitement knotted my stomach

'She stood there… Her back to the silver kitchen sinks with the soft afternoon light to her side cutting the room in half shadow. A young-looking attractive woman with a hard face, tidy short blond hair, engaging hazel/green eyes that searched, and her arms were out. It was on the third floor, in a small flat and the kitchen was tight. She wore jeans and a simple pale cream patterned jumper that clashed with the coloured plates that hung on the walls.

Her smile beckoned. Gerard was looking on and I had gone close to the out stretched arms, the embrace. I had felt the warmth. I had felt the strangeness of her and the little kitchen we all stood in. I had met my surrogate mother…and I felt the hope that all would be ok. There was talk and there was a happiness in the air. Tea was poured, and smiles followed questions. Eyes rolled and searched and enquired. Mrs Doherty and Gerard parked in soft chairs were huddled in their chatter and talk and I sat there. I felt awkward and I wondered. I looked at the place, the tidiness of it, the newness. It was different to what I had known, what I had expected…

I studied the room. Open, not cluttered, clean. There was a grey settee and a chair, a TV and a few prints on the wall. A corner cupboard with glass that housed plates and glass ornaments. There were no toys. A fresh, clean set of spaces easily scrubbed.
'You look well son'. She smiled, still with the searching eyes. 'How was the boat. Good enough the journey I hope. Glad to see you son.'
Gerard nursed his tea.

He was getting ready to leave for the trip back to Ireland.

52

I could see out of the window, to the wooden nets of a large climbing frame on a small green. Tall grey claustrophobic flats tightened in clusters everywhere I looked. I watched the strange woman who was my mother. It was a funny feeling. All was alien, strange. My foster mother's accent had the Irish in it I knew. People outside spoke the clear English I had heard sometimes in Belfast as soldiers would speak. I had a little room next door. Slim and tight. I liked its smallness. The case and the little clothes I had brought had been unpacked. Mrs Doherty, my new mother had helped me. She had said I would be great, showed me the small bathroom, asked what food I liked and said we would sort everything out.

Gerard's departure was hard. Everyone smiled and hugged. A brave face was put on, kisses. We had stood and held each other, and I had felt the moment was somehow similar to when he had told me of Madge's death, that she was gone. He was going down the stairwell outside the flat when I saw him last. He held onto the iron railings and clasped his bag. He looked older, tired. He hid his true feelings I know now. He was away down the stairs and I was struck by my loneliness.

In the background the Roberts rambler stuck in the kitchen played 80's Barbara Streisand and Patti leBelle 'On My Own...'

A man had entered the room with a slight grin. He was a man of few words. A big bear of a man with wide shoulders and massive strong hands. Liam. He was Mrs Doherty's boyfriend. He spoke with the Irish accent she spoke with. He was from the old country back home near Dublin. His family had been farming people who had dairy cattle and other animals and land and like Mrs Doherty he had come to England for work and in search of making a life.

He was an honest man. He built houses and ran gangs of men in all-weather as a foreman. He tried to do his best and be fair. His moods were terrible and controlled the house. Looking back, now with my own children and the great challenges life would bring I understand more. I hold no judgments, but hold responsibility to truth, to the authenticity of my story so that the gift of my life and the great adversities overcome may have a clear voice and record. The Doherty's were a young family starting out in the world. Times were hard, cold. The guns, the bombs, the fears and suspicions had gone from my life. So too had the great warmth I knew. They had been replaced with the isolation of being in a strange environment. Everything was new. All was alien. People, places and things were fresh to my eyes. There was no anchor, no point of recollection or similarity. No comfort, no easy transition. Only coldness, worry, strange places and unrecognisable people.

Alice Doherty tried. There was no money and every penny was spoken for. She had worked as a receptionist but now had to look after me. Liam worked every day he could. Hard and fast as if there was no tomorrow. He had an old Rover 3500 which he would park in the communal bay at the front of the flats. He would come home from work and settle in and eat. Boiled bacon, cabbage, potatoes. Or, there would-be mincemeat. The anxiousness of everything ruled me. I had little understanding of the world, how things worked in England.

As I sit here many years later, an experienced person in the ways of the world, of people. Of the challenges that life continuously presents. That there are decades and different cultures and trends and fads and things change and that ideas and ways of behaving adjust and clash and are proved lacking. That society changes in many ways the same. That like fashion, everything has a shelf life, an important purpose of the moment. That really, we can be driven by things too often outside our control or understanding. That in this rich coloured tapestry of life the central prerequisite is learning and to do that our paradox is to make mistakes and fall short.

Like England, Northern Ireland in the 1970's and early 80's was a place of great pop music and new romantics. The technological age had not yet arrived, music and fashion were big, Margaret Thatcher was British Prime Minister and digital mobile phones were invented. Times were different then and the war in the North of Ireland had shaped people's perceptions. Judgement reigned in many ways amongst and between different groups of the era unjustifiably. People had one goal: to survive and make a life in the best way possible. The people who had made the exodus from the Emerald Isle had imported with them the behaviours and ways of looking at the world taught to them by their parents in Ireland.

Many of those ways had been successfully translated to the UK and worked well. Others did not.

…I had explored the neighbouring flats on the council estate. I had played football with a few of the kids my age. I had gone in goal and gave a great show. They had tried from every angle to score and strangely couldn't. They thought I was a great goalie and they had a strange look in their in their eyes at the way I spoke. A few had asked questions; it was difficult to answer. I had made excuses and run home. Back from the far side school field that backed onto the estate and through the flats and up the stairs holding my football. I tried, but inside there was a yearning, a longing that was to find my true mother and family.

The TV threw moving images. I sat crossed legged on the front room floor. I watched. There were ships, and troops, the sea. Helicopters were in the back ground, and the war correspondent talked about the invasion of Argentina. Alice, was behind me.
She touched me on the hair, a loving gesture. 'How was it out son. I want you to eat now…'
I turned to her smelling soap on her skin.

It was a little plate of sandwiches, ham, cucumber and tomato. I was a small child really. I was about the right height for my age but very thin.

'You need to eat son. You want to fill out now don't you. Too thin you are. Get it ate!'

She had turned on her heels, was away back into the small kitchen that had the woven wooden blind at the window. I ate as best I could. Like a mouse. Since my arrival my body, filled with anxiety did not feel well. I tried and I played. I could not sit still, but I could not eat. Most food my foster mother would cook would make me sick. I would force the food in and it would not stay. Meal times were an ordeal. They would look at me strangely. Their trying would wear thin and annoyance would capture Alice Doherty and she would turn. 'You'll fuckin' get it ate. It's hard enough. Lucky you have food to eat'.

The worst time would be when Liam was there at the end of an evening. Alice would change. The radio would be replaced by the TV and the pot and pans of the kitchen making dinner. She would float in and out like a maid, and I would feel like I shouldn't be there, but was unsure what I should be doing. They would try. There was silence as Liam watched the evening news. I would be rooted to the chair and I would be careful of my behaviour and what I said as the speed and strictness of my punishments frightened me. He had a cushion behind him, at the back. A massive man too big for the chair. There was a tray of food on his lap and a glass of fresh milk on the ledge beside him.

He looked at me. I though he had goodness in him. That he worked hard but he paid a price for the brutal work every day that translated into foul moods. I saw a terrible temper. Knew it was always there and never far beneath the surface. He had the knife and fork in each hand and looked at me eyes balanced. I saw his large hands. I was no stranger to the belt. It would leave red welts that would mark and at times even my mother would intervene to lessen it. He would try deep inside himself, but he would usually lose and the strength of his angry moods would change things. My foster mother, Alice watched me from the kitchen doorway, a tea towel in her hand. I saw they loved each other, Alice and Liam and against the normal worries of that era they would survive.

I went to my room and sat on the bed. I looked out into the falling evening light. There were sounds of people and children outside somewhere. I was alone here. An alien. A stranger, who spoke strange. Apart from, not a part off. Different. Further along the road in the single small houses by themselves was the O'Shea family. There lived Tony and Saoirse, then the kids Roisin and Tommy. They were close cousins of the Doherty's I was told and because it wasn't far it was ok to sleep over. Tommy was my age and we played at all sorts. We had bikes. We had marbles, and we would play fight and roam close to house within watching distance from his mother Saoirse at the back of the house.

I thought of the other kids on the estate. I had had a few silly fights already. I had held my own and felt I was being tested and poked. That because I was different. I stuck out from the rest and because of it got special treatment.

…I loved the sleep over with Aunt Saoirse and Tommy. I loved the warmth and love that shone from Saoirse. A calm presence, she smiled at everything she touched. A tiny woman with a warm face, wavy fair hair and patterned skirts who smoked. She was a kind and gentle soul with bright eyes with mischief, and when Tommy and I would play she would spoil us. She brought light every time I saw her and I wished I could stay.

I heard my foster dad Liam's voice through the thin walls. He was stuck in his ways I had heard Alice Doherty say. He had been treated with the same strictness back home. He had been taught that way. He didn't know any different, it hadn't done him any harm…Alice said something. It mumbled incoherently through the walls. I had become known in the flats amongst the other kids. I had already gained a reputation. I had more freedom now and would run wild up the road at the shops and over the flats. A few times I was brought back home for throwing stones and smashing things and being caught in places where I shouldn't have been...

She had a stern look in her balanced face, 'I need to take you to the school tomorrow, Stephen.' She explained the trouble to get me into the right school. The paperwork, registration. It was because of the address, it had to be a good catholic school. The travelling. I had come from Ireland, The questions, The forms she had had to fill in.

She stopped a moment, white door slightly ajar. Her brown hair fell by her ear and she had a hard face, sure eyes. 'It'll be ok ...You have to go to school and learn...Get an early night. I want you ready for the morning.'

She came in and kissed my forehead. A quick thing more with necessity than with love. 'In the morning, now.'
She had left.

I laid on the bed and my little eyes were fixed on the artexed grey/white of the celling, the cracks. The feeling of being in a strange place was heavy around me. There were still muffled sounds of people's activity somewhere outside. The room was filling with the shadow of late evening as the sun dipped behind the flats...I was wide awake. I yearned for the comfort of sleep. I followed the screeching sound of the kids outside playing as they moved further from our vicinity... A 10-year-old, terribly thin, I lay there eyes wide and I considered my position...And far back, in the corners of my child's mind, was the question of when or how I might find my real mother.

Chapter 3
A landscape of Organised Crime

…As I ran to save myself with the river of fresh blood that ran down the side of my clothes and body, I kept to the darkness and shadows of the street. Camden was a strange manor, I considered. Of the four corners of London there was difference in trends about it that set it apart in my mind. Unlike the harsh and cold council estates of East, North, and South London I knew so well; unlike the busy and glitzy affluent parts of west London - I didn't know it well. I thought of the police passing. I must not be caught on the road like this.

I stumbled forward. It was a cold evening. It was a busy street. Shop lights bathed the footway in luminous half-light. People saw me and jolted as I passed. A couple crossed the road in front of me. A grisly sight I must have projected. I had left my shirt somewhere in the fight at Camden Palace. The blood poured fast from a deep slice wound from the side of my head. Body running red with blood the top of my jeans was saturated by the moisture and dampness of it.

'My god!'
Another woman with a hand to her mouth and feet who moved away from me. No one stopped.

I pushed forward into the unknown, my body hugging and seeking the seclusion of hidden darkness. My eyes had to keep adjusting to the road in front of me as the blood ran freely.

No one helped. I was a man to stay away from. A spectre of trouble that had appeared from the shadows with madness around him and a quickening step. The gushing blood was a clear sign to keep walking. My head spun like the final cycle of a washing machine. I could not believe they had done me…We had been in a gang war with other similar factions who were fighting for control to run the serious crime in certain areas.

They would pay dearly. There was madness in me, anger. I was not of sound mind. I had been released not three months previously from Portland Borstal. I had returned to the streets with no fear and I had learnt the streets had not changed since I had been away. That the east end was as busy as ever with everyone trying to make a pound note, that there was no options or opportunities for me but crime. That you had to eat or be eaten, and everywhere you went you had to be careful. I had travelled on the train from Portland to Bethnal Green in East London. My thoughts on the way back had been positive and hopeful. I would get a decent job, things would be different. I would be able to turn away from my criminality, the gangs, the trouble and the drugs.

I wiped the blood from my eyes. The bottle that one of them had smashed over my head had cut cleanly a deep slice about two inches on the side of my head…I had left youth custody and I had thought the east end would be different. Nostalgia had clouded my reality. The poverty had surrounded me again. Like the old streets and my old acquaintances. I had been pulled easily into the same haunts and patterns of thinking and serious problems, and I had been wrong about my hopes to create a positive future.

Where had the girl gone I wondered? She was pretty and we had gone out for the evening together. We had laughed and were having a great time. We had chosen Camden Palace for the dancing. I had said hello to Lenny who was head of the door and we had got in much quicker than the people who stretched away down the road. My head rushed, was still full of the ecstasy tablet I had taken earlier. My eyes were wide in my head and my body felt light and jumpy…The girl would be back in the club…

It was the roaring early eighties and the age of dance music. The age of crack cocaine, paranoia, people killing each other and standing with their backs against the wall had not yet arrived. It was the time of E's and the dancing love drug ecstasy. A time of getting secret directions out to somewhere in the sticks where there would be thousands of people in a field. All of them out of their nut on varying cocktails of drugs and dancing. The main events of the time were 'Sunrise' and 'Biology'. In those times we were out for days, sometimes seven days at a time, lost in the dance, club and rave scene. We Loved it. But with the lifestyle, came the drugs and money, and with the drugs and need for money came the wars over territory, the enemies, and the violence. We were slick dressers. Always in top designer wear like Armani, Gucci, Aquascutum or Burberry, both casual and smart. Always with the best of trainers, expensive boots and three-quarter length jackets.

I remembered entering the interior of the club. A massive open space that was the main dance floor, swarms of dancing bodies writhing, on the dance floor, on the balconies, by the many bars on the different levels. The dance music thundered Adamski. The smiling, dancing, jumping bodies moved in dim coloured light in unison. Whistles, luminous strips of light and headbands and clothing and makeup moved, shook.

It had started raining slightly from the dark moon lit sky. I moved along the road still looking for a way out, back from the main lights of the street and shops.

'They fuckin done me! 'I barked into the phone. 'I can't believe they had the bollocks to do me!'

'Where are you?' I had known Darren since we were kids. There was a gang of us. We were at war with other gangs like us in London. For this reason, we were usually always together.

'Camden Palace. It happened in the pally. It was that mob from last week, D…I went into the Champaign bar with some soppy bird and the whole lot of them was there…'
'Shit, Stephen. I told you when we go out we should always rave with the firm.'

'I know. I stuck it on them. All of them. I was lucky to get out of there; I can't believe they had the front to do me…!

I kept my voice down as the blood continued to flow from my head and I quickened my pace on the darkened street. My head was low. I told them to come to bring the tools, the guns. I was going to make an example of them and catch them all together when they came out of the club. I touched the cut on my head, the blood. When I had entered the blinding light of the Champaign lounge I had saw them. The main players were there, five or six of them, five white guys and one black well dressed. They had girls with them. The main one was John.
John and I went back years….

Our eyes had locked across the crowded carpet and my mind was filled with how we had left them…We had blocked them in the car. There had been four of them. We had struck quick and hard, scarfs around our faces and guns in our hands. They had been warned with the guns stuck in their ears, they had been robbed and stripped of the money they had. The keys to their car were taken and they had been left stranded in the cold back streets in a part of our manor frightened, mugged off and broken.

They glared over their drinks. One was fat, one had blond hair and a brown suede jacket and held a bottle of beer. The two with darker hair lurked beside them. John, a big fit looking man with sandy hair and flashing blue eyes stood forward.

'You won't leave here tonight without a scare down your face. You watch!' he hissed. He wanted to come forward as he said the words, but he was wary.

'Fuck off. You see what I do to you lot of mugs!' I thanked god for the knife down the side of my sock on my right calf. I always carried one. I had put it down the front of my trousers for the bouncers search on the way in. I had gone to the toilet and transferred it for easy access to be held by the sock on my right foot. Tonight, this action would save my life.

He slunk away from me, a brooding look of menace in his eyes. I felt no fear. I stood my ground. The music thumped around me. The tablet I had taken earlier was kicking in and the acid that had be mixed with the MDMNA spun the room in my mind. My heart beat was alive with the adrenaline that coursed through me. The girl had noticed something was wrong. She had seen the change in my mood and the look on my face. The six of them, at the far side of the lounge some eight feet back, like a pride of lions watched me. I needed to move. My direction was to shift out from the blinding brightness of the place where we were. Out to the sanctuary of the dim light and heavy crowds of the main interior.

I knew they would make their move as soon as I went towards the doorway.

The fat one had manoeuvred himself in front of me. I headbutted him hard on the nose. His face collapsed but a bottle had been swung over the top of people's heads from the side somewhere smashing completely on my head. Colours scattered in my mind. I saw blues, reds, yellow. The force of it had caught me unawares and threw me down towards the floor, but somewhere in the haze and bursting colours in my mind my body knew that to go down was to die. To this day I don't know where I found the strength as my body dipped, bloodied with the force, and in one motion got the knife from my sock firmly in my hand. I rose to face my attackers. They stood there. One with the broken bottle. The blood ran immediately down my face and neck from the cut on my head. The music echoed frightenedly. I jumped towards them. I cut and slashed and thrust. I fought for my life and all I could remember was people had tried to protect me as they had closed in for the kill and I had pushed them away to fight and defend myself.

I had lost my shirt somewhere in the fight. I had fought my way down the packed stairs, ran through dancing people on the main dance floor, made my way to a side fire door by an ally and kicked it open and escaped into the night…

The man was in front of me, suddenly, shielded against the cold by a heavy green tweed jacket and matching tweed cap that shadowed his face. He slightly bumped into me, and I turned. 'You ok, son,' It was the harsh accent of the north of Ireland. I stumbled on, 'Yes, I am.'

Into the night, I forged forward. In my head, lingering a moment was the sound of the accent. In my nostrils, mixed with blood was the damp smell of the man's tweed jacket.

The man watched the figure that dripped blood move forward along the road. It was appropriate that he bump into him, he thought at this time. For a second, a flashing moment he felt to make his move. He smoothed his tweed jacket, put his three fingered hand into his front jeans pocket protecting it from the night. The young man's shadow was waning now, the blood that fell from a wound by his head hidden. A silhouette that stretched into nothingness. He bit his lip. He had missed his chance to act. He had waited a long time for his chance.

Long months that had grown into pulling years as the little boy he had watched and studied had grown into a young man.

He turned into the night and with him took the anger and bitterness that drove him most days. The man known as the Gardener would pick another time. There would be another moment, another dark night of safety and seclusion. Head down he walked, crossed the road and was lost in the London traffic.

The rain was damp and cool on my face. My head throbbed. Unbelievably, it still bled profusely. I had to get away from the lights of the busy street, the people. I saw the bright light and wide-open window of an Indian restaurant. Inside I saw the waiters. One of them locked eyes with me. He saw the blood as I went to come into the shop.

' No. No...Not in here,' his hands were up to shield himself, barring my way forward. People were eating. A woman on a table beside me with her husband looked at me. Her eyes widened at the state of me. I was drenched in blood. Her mouth was open in shock.

'You can't come in here,' the waiter was desperate to get me out of the door. The shock of the people dining had become apparent. Maybe I had not thought this through. I backed out the door, telling the waiter I had wanted to use the washroom to get cleaned up, that I needed help.

He still panicked. It was annoying, me my head spinning, the blood running, no shirt and the anger of revenge upon me. I had looked at him angrily, disappeared into the rising night rain and down the street. I found a cab station. They took me in to the back so I could wash my face, eyes and the blood from the side of my face, body and hair and stem the bleeding.

I had been introduced to the family by the social worker. At eleven it was still proving to be a hard road for me trying to settle in England. It had been eighteen months since my arrival from Belfast. I remained an anxious child. One who had energy to burn and was always in mischief. The house was a normal two story with a tiny garden in front and a slightly bigger and longer one out the back.

Another new family, I thought.

My new foster parents, the young dark-haired parents of a little boy and girl a little younger than me, huddled with the social worker a middle-aged man with a soft voice, brown wavy hair and round spectacles. They were out of ear shot in the little dated but clean kitchen. I watched them from the front room. Across the green carpet through the open white door, I strained to listen.

'Your name, Stephen'? She sat with her brother who was smaller and younger on the settee on the opposite side of the room. Her smile was contagious. A warm trusting that curled with the brightness of her blue eyes and long fair hair.

I was on the chair by the TV. I felt alone with my bags, alone again in my future. 'Yes, I'm, Stephen'. I had been unsure but I found myself matching her smile.

'Great'. The little boy in short trousers and a diamond jumper had jumped up a glint in his eye. 'I'm, Arthur…this is, Ann. So, do you like cars? Racing?' He was already pulling out a toy box full of toys…I felt good about them. They had a real trueness in their smiles and voices that indicated easy trust. Ann gave another engaging smile. She was on the floor with her brother beckoning me to get involved. I moved to join them.

He smiled. The social worker was in the middle of the room. Beside him my new surrogate parents smiled as one. They had soft features, round faces, a calmness that matched the happiness they projected. It had been agreed. They were to be my foster parents while my Mrs Doherty and Liam had my new foster brother or sister. Everything would be ok. My new foster parents had fostered more than 30 other children. They were very experienced. Arthur and Ann were great children who keep me company. I would settle in easy. It would be a good break for me, good fun. I would have a great time. It would not be for long maybe 6 to 9 months. I was not to worry.

The faces smiled. I stood there in my little jeans and black coat and I had questions. It was voluntary…Yes, I would be going home again. Yes, it was only temporary…They were gathering around me and there was talk of dinner and what did I like to eat. Arthur was next to me and I could smell sweets. It was happening fast and I had no control of the situation. My bags were being moved. I was to be shown my room. It was ok. If I needed anything I was just to say…

I watched the social worker out the window go down the path to the car. There were other questions…I was to treat it as my own home. Ann was behind me now as I was guided up the stairs…It was another house, another family. Why was I passed about like a book to be signed in if I was really part of my foster family, I wondered? Ann was beaming. We could play lots of things. There was a special camp in the garden, hidden…I realised my little life was one of instability, I was very unsure of what the future would bring…Ann's excitement was building. We were due to go see her cousin in Wimbledon. He was a footballer and played for Crystal Palace…Arriving at my room, I had my own bed in a shared room with Arthur.

Ann twirled in her white and blue striped dress. Its great she continued, the travelling over to south London I would love. Sometimes we go down the common. There was lots to do there…

I smiled my best smile at her. A soft mirroring engaging sign that curbed my unease. My bags were at my feet. I started to unpack, an uncertainty niggling at my body and thoughts. I would not know it then, but it was beginning of a pattern in my life that would nearly destroy me and would destroy others. A life of possessions in bags, moves, strange places and faces. A surreal reality that presented a future without shape or destination, a half-life of extremes and wandering and adversity where high danger was a central theme and uncertainty a constant. Arthur had joined her and together they grinned. I turned my head from them as I put my clothes in the drawers.

We met to go to look at the guns at a pub in Watney street near Limehouse and the east ends docklands. A close friend who I had known a long time and someone else who was close to them and who knew who I was. A normal looking meeting in a busy pub notorious for the inhabitants who frequented it between three men who were not there to discuss normal things. The Thomas Neale pub in Watney Market was a place I knew well. It was one of a collection of pubs in the Watney Street area like the Hungerford arms or The Dean Swift that were frequented by the Watney street Mob.

I was nineteen and although from Bethnal Green I knew this area well and had many friends here. We stood at the bar talking in hushed tones over our drinks. It was a well-used open plan pub with a separate area at the back near the toilets with pool tables. It was busy, a street office to a few, with eyes that would watch when a stranger was present. Laughing filled the air. Sideways glances looked up from drinks. Banter that weaved with the red carpeted and wooden floor and the stale smell of alcohol and tobacco.

It was great to catch-up. We narrowed our eyes at each other, spoke of a few local known names and the issues around them. There was quarter of a ton of hash that had been hidden in a scrap yard and had gone missing. Talk of the people who were known to us who were looking for it and kicking down doors and threatening local 'faces' to find it. We spoke of the fall out between two friends of ours who were well know east end villains and their wish to kill each other on sight. There was talk of stolen goods that had been hijacked from lorries and were going cheap. There was a discussion about counterfeiters and a mention of problems being caused locally.

We left the bar as quickly as we had met there, the fresh night air hitting our senses as the alcohol rose in our minds. We were in great form. We felt in good company. We had not seen each other and it was good to catch-up. We were so busy in our own problems and affairs that we only met now when there was real business together. Walking through the busy narrow shop filled main walkway of the market, we spoke of the police, reminded ourselves of what we knew of current operations. Who had been nicked, who was suspected of being under observation. Who was a wrong-un. Who to stay away from. Who was flying and doing well with their operations, and making the most money. We took a left towards Limehouse. The overhead bridge for the train was in front of us and one of the exits into Shadwell station. We hurried our pace, focused our minds together as we spoke in the fresh darkness of the late calm evening.

We travelled tight backroads that we knew well. Rows of cold grey, faceless similar streets. Limehouse had got its names from the lime kilns in the area. The potters that crafted products for shipping companies in the East End Docks and the sailors who disembarked from their ships in the old days. The night air was filled with the vibrant sounds of the main roads of commercial road and the Highway. The overhead tube clattered on the track somewhere close. Police sirens raged close. Shouting, laughing, activity from the shops floated in the air. We shuffled more as a tight unit now. Sought the darkness of the shadows the street doorways offered. Our voices had dropped an octave. A left, then a right with a smooth quick pace. We passed near Whitehorse road aiming for my friend's container near ropemakers field, a quite private place on the second floor where no one would disturb us.

'It's a great tool, 'my friend offered.

'A good nine-mil, Steve. I've had no problems with it. There're a few longs. One, is a side by side twelve bore. The other an Uzi. I can give you the Uzi for twenty-two hundred quid, the hand thing thirteen hundred and fifty, the shotgun six hundred – but it's full length you'll have to saw it off yourself. Plenty of ammunition for both bro, and cartridges.' He had turned at me then winking, his face calmed by the alcohol in his blood and happy. 'You wanted a short one, Steve? The nine?'

Matter of fact, measured, I said, 'Yeah, sounds good. Let's me see them all though. But if the nine mil is what I think it is I definitely want it.'

We were close to the 'slaughter', the private place where things could be hidden and clandestine work be done. I wondered why getting this gun had become a sudden priority in my life. I was deep in my usual game of cat and mouse with other known Villains on the manor and other parts of London. There was a list of misdemeanours, a litany of fallouts and all or most of them could cause fatal consequences. Particularly concerning were the Scottish mob from Colombia road. A loose association of serious villains one of them had come to me with a load of money and asked for introduction to buy something heavy in the underworld of my connection. I had facilitated a meeting and unbeknown to me that meeting had gone very badly. I was now very wanted and was hearing stories of certain people travelling around with guns ready to shoot me on sight.

'Stevie, your lot had that lorry down the city. Nice bit of work,' He had very plain features I thought you could easily miss him in the crowd. He put his hands into the side pockets of his blue bomber jacket. 'Had it right off didn't yea!' And he laughed.

'Yeah, nice bit of work. The information was spot on,' I had said it low, guarded.

'Is there anymore of the parcel left. I could move a bit of it out for yah?'

'...Nah, all done only bits left, and they're already placed,' I had sidestepped the answers. People talked too much and didn't think. To say more was to talk out of turn. 'We' had down very well out of it, but the reality of what had actually gone on was a lot different to what they would had imagined.

The 'jump-up' on the lorry down the city was a lorry in transit filled with six hundred thousand pounds worth of Gucci. We had been given great and targeted information. We knew there was the summer collection in there and bags and accessories. We had followed in two cars, and had had the route already worked out for the hijacking.

When the quiet bit of road which we had picked was navigated by the lorry our car had overtaken it and forced it into a grinding hard-stop. The amazed driver had been relieved of the steering-wheel, asked about the tracker at gun-point and put into the boot of our car. One of us had taken the lorry to a spot where the tracker had been quickly disabled and we had driven it another few miles to where another empty lorry waited, and the goods were transferred.

'Ok we're here, it's just inside'. The darkness had become thicker as heavy clouds moved in with the late hours. Up the stairs, through the heavy metal doors with latches and padlocks in darkness following the sounds of the person in front. The door slammed behind us. We were in a room with windows looking out into a desolate yard near an unused part of waste ground by the train track. Half-light from the windows and light from the next room gave us the light we needed. He had retrieved it, from up behind where the plumbing pipes were. It was wrapped in a dirty green cloth. A nine mil'. I took it from his hands. There were black stains on the cloth and I could smell the oil. I felt the weight of the black handgun in my hand, clicked the magazine out.

'15, in the magazine, one in the chamber,' he had brought out a long gun case with the shotgun and unwrapped a brown towel holding the Uzi sub machine gun.

I slammed the clip back into the hand gun. Made sure the safety was on with my thumb.

'This is heavy…beautiful, isn't it,' He had the black metallic, short long, square like Uzi in his two hands with the unfolded stock up and high on his shoulder.

'That was not a fuckin' question,' he swung, a grin chiselled on his features, casting shadows in the half darkness of the room. He stopped at the window pointing out into the unused ground by a derilict building.

'Beautiful, eh. Take out an army with this. But the kick is fierce and if you leave it on fully automatic you'll empty the 32-round clip in seconds!'

I checked the nine millimetres, the Uzi. The shotgun was removed from its protective casing, held, broken open, checked. I liked them all, I already had other weapons, one was a shotgun. I fancied the handgun, it fitted my hand well. The weight was nice. I considered this would need to be concealed. It had to be tested. We were at the window looking into the darkness of the waste ground by the arches that held the overhead train tracks. The roll of money was in my pocket. I could feel it with my hand.

'Only thing automatics are dodgy,' I said. 'Shit for jamming. I prefer revolvers, 38's – you have any of them?'

He hadn't he said. A smith and Wesson special he had had was gone. The nine-mil was proven. He had tested it many times himself. It had never let him down.

I cocked the weapon, put a round into the chamber. The safety catch was eased off.

They were behind me in the shadows as I listened.

'When the next train comes, I'm going to let one go!'

'Aim down by the derelict buildings,' Panic in his voice

I aimed into the shadows of the broken brickwork of the collapsed building, checked it was desolate. 'Well I'm not going to aim it at the fuckin train am I!' I tightened the smile that had arrived on my face, I listened.

They were sniggering at that.

In the distance…coming closer, was the thundering noise of the train.

I took aim, squinted at my target, the top of a length of old wood that rested by the shadowed wall of the derelict building. The years had seen grass and small trees and bushes grow though the concrete and brick work. Their silhouettes peppered the darkness. The train was coming now…Its movements hammered the darkness; the vibration of its passage was on the metal casing of the window. I had the weapon in two hands stretched out in front of me…My finger was on the trigger guard. I aimed.

Two shots split the night… CRACK! CRACK!

I felt the slight recoil kick my grip upwards. Far ahead, the decaying plank of wood was flung back, loose bricks shifted…The train was my cloak. The movement of the train still hammered in the air. I had the weight of the gun in my hands. Two more shots left the gun. The recoil was now under control. I felt I had zeroed the weapon. The train had passed. The noise of its passing held me.

I watched for a moment, a long thundering metal beast that weaved with its lights and noise into the depth of the landscape, and I felt the cold loneliness of secluded fear that was my reality…

…The three men had sat in the car for a while now watching hard the entrance of the club. They knew the nightclub well as they were local and they had been in there many times before. Parked just off Kingsland road in Shoreditch, they knew the club where the target would be found had a beer garden to the side with a fence. Could see that revellers were already there drinking. The overhead bridge ran above them right along and across the road and above the two little main front doors that they studied.

… A train rattled above them. A sharp violating sound that assaulted the ears and body. The road was busy with people. There were bouncers at the door. Large suited figures, a grey back drop against the bright lights of the roadway.

The one in the back, a heavy-set man in black clothing and a cap leaned forward between the front seat of the car, 'What do reckon?'

He had a glove on his right hand and it held tight to the butt of his pistol.

'Looks busy,' in the passenger seat, a thin faced middle-aged man with a rasping voice.

'This place is always busy this time. I couldn't give a shit. Gillen's going anyway. And whoever is with him!' He was wearing a blue three-quarter length coat. Dark short hair and blue eyes were set in strong sharp features.

The handgun rested on his lap

'Be good to catch him here, 'he continued. His eyes strained to the side entrance, back to the main doors. 'They told us he's definitely in there. Him and another fella. They didn't know who he's with… Come on!'

They waited for the traffic, navigated the road crossing together. They had their hands fixed firmly in their pockets and they marched quickly forward with purpose through the cold night air. The bouncers moved for them. The noise of CeCe Penistons 'Finally' echoed everywhere in the interior. They moved, three of them hands tight on the handguns in their pockets, through the packed drinkers. They looked for the face they searched for, for Stephen Gillen. They scanned the people carefully, quickly. Moving into the next room, checking the bars, who stood there with who. The toilets next, smelling the urine and checking the cubicles…They searched the next room, out into the beer garden. Back in the main bar of the club, and saw him. A face from Bethnal green who mixed with everyone. A slim white guy in jeans boots and a grey mac.
'You seen, Stevie Gillen in here?'
'Nah…He was here.'

He had the metal handgun tight in the side pocket of his jacket. 'Where is he now? I need to talk to him important. We have something important to give him?'
'You just missed him. He was here…in the other bar. He left about thirty minutes ago. Think he was going to the Roman road?'
The music had changed. Alison Limerick. They turned from him. They huddled together and they cursed their bad luck at having missed him by minutes.

Nine years earlier…

She stood by the doorway in a red patterned dress and her face was a picture. Ann had dreaded this moment and her downcast features and the twist in her mouth showed it.

'Ann's in love,' teased her brother, Arthur. He danced round her. 'Why the long face.' He stopped now, smiled at her. She was in from the kitchen doorway screaming inside and had wanted to kick out at him. She softened, a half grin playing at her lips.

I watched and I looked at them, saw Ann's eyes and I felt sick inside. My bags were packed beside me and waited on the grey carpet. I had enjoyed it here. I had loved the brightness they would bring, the love. I had enjoyed belonging and having my own brother and sister. I had found a joy inside me as their natural warmth and innocence had pulled me out of my anxiousness. We had laughed and played and fought and sometimes sulked. But we had remained together, we had looked out for each other and we had been kind.

'They'll be here in a minute, Stephen ok. Are you alright?' It was Tracy, the children's mother. Black short hair, a round face with soft brown eyes and a caring demeanour. She had been wonderful. With her husband Kevin they had always been kind, warm, giving in their time and focus to my care. They had listened, and they had smiled their understanding and love. They had seen the great joy of me with Ann and Arthur and they had looked on knowingly. There had been always a safe feeling this last seven months as I stayed with them, and I would miss them all.

I looked out the window and saw the social worker walk up the path. The pensive feeling tightened in my stomach. The door was opened and he stood there. His eyes smiled through his round spectacles and he had not changed.

'Stephen, make sure to come and see us,' Ann was beside me. She held me by the elbow the sadness etched in her eyes.

'I will, I promise…you know I will.' I had a heavy heart; my shoulders were weighty and my stomach turned.

'You better. Do promise.'

'Of course, Arthur. As soon as I can.'

Tracy was there with Kevin. Together they smiled. 'Come back now, Stephen and see us you hear!' They had understanding mixed with concern in their faces. By the front door they watched us go down the path. Ann and Arthur had joined beside them and I questioned how they could keep going through this with children they minded. I had wanted to stay but knew I had to go. They were waving a last goodbye as I put my bags in the back of the car and got in. I smiled as hard as I could as we pulled away. Then the picture of them was gone.

'Stephen, you'll be happy to know everything is ok. You have a brother. I'll let your mother tell you about it.' The car weaved in traffic.

I had heard him, understood. My mind was with the picture of them standing at the door. Of Ann, the softness of her touch, the brightness of her face. Arthur and his laughing. Tracy, Kevin…

'This will be good at home. Oh, your new brothers name is Dominic. A happy, strong little thing…What do you think about that?' He glanced from the road in front, just a moment to gauge my expression.

My face looked ahead into the moving traffic. 'that's great news.' It sounded good but, in my heart, I felt the grip of things. It felt like worry, insecurity, uncertainty. There was the usual anxiousness under the surface. There was fear there, and rejection. Since coming from Ireland years ago it had found a place inside me where it lurked and taunted, poked and haunted. I had carried it, walked with it, slept with it and it had turned into resilience.

The car found the motor way. I would soon be home to Alice, to Liam and new baby, Dominic.

I would meet her and she would be sweet and some of her friends would be there. Rose and her family and Janet, and Liam would be there. In the front room everyone would be soft and smiling and quietly excited and my new little brother would be wrapped in warm brilliant white, wool blankets. In my foster mother's arms, he would be fed a bottle and we would be introduced. I would look at the little figure swaddled and closeted, the tiny fingers and toes and feel amazement and love all at the same time. Everyone would be sitting and standing in the front room with the day light streaming through the big bay windows of my foster mothers' friend's house. The smiles were unanimous and the looks as one. There would be no mention of where I had been for seven months, how things had been there. There would be no real discussion of what, why or when. The time would be erased and the matter would be buried.

The social worker drove carefully. We were in the middle of a good summer. His voice continued about the strain on the care system. Things were better. Foster care was great in some areas.

I had left him to talk…

Words rattled in a monotone over my head but my mind was to my future. Its uncertainty. My inability to settle within myself, my hardship at settling inside my family…at school and outside in the wider world.

The traffic lights changed. I wound down the window and looked out above the passing buildings and into a clear sky. The air was warm and as the sun dipped behind the clear horizon pastel clouds hung in calm clusters. I closed my eyes. The car accelerated beneath me. In the distance the voice of the social worker continued. I centred in on my feelings I felt the well of anxiousness circle and I felt anger growing from deep fear inside me.

Chapter 4
Trauma & the Care System

'I haven't got no money here honestly,' a wiry man with flecked greying hair in a blue tracksuit bottoms and a grubby white tee-shirt. I could see the panic running through him. It was the afternoon, the pub had been closed, but the three of us had walked straight in an open-door way.

We had a knife somewhere but my partner Paul had found a rounders bat behind the bar.

'Expecting trouble? 'he was a big lump Paul. He looked at me and winked.

'...We just have it there, 'the publican said. 'We get trouble some nights, drunks.'

'Are you taking the fuckin' piss?' I was behind him, quick. On purpose so he could feel me near him.

'No, I...'

My eyes flashed, 'You stuck my pals name up. The old Bill are there now...Do you know what they found...'

'I didn't...they just asked a few questions. I told em' I didn't know anything,' he pleaded. His hands moved around and he didn't know where to settle them.

Paul said, 'Cut him!'

The publican folded. Paul had the bat in his hand.

I stepped in. 'Leave him...now I'm not in the mood for your moody bollocks.'

'Fuck this, cut him.' Paul repeated.

'I'm only a publican, I'm not involved in none of this.'

Paul glowered at him. My other pal Zak narrowed his eyes,' The money he,' demanded. 'Where is it?'

I had stepped between them. We were behind the bar rows of bottles with every drink at the side of us.

'Just leave him a minute,' the publicans' eyes were wide. I made them stand back a little more.

'Now I'm telling you,' I had him by the elbow, guided him into the centre of the pub, 'We lost all sorts…the money. We want five grands for our losses…' I looked at Paul, Zak was beside him swinging the knife. 'They'll cut you to ribbons. If I can promise you one thing I can promise you that…Shall.'

A young boy had appeared from the cellar steps. He was about 13 and looked frozen to the spot. I ignored him.

'Ok…Ok,Ok…in the cellar.' The fear dripped from him. A hand rose slightly, shaking, 'I can sort it, I can sort it.'

Zak had locked the front pub doors and watched the boy. We walked, the publican, Paul and I down the cellar steps and under the pub. The concrete floor held a wide-open space stacked with crates, beer barrels, pipes, and tubes to feed the bar. I could smell the dank dust, beer, sense the cobwebs and creepy-crawlies.

The publican opened a safe. There was money counted. It was short. Eighteen hundred pound short. Paul was saying this is bollocks. He was sick of being treated like a mug. He'd brought it on himself the publican. He should keep out of other people's business, keep his mouth shut. He'd be back for the rest next week. He was not to think he was getting away with it. He was happy to pay. The publican, a slippery character, was used to playing Peter against Paul, at playing two ends against the middle. He had taken the piss and he knew it.

He followed us up the stairs, round the side of the pool table. 'I'll see you next week, 'he said. We blanked him on the way out.

Zak was laughing. Paul moaned, said it was a liberty. There was too many people thinking they could have everyone over. I agreed. If you let one person get away with it. There would lists of people lining up. Sure, clean strict boundaries. That's what it was going to be all of em'. We got in the car. The evening was drawing in slightly. We drove through Hackney and Dalston.

The streets were littered with people. The traffic, always fierce around this area thinned a little as we moved closer to Hackney road and Bethnal Green. I watched, rows of flats, streets, a concrete jungle flitted past. Every street had a memory here, I thought. The darkness changed these neighbours. When the last remnants of light were overcome, all would change and metamorphise.

Busy walkways for school children, mothers and professional, would transform into a warren of cops chasing criminals, drug dealers and junkies. The nightmare, hidden in the brightness of daylight, would then descend with nights arrival into no go areas, closed doors, prostitutes, gangsters, racing police cars and crack houses amongst the slums. It was a cold hard place London. East London could be one of the most claustrophobic coldest parts of it.

We were in Hackney road and had stopped at the Joiners Public house. We met Jeff a good friend, Harry his father a short, serious, funny man who owned it. We were stuck around the half bar. I sipped a coke. There was music on. People laughed, watched the TV, held drinks and talked. There was another room with a private bar upstairs. We would use it sometimes for parties, meet ups, planning jobs and discussions.

I left them. We had split the money. We had laughed, and replayed the incident. I had listened. I had a leadership position amongst the group and I kept my self-measured as always, kept my power.

I had said I had to go, left them in a happy mood of drinking and reminded them of things that had still to be done, people who had to be seen and things that had to be seen to.

I had a last look at them, huddled, smiling and laughing at the bar as I left. The evening was still young. The cars passing me on the road beside me had their lights on as the even light of the day waned. I had my head down into the collar of my three-quarter length black mac as I walked forward along the busy road into the fresh evening. The homeless man sat by the off-licence in tattered dirty clothes and a beard. His hand was out and his head down.

I took a hundred quid from the money in my pocket.

'You got to look after yourself my friend,' I said softly.

He looked at the notes I had pushed in his hands. 'God bless you. Really, sir. God bless you!'

I stood and I listened to him. I had seen him before and knew his sad story. In the shop doorway shielding from the drizzling rain. By the entrance to the flats avoiding the cutting wind. I saw him, and I always took the time to stop, talk and give him some food money. I instructed him to get some food. Make sure. To at least find a bed for the night. These streets, hard for all, open to a few, were unforgiving to most.

I took the next right and into the back streets and flats by Colombia road. My mind was filled with the events of the day. The problems of the week. The people, places and things to watch out for. The night two weeks previously outside Camden Palace infiltrated my thoughts. The anger coursed through me. A sudden, uncontrolled and gripping thunder and lightning movement that tingled my body, put a lightness in my stomach and pounding in my head.

I saw my route from the club, no shirt on and blood that wouldn't stop, the cold escape into the night with rising fear and panic. Then the seizing unaltered anger. My friends had come with the guns and weapons to the meeting point. I had cleaned myself of blood in the cab station toilet filling the bin with bloodied green paper napkins, and now looking at the weapons in the opened boot on the corner they had given me a jumper to cover my nakedness and shivers. A pump action, baseball bats, golf clubs. A pistol with a full clip and a flair gun. My three friends had stood and listened with concerned, angry faces.

In the background, far across the main roads above the sound of the traffic, dance music coming from the Palace thumped with the movements of bouncers and people at the front of the club. My mind was crazy. My rage a torrent. I had the flair gun, I was going to wait for them to come out and use the flair gun to burn a hole in the night. We would use the guns. The bats were a back-up. They would pay tonight for nearly taking my life and the revenge of it would be good enough. They had listened and they knew me well. My best friend Darren had said I was not of sound mind. The blood was dripping again heavily from my head. We would all be nicked at this if we persisted. I needed to go to the hospital, stitches. They put their arms around my shoulders. The boot was closed firmly, the weapons transported in one car. I was guided to another that would take me to A & E. They wouldn't get away with it, I had been promised. We knew where they were. They were easy to get.

I walked at a steady pace in the evening air as I remembered. I was aware of the five stitches in the side of my head from the swung bottle two weeks previously. It ached, itched. I had reached the Birdcage pub on the corner of Colombia Road. A busy place of known villains and family friends where we would spend many a private night drinking and dancing. I took the road round and swung into old Bethnal Green road. My mind still wandered.

I thought of them in the pub back in Hackney road. News was, that two close friends of mine had been arrested by National Crime Squad with three hundred thousand pounds worth of counterfeit fifty-pound notes in a hotel room four days ago. It had been a setup by a News of the World investigative reporter and it had been all over the papers. The paper had called them an east London crime family in Italian suits. They were very close to us and when they had told me about the meeting, I had told them it sounded hooky and not to go.

The road grew darker here. Small, dirty cream bricked flats were either side of me. The street lights had dipped and the shadows lengthened. A kid on a bike passed me. I walked, hands deep in my pockets, alone in the night with my thoughts. The sound of my shoes broke the night steadily. My breath was appearing now in front of me. Darkness was here now threatening with a coldness that forced the evening.

…I considered my life. The paper article in the New of The World. Crime families. Gangsters, organised crime…The Underworld. My eyes narrowed with annoyance. They wrote this stuff but the reality was much different. It was more bleak, cold, cruel, emotional and present, deceptive and painful.

The start of criminality was for most due to the adversity of circumstances and environment. For me I had had the nonsense before the knowledge. The stories could be different. In these streets were poverty, pain, emotional baggage, a lack of appropriate role models, adequate knowledge, resources, positive and influentially directed channels, necessary social support systems and meaningful opportunities. A fact of life is that as far back as human beings can go groups and the associations that people had created had built our society and continued now. As history shows us, true long-lasting peace unfortunately is forged by war, not by trusting others to do the right things and abide by the rules. As we had become more advanced at converting our environments into populated cities from the ancient feudal systems of the past the 'haves' had become less, and the 'have nots' vastly more.

I walked. My watch made me hurry my pace. On old Bethnal green road, and the tall grey flats of Charles Dickens house rose high in front of me. Lights from people's flats littered it clustered in the darkness. I kept going, up towards Shoreditch and The Boundary estate.

...People were naturally territorial. They had a problem fully trusting the unknown and stuck with people and places they knew. The unknown meant uncertainty, I thought and change was always uncomfortable. They called it the underworld. Mafia. Organized Crime.

I walked, kicked a stone in front of me.

I knew the criminal families of east London, of the wider city and beyond were made, not born. They congregated together in their actions and thinking. In this loosely connected labyrinth some were more prominent than others, more resourceful and skilled. Some would have worked together, some would know each other. Others would have heard of each other, many would be close to people and family members in the same circles. Many prominent criminal families in the east end would have gone to school together forging the relationships and circumstances that would stretch out like the branches of a tree into other boroughs where these wider relationships and alliances would repeat themselves.

I had heard it said that there were approximately 1100 criminal gangs in London. Some of them had hierarchy, internal rules, structures, and were highly organized. Like a corporation with different divisions, a hierarchy and levels of leadership and skill, the criminal fraternity would stretch out across London. Across the country, city to city and gang to gang. Then from nation to nation like stock and bonds and commodities.

I had crossed the little green in the middle of the high flats. Past the wooden benches where people hung out drinking and smoking, by the tall wire and fencing of the small football pitch, over the grass and stood at the little wooden gate at the ground floor flat on the Boundary estate.
'Look who it is, 'she grinned. 'Long time no see,' and her steady laugh filled the night air.
I smiled. We had always been the deepest of friends. She had always looked out for me.
There were three of them.

They sat just in the concreted garden, by the short wall on two deck chairs. Lily, brown eyes shining, well-kept mousey brown hair hanging at her shoulders and a cup of tea being nursed in her hands. Harry, was beside her. A big man with a presence and always immaculate, the light above them bounced off his sliver grey hair and highlighted the smoke in the air from the cigarette he smoked.
'

Alright, Steven,' He smiled, a cheeky smile that showed mischief. Harry Draper was well known in London. A half traveller from South London, him and his brother Alfie had fought through life the hard way. They were fierce fighting men. They had had many businesses and were now in the furniture and welding business with outlets all over London. I stood there, it was a safe place, protected. They were like family. Harry had always treated me just like one of his own kids, and I had respected him very much for it.

The door was ajar.

Callum appeared, in an expensive dark blue suit, a white shirt opened at the neck, his dark brown hair gelled back. He pushed through them at the door and his dark eyes glared at me. 'Alright, Steve. I was waiting for you. We need to talk.' He was up the path and his hand squeezed the side of my arm slightly. 'How you been, OK?'

'Where you going, Callum?' came sharply. It was Lily, an engaging grin on her mouth, enquiring eyes.

We were at the black Mercedes and looked back towards them. 'Got to go somewhere. Just down the road.'

'Bye Stephen, look after yourself now,' she was at the other side of the gate in jeans, hands pulling tight a red coat against the chill of the night. She smiled widely. Bright red lips that arched. Her eyes searched mine with a knowing look.

'I will, Lily...'

The car flew forward. I saw a last look at her behind me, the night swallowing her as we raced forward.

There was incredulity in Callum. A laugh at his lips, anger in his voice.

'They're on to us! 'he roared.

'What?'

'The other people. I'm telling ya...I was in the flat with the Tandy listening to Bethnal Green police station.' He spat the words out. We joined the flowing traffic. 'We're under observation I'm telling you I can feel it.' He continued.

'Callum, strange things have been happening. You reckon they're there?'

'Steve, I know they fuckin are. I was down with that fuckin Robert at the club the other day...Flash sod, there's going to be a lot of trouble. I'm not sure I want to be part of a few things out here. He turned from the steering wheel, an unsettled look on his face.

I answered, 'Is he for fuckin' real'.

'Stephen, there were terrible rows.' He added, 'I said I have something better, diamonds and bullion in Hatton Garden...'

He put his foot down and overtook a car in the fast-moving traffic. He was angry. His face in the half light of the car painted a worried picture.

'I bet they're bugging, Callum, 'I offered. 'We'd better sweep everything. Got to stop meeting that mob down there'. My head was in overdrive. I was watching the cars all around us. A feeling of being closed in settled over me.

Callum raged, he talked about the boys from Whitecross market, Old Street, 'I told 'em you have another one of them and we're going to be nicked!'

My watch said 10pm. I felt open, vulnerable. I needed to seek sanctuary. 'Callum, we're going to have to watch the meetings. Be careful. Watch the other mob, stay away from them. '

We were near Spitalfields and I tightened the button on my mac. 'Callum, drop me off in Kingsland.'

'Where you going?'

'I'm going to pop into the 'Weigh IN' club a minute.'

'The Weigh IN...Fuck that! I'm staying away from that gaff'

We had pulled in to the side of the road. A train thundered along the overhead above me. The cold night air was in my lungs, the main door of the club with its bouncers across the road. At the wound down car window, over the deafening screech of the train,' Callum be careful. Get everything swept. Watch talking anywhere. I'll phone you.'

He was there, a moment, a wide smile splitting his face, serious eyes and hands that made ready the car. 'Don't be in there too long,' he said.

It had been a quick visit to the club. I wanted to see was Bob the owner in as a friend of his, Dickie had asked me to pass on a message and ask him to do something. I had wanted to break the day, have one or two drinks as I accessed everything. I was on the manor. I knew people, it suited. I had got chatting to someone I knew from north London a moment outside. We had navigated the drinkers and with a drink found a place to sit and talk. The music was belting my ears, I couldn't hear properly and was thinking of what Callum had said in the car. Then the trouble came, a man staggering with his drink had barged into us, stood on my boots and peppered the bottom of my jacked with spilt alcohol. I had pushed him back and told him to Fuckin' mind, and because of it I had left the club early. The busy street was the same outside. There was a crowd at the kebab shop across the road. I had moved quickly, along Kingsland road, hands in my pockets watching the people who paraded past me and were out for the night. As I swung into Hackney road I was unaware of the car with three men that came from Hoxton. Unaware that it was pulling into a side street on the opposite side of the road to the club. I was unaware that they searched for me and had firearms to shoot me on sight.

I felt the coldness of the evening wrap around me now. I should have brought a scarf. I thought of the conversation with the publican. The money he owed. There was the dull pain of the wound on the side of my head from Camden Palace. I thought of Lily, Harry and his attacking smile. The police, the observation. I walked on into Hackney road by the bingo hall.

...I was unaware of the car behind me that waited. The nature of the men in it, of their intent. They were parked by the shadow of the bridge, and they watched for me with eagle eyes. I could not hear the men who mentioned my name, could not see the guns they concealed, that they searched for me and were ready to use them.

On the road ahead of me along the dirty street pavement an old woman in the headscarf walked. I watched her back as she moved away in front of me, the headscarf that was knotted tight at her face to shield her from the weather. There had been another time, another woman. She had walked with a headscarf and she had been taken from me when I had needed her the most. The sadness was at my eyes, a tugging at my heart, a longing in my mind. Head down, I walked.

…The move had been easy and the new house was much larger. A three bedroom with a tiny postage stamp of a crazy-paved garden at the front. Behind a tiny little wall, it was a new start. On a normal similarly house lined street, on a normal estate, in Stepney it was unremarkable. Dominic was a baby on his feet and my mother was pregnant again with what would be my brother Jimmy.

It was a calm place where I would ride my BMX bike and wander the estates. Down the road was my foster mother's sister, Gloria and her husband Michael. Michael was a fighting man, a big seriously hardy character from Cork who had been to prison and hated the law. They had a busy house where we all congregated. Together with our little friends from the estate we would be in and out of there. Then there was my cousins Eilish, John and Christopher.

Gloria, was a happy soft but feisty woman with dark black hair who would drink endless coffee, work from home and chase us for fighting and arguing and not being respectful. My foster Uncle Michael would work on building sites. He was banned from the working-man's club for fighting and wrecking it whole drunk. He would take a good lot of drink then be in bed. When we played at their house he'd bang the celling with a stick on the floor upstairs, and tell us to quiet our noise. We would fight, my foster cousins and I. Long, bitter sharp fights where hair was dragged, eyes gouged and bodies punched and kicked.

The good Catholic school, St Michaels, was over in Hoxton. Every morning I would walk with my foster cousins and friends down the busy street, cut through the estate and up the lane. We would laugh and play and I was still only twelve but would be fighting over my funny accent. I had only been in the school a short while and had had three fights already. Two in class rooms over desks with metal chairs scattering. One on the main field at lunch time while a circle formed round us and a great crowd watched. We had grappled and tore. We had punched and kicked. I had tripped and pulled the bigger lad to the grass, bit into his cheek as hard as I could. It had been broken up as teachers approached and I had stood outside the head masters office being blamed for the lot and suspended for two weeks.

The house door was open, my brother Dominic played on the floor, and Alice Doherty screamed:
'You will eat it. Open your mouth.' We were in the small kitchen at the back of the house. There was a small brown breakfast bar by the sink and cooker, brown patterned lino on the floor that split the room where at the far side there was a wooden round table and chairs.
I gaged, the mincemeat, onions and cooked tomatoes sliding down the side of my mouth and face.
She was at her wits end. 'The fuckin' mess. I cook this good food and you don't eat.'
She had another handful of food from the white bowl on the table and she rammed it over my mouth. Tried to push in down. I coughed, gasping from breath, spraying food on the pale cream walls. It dropped around me, over my jumper and jeans.

She stood there now screaming, eyes wide, dark hair jumping in her anger. 'You fuckin little shit. You will eat it! You're lucky to have a dinner!'

'Alice...'I spluttered. 'I, can't...'

'You fuckin can'. We work hard for this food.'

I was choking, twisting, turning from her grip. I managed to turn my head and slip away from the weight of her hands and body cornering me at the table. The bowl of mince meat and potatoes smashed on the floor. The silver fork span on the table.

'Get back here!'

My side hit the corner of the breakfast bar as I flew into the front hallway.

'You little bastard!' She screeched now. It had built in her this rage for many months as I had struggled to eat the food she cooked and hid it strange places like behind the bin in the kitchen or the chair in the lounge.

She was behind me as I flew through the open front door, out outside into the daylight. I could feel her and the rage inside her. Knew her flashing eyes trailed me. My brother Dominic bawled. It had started when the bowl had crashed and my Foster mothers voice had rose and the chair had scraped and fell at my escape.

'You wait till you come back here! You will fuckin' eat...You're nothing but trouble!'

I was out in the air running, over the little stretch of grass, past my bike in front of the house. Her voice died behind me. I ran. I wanted my place of safety by the side of the shops that was a fenced area that housed a small iron electric transformer for the council. There was a gap in the fence where a panel had been removed and it was shrouded in bushes and tall trees. I wiped the old food Alice, my foster mother had tried to force down my throat from my face, my cheeks. I gasped for air. I would go to the place of safety, crawl through the opening. There, shielded from the road by the canopy of the high trees and the green of the shrubs and bushes, I would have peace. I would have quiet, I would have safety and I would make myself calm and regather my thoughts.

❧

The schoolteacher, a young, mousy haired man with a thin spotty face, slammed the book on his desk.

'Enough! Now you will listen. Class, again, the square route of twenty-five?'

The class was small. White tiles, six wooden desks, to the right filtered light that streamed through a large bank of metal framed windows. A selection of coloured drawings on the wall. There was a small globe of the world on the table near a tiny sink in the corner. A wide wooden desk, stacked with blue exercise books, in front of the oblong blackboard for the teacher

He turned again from the blackboard, frustrated eyes, chalk poised.

'three hundred past six, Sir!' She had tight fair pig tails, a turned mouth, laughter in her eyes and rebellion in her face. She was one of two girls in this class of six. A special class. For special children. Ones who had been so unruly every school had nominated the rotten eggs should be put in one heavy basket.

'A thousand over twelve'. The boy to my left. A friend, annoying with short ginger hair and freckly cheeks.

Sniggers rose, erupted quickly.

The teacher stamped now. Up and down in front of us. 'Bloody well enjoying this aren't you,' the chalk was tight in his swinging hand. 'No one? Not one for What is the square route of twenty-five...?'

I looked around me. They pissed themselves laughing. My stomach ached with it. I couldn't help myself.

The teacher paced. His transparent eyes blinked behind his square glasses. He dipped his head to the side. A frown developed hard on his brow.

'Not One…for?'

It was a rubber, thrown with great speed and accuracy. It had stopped him in mid-sentence, hit him on the head and bounced from the side of the black board.

His anger flared.

The laughing raised, giggling shattering the space. A contagious spillage of noise that rippled.

He sat at the chair in front of his desk. He was used to the torment. Trained in the specialist manner of managing delinquents. Overcoming the frustration and anger was key.

A slow voice, soft but commanding, 'You lot are well aware of the line. There is a line here now. It is in front of this desk and the repercussions for crossing it are dire.'

The rubber moved between his fingers. 'This is assault'.

'That algebra we're learning on the board is assault, Mr Denning,' I pulled a funny face. Slinked back laughing to my chair. I had forced the sentence out, hadn't been able to resist the rhythm of it.

They fell about their desks beside me laughing.

I felt in these moments alive. There was a loose freedom that I couldn't explain. I had always felt different. Here in the class we were different together, special.

It was a comfort to me that others were different too, and in being different together being different could be mitigated. The laughing continued. Hands were covering stomachs that quivered and turned and rolled. A boy held his ears back, twisted his face, stuck out his tongue and rolled his eyes to the back of his head.

The teacher shifted round, narrowed his eyes. A piercing look that could shatter concrete but had no effect.

'five,' He spat. 'Five, is the square route of twenty-five...'

'But of course, 'One of the boys said. Just managed to get it out, monosyllabic like, between his giggling.

I felt it then. That in the midst of trouble and pain, laughter could be found. That in the shame of being branded bad and different and not worthy, a light could be found and held onto. That the terrible feelings that settled in me could be transmuted to fun. I smiled with them. Together we were one. We had twisted shame, turned trouble, upset bad feelings and found better times. I settled in my chair. Elation was circulating inside me. My anxiety had been diluted by excitement. Fear was further away, and the great anger that had started to grow deep inside me was stable.

I sat there. The laughing had subsided. The teacher rose to the board. My face moved. The tiny unseen nuances of hope, anguish, rage, love, insecurity...fear...

I fidgeted. Held myself back from them

Excitement was with me again, overpowering my deliberations. My lips tightened. It was inside me these movements and they were unseen. I lowered my head. My hands were in my lap and I looked at them.

...The square mile of the City of London had pulled tighter the leash of its security. The IRA had been stepping up its mainland bombing campaign and the security forces up and down the country were on high alert.

In the passenger seat of the XR3I my eyes scanned the traffic around us. My senses were heightened. I looked behind everything. People, places and things. The afternoon was bright. The day busy. There were three of us in the moving car as it moved sleekly through the winding east end traffic, but I knew I was more aware to the dangers than the other. There were weapons in the car. On my lap my blue/green jumper covered the sawn-off shotgun I held in my lap. The shops, moving people, cars and the cracking light and shadow of the hovering sun behind the buildings filtered past me. I kept watch and controlled my mind.

I watched. There were people gathered outside shops. I looked in the rear-view mirror. The black BMW had not long slotted in behind us. The red Volvo, soft top Audi, each car following far behind us was checked, recognised, remembered. I watched the smooth movements of the cars and their occupants a moment longer in the mirrors. A sign of nervousness, of haste and edging forward out of the line of traffic unnecessarily, of not belonging and going about normal business. A feeling. An instinct of eyes that stared too hard or for too long. Signs had become my life. Reading them well and correctly was keeping me alive.

I searched for the sign of a trap. Observation that worked in the background, constrained by what the eye could see.

There was something wrong. The car jolted forward as the driver changed gear. Silence. Strange things were happening round me. The cars that pulled out when I did, the noise of walky-talkies in the air, weird vans parked everywhere I went. It was in the air. A difference that dictated caution. My senses spiked now. It was in the churning in my gut, the light paranoia always in my thoughts, the shiftiness of my movements, the darting way my eyes travelled. I always felt like this when they watched me, when I was under observation. We had driven around the roundabouts a few times to draw them out, darted through the traffic lanes, changed vehicles under the flats in the underground carpark and pulled back slowly from suspect cars. Anti-surveillance techniques always needed to be used consistently.

'Over there,' From John sitting in the back seat. His face turned. A hard face with a chiselled chin and a thin scar near his ear.

The blue Securicor van had just made its drop. The helmeted guard slid the black box through the hatch at the back of the van, thumped the back of it with an open hand.

I studied the scene.

'I see it,' I said. 'Looks like his first run. Bet it's a dummy. This is not brinks -mat, they don't carry fifty. This crowd are only insured to take twenty-five grand across the pavement'.

I imagined the guard behind the armoured interior. Inside, with the money cages.

The guard outside at the back was joined by another and together they waited, preparing to receive the boxes that were to come back to them produced from inside the van.

Ian had slowed the car as much as he could in the traffic. He stopped, made a 'u' turn so we could be close to the bank.

I studied the movement of the guards, the confidence of their walk, how synchronised their movements were. In front of the blue Securicor van, a box van unloaded crates from its elevator at the back. Behind it cars looked parked badly. The shops either side of the bank, a baker's, a supermarket had a sporadic flow of moving customers.

'One Box..Two…Three' I counted aloud. I watched the guards turn for the bank. What was wrong with this picture?

We had to position ourselves better. The next run would be the best. The trick was to be on them with force before they knew it, drag them both with guns to their heads quickly to the side of the van where the guard inside could see them. John would hold back the public at gun point. Holding one guard I would bang hard on the side of the van by the hatch. The guards would be pushed to the floor. We would shout to the crew inside that we had their colleagues.

They were to throw out all the money bags at the back of the van. They would execute our instructions or we would shoot.

Our car was turning in the road, quickly seeking the right spot for the ambush. There was traffic in front of us and behind, stationary. They awaited our final manoeuvre. The feeling of high fear mixed with propelling excitement thundered through my body. Like electricity it sparked and frizzled in my mind. Adrenaline hammered behind my eyes. Our car stopped, reversed. I looked at the front of the bank, the open glass doors…

I was imagining it in my head. The picture of it replayed clearly in my mind. They would soon appear. Walking holding the long black boxes. Inside would be a tagged hard plastic pouch that held the separate denominations of notes and sometimes cheques. We would catch them quickly on the pavement. People would scream and gasp. Guns would be pointed and orders given. Cars would stop. It would pass in slow motion. Primitive feelings would be evoked deep inside me, panic, fear, survival, anger and excitement. There would be a moment, like the flicking of a light switch and there would be no way back. Only forward to the end.

Our car had found a position. Ian had his hand on the gear stick for the last manoeuvre. I could feel John's readiness behind me. He slipped the baseball cap on his head. I quickly put the ginger wig on my head, fixed the scarf over my mouth. The open glass doorway of the bank remained empty. I watched it, focusing my gaze hard into the dimness. The shape of the guards was appearing.
'That's us. Quick.' I shouted. My hand was on the inside of the car door. I felt the metal weight of the sawn-off shotgun in my other hand…

All hell broke loose.

…The crashing sound of the car that rammed us was the first thing I felt. The force of it had hit us on the back corner of the car making the backend swing and the car jolt violently. My head rolled, hit the side of the interior of the car and my body twisted. The sound infiltrated then. My mind a fractured jumble of screeching tires, loud shouts, a hurried panicking. Shattering glass. I could smell the leather of the car interior, stale oil, the burning of rubber car tires.

'What the fuck!' Ian had acted quickly as the car had spun, had pre-empted it. The car that had rammed us, a white caddy van had appeared from nowhere.

Ian smashed the gear stick in reverse. His foot hit the accelerator hard. The smoke of the tires spinning sent burning rubber in the air around us. They screeched. The car behind that had hit us was forced back, away to the side. The guards had withdrawn into the safety of the bank.

'MOVE! To the RIGHT…!' I shouted in desperation. I saw the obstacle of the parked blue hatchback to our left. Panic was in the car. We looked in fear for the armed police that might be there.

The car jumped forward crashing into the car in front of us. The gears crunched. The wheels of the car spun again. We straightened the car to make our escape. Smoke rose amongst the sound of twisting metal and smashing headlights. A car horn, stuck pierced the autumn daylight.

It had all taken a moment.

We were out from the barrier of the cars in front and behind us. Police sirens flooded the air all around us. Ian changed gear again. The car jumped forward. We infiltrated the moving traffic seamlessly.

We were moving in busy traffic towards a rushing Liverpool street and the police were pulling further forward in the traffic behind us. Two cars. Sirens screaming.

'Shit, what the fuck happened there?' There was panic in Johns voice as he realised his predicament.

The traffic was slowing.

Ian slung the car veering into the middle of the carriageway inches to the side of oncoming traffic. I pulled the scarf down from my face. The car continued accelerating, the speedometer climbed.

'Don't know,' I rushed. 'I thought old Bill, but they would have been there with armed police?'

'It was a fucken' jobs worth have a go hero,' Ian come down a gear. Looked at me side wards. His hand lingered on the gear stick ready to replace it hard back into a higher gear. His food hit the clutch, hand found another gear, foot hit the accelerator.

The car lunged forward again. I glanced back at the police cars. They weaved in and out of the traffic behind us. They closed tighter now. A van had joined them in pursuit. We managed to take a swift, swerving right through moving fast flowing traffic.

I looked at the roads to either side of us. High grey corporate buildings blocked the natural light. Rows of offices with heavy front doors and security. Drab old worn rendering that held concrete statues and gargoyles. The sidewalks were wider here, busy. The Police cars behind us were growing. Sirens howling, they coordinated their web of planning behind us with a sure urgency.

The road way in front of us was filling with standing traffic. 'Ian, pull over!' I roared urgently. I pointed to a break in the buildings. With relief. I saw there was an alley.

'Over there!' I demanded.

We looked at each other. A moment frozen as the car screeched to a halt. There was panic in Ian's wide hazel watery eyes, sweat gathering around his forehead under his baseball cap.

I swung open my car door. My heart thumped in my chest. My body was clammy under my clothes. I was on autopilot. Fear was going through me. Panic was close. The Police cars had seen us now. Blue sirens flashed. The noise was closer, deafening and alive in my ears. I had used the jumper on my lap to shield me as in one motion I kicked the gun under the car.

Our feet hit the ground running.

The police cars screeched behind us. We scattered in different directions. I ran to the alley. The sirens were all around us. I passed city people. A man in a three-piece suit pulled back. Two smart women with folders. A man in a rain coat with a briefcase. They grimaced. Stopped in shock. The pavement of the ally turned and curved to the left. I could feel the activity and the preparation of the police response behind me. The structured noise. I prayed for escape. The thought of prison, of being caught pushed me. There were black iron railings beside me. The grey façade of the buildings grew tighter here. There was a gap in the railings that looked like a way out. The sweat was on my face. Warm epinephrine exploded in my head. Desperate thoughts rebounded in my mind. I bounded forward, breath panting in my chest as I ran.

∂

The night wrapped around us like a cloak. I looked at Tony beside who was trying to drive the old blue ford escort. He was a year older than me at fourteen. A rebel with short blond combed hair, a strong quiet way and scarred cheeks from acne. It was the early hours. A bright far moon high but clear broke the blackness with its ghostly yellow glare. The gears rattled unhealthily, jammed again, then found a correct position. The car shot forward climbing wildly in speed. We peered out of the windscreen into the rushing darkness that rose to meet us. Tony turned. A slight movement with an unsure grin then returned to the blackness in front of us.

It was a quiet road in North London and a small roundabout with a grassed hill beckoned ahead. I had stolen cars with Tony a few times. Out with the big bunch of car keys jiggling locks, unlocking steering columns, accelerating at high speeds in stolen vehicles and getting chased by the police.

We came too fast as we hit the silent roundabout. Tony had mistimed again the gear change. His hand struggled to find an appropriate gear and the gear stick kicked back rattling.
'Oh Jesus God!' I had my hands at either side of me. They gripped hard the edge of the black leather passenger seat.

Tony tried to turn the steering wheel in a last-ditch attempt to control the car, to slow down and stop the impending doom.
The car lunged forward. Sixty miles an hour, no brakes. The car cut into the road of the roundabout, threw and jolted our bodies upwards as it mounted the kerbs of the small mound. My eyes widened. Fear and panic advanced with breakneck certainty in the centre of me. It was a split second, but it stayed with me hitting wildly my mind and body with one explosion. The car raced over the grassed mount of the hill. I could only hold on and look at what was in front on me. The car smelt old and oily, damp, rusty. The tapping of fast-moving undergrowth against the car's bodywork filled my ears. A crackling, snapping, tinkling that mesmerised me.

'Holy Shit,' I spoke loudly.

Although slowed slightly by the mount, the car still moved with increased pace. Down the other side of the mount we hit a road sign, then the curved tarmac of the other side of the roundabout. The car jumped from the ground, jolted, vaulting the linear concrete kerbs of the footway. We flew in a leaping motion, over a grass verge and hit a slim concrete post that steadied a wired fence.

Our bodies shook a moment with the impact. We looked

at each other quickly. Blank faces that had realized how close they had come. We had hit the fence post with force. The front of the car was buckled. Steam rose from the engine, hissing.

Tony was out of the car door in a second.
I was out fast and ran around the car to join him. We ran in spurts. The cold moonlit air hit our lungs. It mingled with the spiked body chemicals and the gratitude of our close shave. We sprinted from the scene. We had been lucky, no one had seen us or had been hurt. I was thankful. Down a house lined street, sprinting as fast as we could. Our breathing, deep gulps, recreated into mist in front of us. We swung a left into another similar road, then a right to the lights of a row of closed shops.

We continued running through the moonlight until we felt safe from capture. Hurriedly we had zigzagged through old streets. They were lined with houses and flats and ran beside the high black wrought iron railings of a tree bordered park. We climbed over the closed park gates and fell to the other side. It was late, darkness ruled with silence in these hours, but traffic from the busy road arterials on either side of us still appeared. We quietened our pace, relieved, as we covered the outer grass verge of the park towards the inner darker, silence and the cover of the tall trees. The wind rose. The swaying arm branches of the fern trees shifted together as if in an orchestra.

Tony's head was down as he walked.
'We should be fine now. The accident is far behind us…?' I noticed my clothing. Only jeans, trainers, a tee-shirt underneath a worn thin jumper and a black tracksuit top. 'It's cold here.' I continued. 'It'll be freezing later!'
He was slightly ahead, head still down. No sound, still walking.
'Over there, Tony,' I pointed to a slim winding man made path.' Let's sit at the benches a while…'

He turned a moment in the shadow of the trees, a grin on his face.

I followed behind him. He was in the same kind of clothes as me and wouldn't fare much better in the coldness of this night, I thought.

The trees surrounded us. Tall, cloaking, swaying creatures, ancient and whispering. Resting birds in the treeline shuffled. A large bird bolted in the tree blackened interior. A sudden flapping rush that scraped and moved leaves and branches.

'I don't know what happened. One minute I had it, then lost the car completely,' Tony said. He didn't turn, kept his head in front with the words. We were coming into the tree bordered pathway.

'The gears were tough, 'he continued.
'Your legs were not long enough to touch the pedals. Your problem, Tony is you need to get a driving licence', I offered. He turned. In the dark moonlight. A silence. Our eyes locked and I had a light in my eyes, a creased brow and the sarcasm on my face and chin and curling my mouth

Tony looked at me, eyes blinking, a stretched face that tightened.
He laughed. A deep, genuine long hearty sound that vibrated. I was with him. We were looking at each other our eyes watering with laughter, structured giggles rolling across us as we gasped for more air.

We found one of the wooden benches that lined the pathway. We sat. Tony had his hand on my shoulder. The relief was needed. The great laughter a tonic to our pain and worry, and we wished it could go on for ever. I had always liked Tony. I took to him the first time they had taken me to the children's home. He had stood there in the reception area, a cap on his head, looking older and more mature than the rest, more alone, and with a quiet strength that singled him out.

Fieldhill Children's home was run by the local authority as a care home for vulnerable children. In reality, behind the closed doors of the two buildings that held about 40 children, it was the last stop before prison for many. Holding a Secure Unit for special security cases which had the corners of every room rounded, and twenty-four hour a day surveillance in case of suicide, it was a place of violent containment for small children who were treated like adults.

On the bench, we looked ahead into the dark shrubbery on the far side of the trees. The wind had picked up and the shivers through my exposed skin were reacting to were increasing.
'What we going to do?' Tony sat, legs swinging below the bench, hands clasping the bench framework either side of his knees.
'I don't want go back,' he continued. 'I'd rather stay here. He moved his head, indicated the space around us.
'We won't have to. Don't worry,' At the moment the great pain in my shoulder and arm elevated.
'We need food, Stephen. What we going to do. I'm hungry?'
'We'll find something. We're not going back,' I answered. The pain had moved, it travelled now down the right side of my body. I felt the anger rise to a peak in me.

I had been in the dining room at the care home. Sat at one of the little wooden tables that each held six children and one or two staff members, on a wooden chair. Mr Cooper, a big tall barrel of a man with wispy thinning black greasy hair had been at the table growling his orders. There were a few nasty bullies in there. In my opinion he was right at the top of the list.

One of the smaller girls, a tiny slim little thing with slight sandy hair had sat and cried. The pain of her sniffles had mixed with her running tears chapping her face, and he had forced her to eat. Slammed the plastic cup filled with orange on the table in the middle of us and my anger had erupted. He had pushed and pushed the girl, who we had heard had been abused and kicked and thrown out by a dysfunctional family. My eyes had filled, my heart going out to help her, and my little fists had hurt as I clenched the silver cutlery in my hands with seething rage.

'How's your arm,' breaking my chain of thought, Tony looked concerned with pained eyes.
'Cooper…I was just thinking of him…Its OK, bit of a sharp pain at the top of my shoulder,' I moved my arm as if to confirm the words. Pain shot through my side again. A twisting, stabbing fire that disappeared then resumed.
My mind was back with the girl. The rage. The place where terrible things were done and no one helped.

The little small girl had sat there in her creased dress printed with bright flowers, and he had forced her to a silent, torture that saw her gasp for breath and choke her pain and control her air blocking sniffles. The kids on the table had kept their heads down not wanting to be involved or draw attention to themselves. I had watched his treatment of the girl, her lonely desperation, and the curl of his cruel mouth and I had jumped up and flung my whole plate of dinner in his face. Fish, gravy, carrots and mashed potatoes had been my shout in the dark.

The whole dining hall was aware of it. Heads turned, jaws dropped and eyes glazed. I had the silver fork in my hand. Small and thin for my age at thirteen I stood to face him as tall as I could. The people at my table had moved back. The little girl, widened her tear-filled eyes.

The sound of the chair screeching back assaulted the air as Cooper stood from the table. Mash potatoes mixed with brown gravy slid down the side of his neck. His eyes were wild. They stared violently at me as his large frame moved in one movement around the table. Like a big black bear with a freshly caught deer salmon he claimed me. Wiped me from my feet. I punched out and tried to use my slight weight and kicked.

I pulled at him at the elbow of his jumper. He had me round the neck in a vicelike grip with one arm. He squeezed. He held me tighter, twisting his arm, and my body was lifted as we walked backwards, his body and arm dragging me behind him. I choked, tried to breath, fought him with all my strength. We were out of the dining room, into the pale white walls of the slim corridor that led further into the centre of the main building.

He dragged me, still struggling for breath. My trainers twisted on the light blue lino floor tiles. I tried to get a position of leverage. To gasp breath, find needed air, to hurt him back I twisted my body hard. He tightened harder his strong grip. He pulled and dragged me. Words were on my lips. I cursed him, swear words, spoken in broken and strangled syllables. We were up the hall. I looked back and I saw the face of the girl. She had left her little chair. She no longer cried. She hugged the doorframe of the dining hall. There was no expression on her face as she watched.

We had navigated the corner. Out of sight of everyone now he tightened his vice like grip till I couldn't breathe. He pulled me, more lifeless now through a communal area. He said something, threats. Flecks of spit sprayed the side of my face, stale unkept breath filled my nostrils as he shouted his anger. I pulled at his hair, clawed at his ears. He let go and I clawed at him again before his big hands found me once more. They grappled, held, pulled, swung me forcefully into the wall. My head hit the corner of the brickwork, the pain soared through me, crippling my resistance. In a pathetic motion, my hands were up, but it was a token defence as his weight covered me. I was on the floor. He manhandled me, dragging and wrenching me out onto the concrete of a space behind the building. My face was black and blue and my cheeks puffed by the beating. He dragged me along the uneven floor, and I lost consciousness.

'Come on. Let's go, Stephen…Lets move. We need to find somewhere. It's so cold!' Tony was up and looking at where to go in the tree line.

My teeth were chattering beneath my lips. I had paused a moment there and where my real mother might be had visited my thoughts. A wind scattered the trees faster now, and with its quick movement into the night had summoned a freezing cold early morning air. It had helped to remove the terror of not wanting to go back. The waiting, walking, sleeping nightmare and the constant violent daily battles that we would have to endure. I thought of the other children left behind. Some would run away from time to time like us - most would stay. I thought of the little ten-year-old girl…I wondered if she was ok. If they left her alone and if she played with dolls and glitter, if she had started eating and if she was happier.

The rising winds crashing in from the east of the city had moved the cloud cover. The moonlight, tempered by fast moving dark weather, shone intermittently high behind the treeline. We walked together into the blackness following the slim winding path. We shivered against the night. We were silent. We were together, though alone with the turmoil of our thoughts.

I lay in the police cell in the white paper forensic jump suit on the thin plastic mattress and listened hard to the hum of a near generator. My eyes travelled the spartan white walls and ceiling, the blue floor, the inside of the metal green painted cell door.
The metal hatch on the door clashed back.
'Gillen…?'

I didn't move from my place laid out on the thin blue cell mattress. I could see at least two of them outside, faces shielded by the door grate.

'We found the gun under the car.' Outside the door they stood. They waited for a response.

'The gun, a 12 bore shotgun illegally sawn-off, 'the gruff crackling voice continued. 'You were arrested hiding in the bin area of a block of flats close by. Two others have been arrested. John Jefferies. Ian Thompson…Do you know, Ian Thompson?'

I moved to the door. Someone banged the metal cell door further down the hall, shouted for attention through the side of it. I stood by the door frame, peered outside to see who was speaking.

'You're going to be charged, Gillen with conspiracy to rob. Firearms offences. Traffic offences.'

He stood in the plain clothes of a zipped wind sheeter and trousers. Tall with brown greying hair, bushy eyebrows, green searching eyes and a grizzled worn face. He continued in a rasping hiss, 'You're going to prison for a long, long time, Gillen. This time you…'

I looked at him, at the tight forced lips he spoke with.

'We know what you were doing at the bank near the Securicor van, 'Interrupted the other policeman. A tall man, with a large wide frame in a blue Barbour jacket his fierce features zeroed in on me. Clear blue eyes, set in a hard-chiselled face stared at me. His bald head with trimmed fair head hovered closer to the open hatch.

'My name is DI Sixsmith. I'm with SO8, Gillen, Scotland Yard Flying Squad. We know what you're up to, who your friends are. We know what you were planning today.'

'You've lost me. I was urinating by the bins and your lot picked me up. No evidence, a fucking liberty.' I stood back from the metal opening. They were trying to trap me. Engage me in conversation and trip me up.

'Anyway, I have no comment. My solicitor has advised me to answer no comment to all questions.' I moved to the back of the cell. Sat near the small toilet on the thin blue mattress.

The metal flap clunked with force as the policeman's face moved closer. It was the Detective Inspector He pushed his clear blue narrowing eyes to the metal cell opening.

'You think you're a big man with a big gun…. We're going to fix you, Gillen…You watch' The eyes lingered a moment as he looked in the cell. The open metal cell hatch was slammed closed with a finality. I heard them outside as they moved away from the cell door and walked up the shiny hall away from me.

෨

The children's home was shrouded in gathering darkness when the police car turned into the concrete car park at the top of the hill. The two buildings, one the main and another the annex were close together, split only by a small patch of grass and a slim winding path of block paving. Sharp anxiety was inside me turning in the pit of my stomach, my heart was beating fast and on my face was etched a frown of great apprehension. It had been two days since we had wrapped the stolen Cortina around the fence post. We had tried our best to stay free, taking bread from the back of bakers in the early hours and stealing little things to eat like chocolate to stave the hunger pains. We had wandered hanging round the shops and streets of London passing time and looking for opportunities. We had searched for hope. The evenings had brought their lonely icy cold and we had struggled, getting into any place we could to shelter our young bodies from the unforgiving freeze, our shivering limbs, numbed brains and chattering teeth.

Tony had his head down laden with dark thoughts as we exited the back of the police car. There were lights on in some windows, small lights over the building illuminating the pathway into the middle of the yard between the houses towards the main entrance doors...I remained silent thinking as we walked...We had tried to remain away with the freedom we had taken. It had been hard. We had had another adventure together and excitement and adversity. We had felt joy at our independence from this place and we had laughed because of it, even when we had nearly killed ourselves in the car crash, when we had felt the icy night wind torture our bodies, when the hunger had pulled at us and we had searched for shelter from the early hours, we had felt joy.

The brightly lit main doors loomed forebodingly as the two police officers motioned us forward. We felt the warmth hit us in the main reception as we stood on the grey carpet. Mr Cooper was with the police officers. He glared at us as he talked to them. Two other staff members were with them, old Miss Clark and young Mr Burrous. They glanced side wards as the police officers left.

ತಾ

...The man who was well known and thought about and was from the west part of Belfast had received the address of the children's home from a trusted contact in the old country. Far back, hidden by the covering bushes and tight tree line his week of daily vigils was paying off. He had done research and reconnaissance. on the children's home and the staff who ran it. He had come from his digs close by every day for hours at different times painting a picture in his mind and he had watched closely for signs of the boy. For days, at the different vantage points he had chosen, he had sat and waited and searched for signs of the boy.

From his hide, he had watched through the trees as the police car had parked and opened the doors for the children and escorted them to the main entrance, and he had seen at last the face of the boy he had trailed from Ireland. With his three fingered hand he dipped into the deep pocket of his jacket and looked at the white paper with the written words, addresses and descriptions. It was there, written in a scrawled hand that needed to rush. He looked at the top line. It was the name of the boy, Stephen Gillen.

❧

I saw Cooper. He approached, the other two behind him. Cooper's eye's flashed anger. The tight lips that were surrounded by a black beard said words dripped with sarcasm.

'Well, glad to have you back. Sure, you are happy to have arrived back safely. You've caused more trouble of course...'

He pushed us, me first then Tony. A forceful movement on the centre of the back that reinstated his supreme authority.

'Move. Get upstairs to your rooms!'

It was 2am. Through the silent corridors on the first floor, by the games room, the pool room. TV room to the left next door to it, past the main staff room. Along the hall, the dimmed lights adding to our mood of subdued silence. The staff were behind us as we were marched. I was aware of their heavy silence and tight faces, of Cooper's eagerness to lash out at any slight misdemeanour. Up the blue carpeted steps to the second-floor dorms, round the white walled corner corridor through a fire door and onto our main landing.

Tony was pushed into his room and the door slammed.

They walked me further down. I opened the white glossed wooden door to my room, into its blackness. Violently a hand pushed me in.

'Get in, Gillen. The fun's just starting. You try to leave here tonight and you will see what will happen to you.'

I turned in the shadowed space of my room towards the light. Towards the voice that growled, the faces that showed malice in the crack of the door. It was Cooper again, and he spat it out, 'You'll be seen in the morning, both of you...for your little outing. You'll be watched and lose everything for a month!'

The sarcastic psychopathic grin broke along his lips and face, 'It's great that your back safe as I was saying. You're nothing but trouble, Gillen. But whether you like it or not you were sent here by the local authority and this is where you'll stay...This is your home!'

The door slammed and I was left in silence. I stood there a moment, checking the squeaking of the hall to confirm they had indeed left the landing. It was a habit. Listening and checking the noises of the landing and of the movements of the building in the night to check for staff via footfall. I sat on my bed, a little low single with starched sheets and blankets. I had a window behind me that looked out into the woods at the back, a little cupboard, side locker with a chair and some books and comics. I looked at the book spines. My eyes had adjusted in the darkness with the light of the night that streamed from my closed window. One of the volumes was a geography book from where they schooled us in the back of the Care Home annex. I opened it, flicked the pages. I felt the sharp edges of the pages as they turned. There was an index and my finger moved down the glossy paper as I tracked the words.

'Countries of the world, 'whispered.

I was searching quicker, passing a map of the globe until I arrived at it. It was Ireland, the pictures showed me green pastures, fields. There was blue/grey mountain rock and high hills, loughs and deep rivers painted in riveting colours. I flicked the pages. Dublin, it said. It had the picture of a long winding river, the Liffey. The low drab buildings of a tight city bordered and collected around it, and there were small boats and a longing for scenes set in older times.

I listened. Silence. Only in the background was the faint hum of the generator that fed the kitchens. I moved back on the bed. I had kicked off my trainers and, cross legged, using the shadowy light from the small window, searched the pictures of the book eagerly with my eyes. I flicked the page. It talked about the free State, the Republic. Then there was the union jack and the end of gabled walls I remember it said Northern Ireland & The Troubles. I could not understand all the words but I knew the pictures. The grey, cold drab streets with the armoured vans, the checkpoints, the police, in the distance rolling hills, and grey streets that had flaming lit skies.

Compelled, I looked hard at the photos in the book. There were buses and cars being used as barricades. Groups of people throwing petrol bombs. There were graphic pictures of the soldiers, their guns. There were coffins being carried to a cemetery called Milltown, balaclavas and painted murals. I searched closer in the detail of the pictures as the crunching feeling gripped my insides, the deep feelings that stirred deep inside me were remembered and translated to a taunting vice-like pressure inside my head.... I held the book. I felt an icy chill spin down my back. There was a panic in me as I saw the face of the boy, was transported in time back to the scene of the bullets and the night fires and the calling for a mother who was not there.

Sweat was beginning to appear from the pores high on my hair line. 'Please, mother. God, mother please.'

The chill in my back was like a blow. I felt it, my little hands clawing in the cold damp mud as a distraction from what I witnessed. The lids of eyes tightening. The smell of cordite and petrol and burning in the air as petrol bombs spread fire and the tracer rounds riddled the evening...I was on the bed my breathing constricted by fear…I had dropped the book to the floor. I lay on my bed and put my arm across my eyes to hide from images that danced in my head. The sorrow was a wave over me and through me and the tears were in my eyes. The feeling, hard to control washed along me and I was in the corner of the bed, coiled in a protective ring, curled, screaming for warmth…

And I heard it in my mind, a soft loving voice that had a hint of mystery.

'…And the great *Monkey Puzzle Tree* stood tall and strong and resilient in the light of the fine morning. It was said they were magical, that they come from a faraway land that no one had ever visited or found. That the Gods in their great wisdom knew a place that was in dire need of their magic and their strength and their courageous ways so they were brought to us here to help and to watch and to add their magic to the soil of the land. It is said they can live to be a thousand years old and still be strong, that they are a beacon of hope where ever they live and that they can see and hear all people, places and things. But what is even more extraordinary is their unique way of knowing special people with special gifts like themselves…And at special times, and on magical occasions…'

My thundering emotions had calmed. The pictures and the face of the boy were lost. The dampness of my tears was slowing.

'Stephen, 'I heard it, a girl's quiet voice in my room. My senses were pulled back to the reality of the darkness, the window that spilled soft light from outside. My body was clammy. There were sniffles in my nose and I wiped the tears at my eyes.

'Stephen…?'

I focussed my eyes deeper into the space by the door. She stood there.

A short shadow in a light pink dressing gown tied with a belt at the waist, fair hair falling and tangled haphazardly at her shoulders, eyes that blinked in the darkness and a little voice that had enquired.

'Debbie?

'Yes, Stephen it's me,' She was at my bed, in from the shadows and I saw her cheeky curved wide smile. She had smashed again the little round glass of the fire door that separated the girl's rooms from the boys. 'Are you ok. God, I missed you, we were all worried. Where did you go?' On the bed, she sat and her face had the brightness of longing and the beginning of questions. 'We thought you were really in trouble. you and Tony were not coming back? Cooper said the police was all out looking for you and you were going to prison. I said you were too young to go to prison. He laughed, he said we were all going to prison here...he'

I had my arm around her shoulder. My voice calmed her.

'We're fine. We're back right. I'm here'

'But you have to go to court, you...?'

'It will be fine,' My heart was recovering. Now it re-stretched, a warm sorrowful experience, as I saw her face crumble. Debbie, a leading girl in the home, herself only fourteen was prominent and protective towards the other kids. I had watched her once fight injustice in this place like me biting and scratching and pulling, and she would try to give as good as she got. The silence of the night was around us. We listened a moment checking for noise disturbance. Whispering she continued,' I don't want you to go, Stephen. We are all a family now. Little Anabelle was so thankful for what you done for her in the dining hall. But you must not get in trouble she says.'

I felt her little body close by. I could smell the shampoo in her hair and see the light in her eyes, the concern at her mouth. I looked into her face a moment. I didn't know what to say. I didn't want to leave the family I had made here. It was terrible, it was violent, cold. It was all of these things, but there was a togetherness at moments like this.

I thought of my upcoming court case. It was just after my fourteenth birthday. The juvenile court had been adamant in its decision last time I was there. There had been a difference in their manner, in the way they looked at me and how efficiently things had been shuffled back. I had a premonition of trouble then. It returned, a deep stab in my solar plexus and in the centre of my forehead. We sat, in the shadows. She had my hand in hers and I was glad of the warmth, that we were together a moment.

…I thought of Debbie. I thought of Annabelle the little girl who had problems and the other children who had emotional baggage and behavioural issues. I thought about my overwhelming anger. I thought of Cooper and the people who were controlling my life and I wondered if when I went to court just after my fourteenth birthday in two weeks if they would send me to prison for the first time.

Chapter 5
Serious Crime & Prison

The blue flashing lights and screaming sirens of the police escort exploded into the busy early morning air of the city of London as the motorcade navigated quickly the tight streets.

The white level 2 escort transportation van that held the dangerous prisoners was long and bomb proof with distinguishing think black numbers on the roof and a thick bright orange stripe along its side so it could be watched and continuously observed from the ground and air.

Police snipers from the vantage points across the road on the top of buildings watched as the four armed police vehicles and two lead police motorcycles created a floating box manoeuvre and sealed the roads and access at every side as the van as it disappeared into the downward tunnel to the Old Bailey.

We had started earlier in the day from the high security Unit in Brixton Prison, South London. We had been searched in the sterile area in the prison within a prison, taken through the air-lock doors and guided by a bolstered prison staff and barking dogs into the van which had pulled tight into the side yard. The van had joined the police escort as it left the prison gates and it had not stopped at traffic lights, just roared and screamed through the early morning traffic. My mind was travelling. The attempted robbery that had put me here. The ramming of our car from behind to the member of the public in front of the Securicor van. The car chase. The city of London. The cells at Snowhill. DI

Sixsmith and the warning of his cold voice through a metal grate in the green cell door.

Then, inside the van, opened in my mind. It was three weeks ago and I saw It clearly. Could smell the freshness and the crisp air and could hear the softness of the conversation in my ear and the snap of the young horse as its legs ran…

…We were together… and we watched the young fieriness of the young black foal run in the paddock. I could visualise it as my eyes closed against the eagerness of the police motorcade and the stabbing of the sirens surrounding me.

Our arms were draped over the wooden frame of the outer ring and in the steady weather of a fair and level afternoon we talked quietly. Happily, like a father and son as we studied the progress of the young wild horse. Showing its youth and immaturity it ran and pulled and tugged on the rope around its neck testing the man who held it. Near the centre of the circular training paddock, the man who skilfully worked the rope stuck hard his heel into the soft ground to facilitate the good positioning he needed, the proper leverage against the pull of the horse.

A little and quick gazelle, the young foal shook its sleek, silky black main, swung the wet blackness of its nose. It opened wide hazel eyes, dipped its head with strength, breath snorting finely as it was bucked and ran.

He stood resting on the wooden frame of the paddock, relaxed beside. A big fat man with slight deep and rich dark hair, a big name and a specialised experience of life, great wealth and influence. A fighting man known far and wide. A gypsy from the old school who was head of a highly respected family.

'His father was a great race horse, 'he said in a soft voice as he watched the horse stop and steady its self a moment.

'We have great hopes for him just the same. But he sweats out a bit early. This is how we train them, Stephen.'

I was silent but felt compelled in the company of this man to speak.' They're beautiful. What an animal. Really something,' I said.

He smiled. A genuine soft smile like that to a young son who was wet behind the ears. I knew behind the smile was a wide, striking cunning and knowing. A hard upbringing that had forged and moulded and kicked and polished him toward the finished article that now stood before me. He moved again with an unassuming manner and objective measured eyes.

We turned. We said goodbye to the trainer. We strolled to the black Mercedes sports we had arrived in. I had travelled down the night before with his son James who was a professional boxer and a close friend of mine and I had stayed the night at their family home in Newmarket. I had been welcomed in the house with a unique family that was fierce and wise with no airs and graces but active and I was treated like one of the family...

ॐ

The raging sirens woke me. The police and the van manoeuvred through an obstacle in the traffic lanes.

I sat on the plastic box that was my seat. Inside the van, in my cage, a claustrophobic space that you could just about stand in, I watched the police escort outside from my tinted window. I had a splitting headache as the sirens of the screaming motorcade were worse inside the van. A splitting, relentless turning and vibrating screech that affected the heart and soul, hammered the head. I pushed back the bright yellow and green of the prison jump suit I was being transported in revealing my watch. The Black and gold round face of the IWC logo shone and glinted. As a category A prisoner, I would only be given my pressed blue suit, white shirt and tie when safely inside the building.

A reminder, my watch, I realised, of finer things and happier moments in the torrent of a hells storm.

Twenty minutes, I thought…It had taken us twenty minutes from Brixton to the City of London. A bloody miracle. I sighed. A long gasping inhaling sound that helped release the tight muscles in my neck and shoulders. The image played, dissipated. The young foal, its playful jumping, the brightness of the day I had spent in Newmarket not three weeks before…was gone. My heart crashed. Hitting waves of despair, it ebbed like a withdrawing ocean on the sand and seashells or regret and longing.

The light of the outside world left us, as we drove down into the deep recesses of the building.

At the bottom of the enclosed tunnel the armoured Category A van came to a grinding halt in the sheltered light as the massive turntable twisted the whole vehicle around towards where we would be walked to the cells.

The grudging dim lights spoke greyness and doom. The dark blue uniforms of the prison officer that waited for the handover. The worn dirty grey of the concrete all around us. The keys that swung and hung and were handled on long key chains. I watched and heard it all. Inside the prison jumpsuit I wore my heart was heavy. My body ached with stress and anxiety. My body was weaker with the terrible diet and sleepless nights. There were three of us in the van. An IRA prisoner linked to bombings and a Colombian drug smuggler arrested with a ton and a half of cocaine linked to a cartel.

From inside the van through the little white metal grate on the door I watched them shuffle past. They opened my door and I felt the gratitude of my legs and my body to stretch and move and my feet as my black shoes hit the concrete of the concourse outside. The dim aura of old concrete, ancient history and grim turbulence clasped around me as I walked. Up the steps into a holding cell. Then it was up a set of stairs, through more metal sets of barred gates on my way to the Category A Suite. The sound of keys, banging metal doors, shouts and talking accompanied me. The stale smell of the old building, a damp foreboding nausea attack that mixed architecture, paperwork, rancid food and metal, hit my senses filling me with dread.

In the western part of the City of London, opened in February in 1907 and designed by E W Mountford the Central Criminal Court, also known as the Old Bailey or Justice Hall, was built on the site of the infamous Newgate Prison and over the centuries had been periodically remodelled.

… The Cat A suite comprised of six cells. Mostly single cells, with extra officers and two extra metal gates on either side of a small tight area closer to the main most prominent and infamous high security courtrooms in the massive building. The area was the most secure part of the Central Criminal Court. The cell door closed behind me. I was in a slightly bigger cell that could hold six people. Two people sat on the long wooden bench at the back of a small claustrophobic space. I stood, exchanged nods with my cell mates, put the see-through plastic bag that held my depositions, strategy notes and defence correspondence on the bench. I attempted to rub the tiredness from my eyes, my nostrils filled with the damp decay of the building. There was graffiti all over the walls, names and signs and slogans scratched and scrawled and drawn. I viewed the filthy pale-yellow walls of the cell, the ceiling and a depressing, painful sigh scattered the energy inside me.

Detective Inspector Albert Sixsmith and Detective Sergeant David Truman walked briskly down the corridor. The building, a drab discreet four storey grey- windowed monolith imposed upon a busy back street in East London, it comprised twenty-five officers of the Specialist Crime Directorate 7, S08 Scotland Yard Flying Squad, and was one of the four similar units that were positioned to police east, north, south and west London to combat armed robbery, Organised Crime and the gangster problem.

A white long, tight busy corridor with windows stretching to the left matching the crispness of the mid-morning.

DS Truman, matched his Detective Inspectors quickening pace. A short man with a lazy eye, short black curly hair and a strong pitted expression, he buttoned his blue Barbour as he pressed forward.

'We're hearing intelligence from Bethnal Green and Bow, Guv.,' he said. 'It's been checked with a few of our informants…A new firm, showing lots of money. The usual, there's a gang of them. Well known scallywags in the area, everyone's scared of them. New nutters on the block apparently. Didn't have big league money. Originally from south London. Ages range from 20/21 to 30…Now they're driving round in top of the range Mercs, buying businesses, coming up in the world. Don't work. Haven't done a day's work between them it seems…Interesting crowd. Could be a fit for the Security Van hijacking last week by the docklands?'

DI Sixsmith grunted. A deep chesty sound that commanded authority and showed boredom. He had been a wrestler when he was younger and growing up in Glasgow never showed his real feelings, always sent people the wrong way and set traps so that they should reveal and speak more.

He said, '…Were talking about the Robbery last week Where they hijacked the van driver from his home, drove him round at gun point threatening him with pictures of his wife at work…the one where they used black tape to attach a bug on his ankle and then sent him transfixed with instructions to say nothing till he had the van on the road?"

'Yes, Sir. The one where they listened to the crew, told him not to say nothing to them till they were on the road. Then a motorbike appeared in the traffic and they were instructed to follow it. The van was escorted to a quiet warehouse by the docklands where four other gang members waited and they cleared a Securicor van of three hundred and eight five thousand pounds of cash…Gov. We'.

'Quite a sophisticated robbery then… Do we have anything more, DS Truman? Something to collaborate?' He powered forward.

Sixsmith took his job, his profile very seriously. He thought of it a compliment that the organised criminals he pursued thought him a bastard, an ogre. He wanted to hunt them down, infiltrate their dreams with the nightmares they were bestowing on other people. "An eye for an eye, he mumbled.
'Sorry, Sir, 'Truman stuck tight, like a trained dog to its master.
'An eye for?'
'You know exactly what I mean! Don't chew it. The ends justifies the means, Truman. We're in a war here. They're on the back foot, and I intend pushing them into the sea, and to the bottom of it…!'
'Of course, Gov. Shall I put surveillance on them…?'
Sixsmith could see the swinging grey double doors at the end of the hall. They were trying to hang him out for the vultures.

He considered his options.

The Flying squad originally formed on an experimental basis by Detective Chief Inspector Fredrick Wensley way back in 1919, had been plagued by shouts of foul play and corruption. They hit the wooden grey doors at the end of the next corridor.

They waited for him, he knew, beyond the heavy chestnut doors at the end. His team, ready for the de-brief of what needed to be done next. He thought of the whispers he had been hearing. Warnings of his squad being investigated for their unconventional methods. Threats of the 'ghost squad', Scotland yard's internal police investigative unit being interested in a few cases.

He sighed, it was deep inside him and if he was honest twinged with the slight fear of discovery. It was not long past the 1977 bribery and corruption scandal that saw Detective Chief

Superintend Kenneth Drury imprisoned for eight years.

The noise of the typist and the offices was denser now, fading. The noise of the typewriters, the office girls laughing, paper being shifted.

He turned to DS Truman.

'Keep all our records tight, the surveillance logs succinct, ok? As always, I don't want any holes in any of our cases, our work…about this little firm now around east London, do we have names?'

Ds Truman stood a moment, his lazy eye twisting his features, his mouth turning and his lips thinning tightly. He said, 'A few, Gov. Couple of them are brothers. Others may know each other from school and prison it seems. One name that's come up is Stephen something G, another Con from South of the water. We've been getting reports about him. Two up and coming nutters. Hangs around with the south London lot too were hearing. The Bermondsey boys from the blue…That Bermondsey triangle thing.

DI Sixsmith ears picked up. The notorious Bermondsey triangle, he thought. Termed so by the flying squad because it was suspected to harbour more of London's top-drawer and elite armed robbers in that square mile than the rest of London put together.

He could again feel the thrill of the chase in him. The ambush trap to catch wolves. The snare that was layered and waited for and tightened and structured so that eagles could fly into a net. He hit the doors and was welcomed with the noise of the team.

He said, 'Ok. Great. Let's put a team on them and see what this lot are up to…'

☙

'...It is good that you have your accompanying adult and guardian with you from the Care home representing the Local authority, Master Gillen for what we are about to say to you...'

There were three of them. A man with horn rimmed glasses and two stern looking women magistrates on either side of him. They had heard the charges against me. They had looked shocked and stern and angry and business like. They had huddled for what seemed ages whispering and toing and froing and deliberating and had stopped to focus on me tidying the papers in front of them with a cold-eyed precision.

I sat in a chair in the small room in the middle of two long tables either side of me. An old court room in Hertfordshire with much dark stained wood on the walls and floors and parts of celling. A dusty environment, with unkempt heavy blue curtains at stained windows. The dank smell of disinfectant filled my nostrils and an impending doom clutched my insides in a prickly piercing grip.

They were on the long table at the bottom stretched along the two others either side of me. 'Stand up, Master Gillen...We have looked in-depth at these charges...'

The paper was in his hand as he looked down at it, 'Taking and Driving Away without consent. Theft, criminal damage. There are many counts which we have taken into consideration. We must say at this point, we feel much has been tried with you. Everything in the way of correcting your behaviour thus far has failed. You have consistently shown a disregard for the law, the public and the Local authority which has guardianship of you. You being already under a care order...'

I stood there, shoulders dropped and bowed, the weight of expectation churning in me, my hands behind my back fiddling in my anxiousness. I had turned fourteen a week previous. A small boy for my age, I thought, now loose and out at sea without a paddle or a star to follow home as there was no home. There was a brave mask on the crumbling emotion cascading around inside me. I tried desperately to stem my tearful eyes as I continued listening.

'…Under these conditions we have a clear responsibility to the protection of the public and the rule of law. You are now fourteen and therefore can be sent to a young offender Detention Centre and held in custody. We feel that a detention order of this kind in this case is justified. We therefore take into consideration all the charges we have been asked to and will proceed on the others on which you be sentenced on today…'

My hands tightened into a clenched fist. My breathing slowed, ears straining, stomach tumbling down the hill of suspense and overcoming apprehension. Fear was cartwheeling in me. I could feel a lightness in my limbs, a dryness in my throat. Eyes widening, my brain was navigating a fast-approaching internal filled panic. My anxiety heightened, throat clenched.

'We have tried, Master Gillen. All of the people charged with your care have tried. Us included…'

He stopped a moment. A cliff hanger of a pause that stretched too long with menace and hung too high with silence upon the room and in front of me.

'…It is therefore our collective decision, and the decision of this court that it has to be a custodial sentence at this point. We sentence you to eight weeks in Detention Centre. So, you will go now and be taken from this court to your place of custody where you will serve your sentence…We would hope this would be the last time we see you here, Master Gillen…'

The burly short sleeved white shirts of the two jailers were at my sides. They held my elbows, turned me and cuffed me. I was out toward the doors and heading to cells.

Behind me they continued in a raised sharp final voice, 'We also very much hope that this may serve as the needed deterrent to stop you committing further of these offences…!'

The accompanying social worker from Woodside who had taken me to court, a kindly man with bushy brown beard and casual clothes bounced beside me as I was escorted. His face tried to make a terrible time much better.

'Sorry to hear about this, Stephen. Don't worry, it'll soon be over.'

I was through the door and I saw him but couldn't channel the fractured emotions accelerating inside me into anything meaningful. His face was disappearing behind the closing heavy wooden doors.

'I'll handle everything, Stephen...I'

The doom filled me. I had entered a state of melt down in my present levels of anxiety. Around the corner, an echolike place of filthy, silky cream walls. Through two sets of old worn iron barred gates. They marched me, faces unmoving, our footsteps in my head, panic fear in my stomach, moving water in my eyes.

The cell door closed behind me. A reverberating silence forced through me. I looked at the green closed cell door. It was a milestone, I knew that. I was going where I had never gone before, and all I could see, feel, experience, smell and hear – was the gripping fear.

The morning of my release had swept in before I knew it and all I could think was of my beautiful boy Terry. As I had sat in my cell in the high security prison in Brixton, the most secure prison unit in the UK, I had turned inside me the enormous knowledge of having a child. As I had travelled back and forth to the old Bailey and the Category A Suite and the high drama of my court case it had filled me. I had been aware of the change within me, the pulling responsibility, the pensive joy. A new father. It was new season in my life.

I was in the air lock area between the two massive metal front gates of the Prison. The bullet proof windows of the gate house were to my left. There was a metal drawer where escorts coming in and out of the prison would leave & pick up their keys, a row of metal grey lockers. Over me was a big mirror on the high concrete celling to check there were no prisoners clinging to the top of vans, lorries or other vehicles. It was a sterile area where a generator hummed.

I had been here like this too many times, I recalled as I watched the massive grey front gate slide open. In front, the beginning lightness of a fresh morning streamed in. The noise of birds, traffic in the car park, the hustle and bustle of the outside world. I griped the see-through prison bag in my hand tighter. I had seven days. In front of me was the home leave I had been given to see a baby boy just born who was beautiful and gorgeous. Six months old having been born in the London Hospital Whitechapel.

I walked into the light of the morning remembering the journey that had brought me to this point. The spinning car. Being rammed beside the Securicor van. The police chase and arrest. Dirty cells and depression in the city of London, the high Security Unit in Brixton, The Old Bailey. Screaming armed police escorts, headaches and regrets and worry and legal meetings and court battles fighting for my life. The gates had pulled completely open. Fresh air and stoic brightness beckoned. I breathed in deeply. A grateful, hopeful movement that entered my lungs and brain travelling deep into the centre of me revitalising a freshness in my core.

I stood. Alone. A moment encapsulated in time, the air and the birdsong floating in the morning. Amazing it was, to me the stark contrast of my existence, I thought. No hammering sirens here, the rush of armed police escorts. No low flying helicopters, high security or smirking flying squad, no rattling of silver keys. I was filled with the hope again of a beautiful future. A good energy. That was freeing and non-combative and joyous and open, one which built and created didn't pull-down and destroy. A positive place of good people, places and things.

I cast my mind back to the last fourteen months. I had gripped unsteadily as they had rocked and kicked me through the higher end of the judicial system. I had strategized good fortune at my Old Bailey trail beating a conspiracy to rob charge. My lighter punishment of two and a half years for prosession of a firearm was still a shock. I had already served nine months on remand and the low sentence had demanded they remove my high security Category status. B Category then C had followed seamlessly. I had navigated fourteen months of this rollercoaster ride and a big difference had been the baby boy who waited outside.

'There he is! The man himself' It was him. Callum Draper, a wide smile shining out to the world, eyes glinting. In grey trousers a crisp white shirt and blue cashmere jumper. Immaculate he had his arms stretched out fingers beckoning. He shook the bottle of champagne, cracked its cork into the air.

'Great to see you bruv. If I don't see you through the week I'll see you through the window. Now I'll need to ask you a few security questions, make sure it's you?'

The bubbles shot from the bottle. He was in stiches of laughter and the strength of it was splitting his face in a wide-open brightness. He continued,' It's fuckin home time.'
We embraced. A brotherly feeling that was warm and all arms and shoulders and backs and comforting.

The glint was at the side of his brown eyes. A smile lifted, curled. 'Great to have you home, Steve'. He had the glasses from the back of the car and with them on the concrete ground of the stoned carpark poured us both a tall glass.

It was behind me. Wayland Prison, its long stretching corridors, camp-like dorms, it's strange people and energies and regime. With a final metal clunk, the prison gates closed far back behind me.

'God, it's good to be home. Amazing. If I can't see you in the spring I'll see you through the mattress.' It was one of our old sayings and he loved it and we were bent double together in laughter and we remembered.

'Can't wait to see my boy, I added. 'Imagine the little thing'. We opened the door to the black Mercedes. We sat a moment with the drinks at our lips. We would have a few hours' drive to London.

'…He's beautiful, a real beautiful boy. A blinder'. I said and the feel of his little fingers were in mine. He stood and jumped and bounced on unsteady legs and stood on my feet tall in front of my face and his smile melted me. My first born. Terry.

Behind, his grandfather, Christopher who had brought him and the social worker who had facilitated the meeting smiled. Christopher, a good man who was a black cab driver from the Roman Road was unsure and guarded and watched with no judgement, hopeful. The woman case worker had her hands resting on her lap.

'   Our wish is you can be a father too, Terry, Stephen under supervised conditions at first.'

My focus was on the miracle that jumped in front of me. The soft new born skin of a life and the face that resembled mine. The chiselled chin, intense features. The same hazel all-knowing eyes that danced and jumped and engaged and smiled and seduced. His little hands gripped my fingers, feet kicked and sprung and twisted. A mesmerising bonding smile linked us. Love at first sight.

The case worker continued,' We hope this can be relaxed as we go on and more and easier visiting rights can be arranged.' I said,' I do hope so. I have great plans for a wonderful future ahead. I'm studying an OU business degree in prison…'

She cut in, 'you have seven days home leave and are due for release in three months is that right?'

'Yes'. Again measured tones, but inside I beamed.

'Ok, then we can hope to arrange something for then maybe.' She was up and her indication was the baby should be handed back to his grandfather and it had gone great but the two hours were up and it was her remit to be a stickler for time and her fingers were rattling the handle of the door. A reassuring tight smile streaming across the lines on her face.

'I'll see you soon, Terry ok! See you soon boy,' Our eyes were aligned then. A moment of knowing reserved for people of the same bloodline. Soft kisses on cotton wool skin, excited eyes, warm cuddles, a tight hug that lingered. It was terrible to go. The door was open and the sign was to go through it. I left, my teeth clenched in frustration. A stab of longing in my heart and welling tears in my eyes.

The quietness of the grey street over the back of Vallance road hit me. I stood outside the social service building in Underwood road Bethnal Green.

'Alright?'

My head turned to adjust from my thoughts.

Through the wound down car passenger window, in the black Mercedes across the road, it was Callum who had been waiting for me. I buckled my seat belt. The car pulled easily into the slow-moving traffic in Vallance road. We went under the overhead past the old place where the Kray Twins were brought up, into Bethnal Green road.

A right and, 'Glad that went ok, Steve. They're another load of spies them people,' Callum spoke. He tipped the ash from his fag out the window adding, 'Things are proper paranoid out here, Steven I'm telling ya. They're all over us. I know they're there the other people. We'll go to my gaff. We bought all the police passwords for their frequencies. Bow Road is Hotel Tango Two.

I've got the Tandy's receiver on indoors all the time. Been some interesting conversation between 'em let me tell you...'

The car accelerated forward in the traffic. The busy shops of Bethnal Green road slipping by us to either side. The market stall, pubs, Kelly's the pie and mash shop, a throng of people on the pavements that walked and jostled and weaved and pressed business.

'I've got your money at home, Steve. Sorry you have to come home to this madness'.

I lit a cigarette, inhaled. The smoke making me feel better. 'They still having that work? what's about? Callum...Even though I'm just out I could do with a few quid. Got this baby now, Callum.' He listened. Threw his cigarette out the window into the roadway. We were down in Bow at the back of Roman Road. He was getting ready to turn the car.

He told me to listen.

I was told there were bits about. To take it easy.

We were at the back of St Stephen's Road. The garages where a bike was hidden to be used and bullets were made was pointed out. A small enclave of green doors that housed six small garages either side of a concreted entrance.

There was too much activity. We would need to be doubly aware. It was said to me. Do anti-surveillance. There were strange things, couldn't put a finger on it. Strange feelings and movements and it was making everyone paranoid. I was not to worry. I was home. I was with family. Blood was thicker than water, right. I was not to think on it twice. Everything was sorted. People couldn't wait to meet me. Take a few days, but be vigilant to the people, places and movements around me as there was something big coming up...

We parked the car by the small back street roundabout and took the concrete stairs to the third floor where we stopped a while on the slim tight passage way to the flat looking at the surrounding street, the places of cover, vantage points of interest and ways of entrance and exit for traffic.

'…whiskey tango we have two IC ones at the end of Broadway tampering with a car. Other youths are attending the scene, copy.'

The radio receiver crackled in the corner. A walk talkie looking device it had two black buttons on the top for the fine tuning of frequencies that the buttons on the front had pulled in from the air.

We were in Callum's front room. A clean expensive spread of new pale grey carpets, crisp cream décor and matching settee, chairs and furniture. Classic professionally taken pictures, graced the walls. Callum with his daughter May and son Mark. A family pose of him, and his wife Dawn, Another of May in black and white. Colour photos of the wedding. Old photos of his much-missed aunt Libby.

I sat in the chair and looked at the silent TV that played and my mind was alive with pictures of the baby. My son with the vulnerable eyes, the jumping legs and the wide grin.

'Here, that's what I was keeping for you,' He threw it, the plastic bag with ten thousand pounds in used bank notes. 'This will keep you going right?'

More of a question, but he was at the radio receiver and he turned it up. His hand was up to quieten me and he listened. 'Shhh…I just heard something?'

'…Over, over.'

Two voices, sharp, pointed, drilling an exchange on a line that was meant to be secure but crackled with not a full clear background.

'…Yes, over?'

'Target one and target four sighted. In flat. Target one with another suspect. Request hard stop for tango bravo Charlie. Known associate. Request execute warrant for questioning?'

Another voice barked.

'Denied! Charlie two, over? Denied. Repeat Charlie Two…This is a sophisticated Divisional operation. Repeat this is a separate Divisional operation involved to secure targets in Operation Nemesis. Not to be stopped. Declined to be hard stop, Repeat.

We stood there, our ears straining for more, incredulous. Breathing thinning, eyes wide. Our heads were close to the cabinet where the receiver rested. We listened closer. In the back ground of the police conversation we could hear the clatter of a train as it passed, the passage of its journey covering tracks. We looked at each other, eyes questioning. We knew what we were hearing. We understood the seriousness of what was being discussed. We were aware that a hard stop was the barricading ambush of armed police on suspects suspected of being involved with or carrying firearms as they were mobile in their vehicles. We had the verified code word for Bow Road Police Station, Hotel Tango Two. We had the receiver to listen to police frequencies. Harder, we strained as the exchange continued.

'…Charlie two asking permission to close in further on targets.'

We listened intently. In the background, behind the voices we could make out the noise of the train going on its journey.
We rushed to the balcony and looked out into east London, into the grey smog filled afternoon air. Our hands were on the black metal of the balcony. They tightened into the metal as we stood rooted to the spot.

We watched. We saw it and we knew. Just across from us not two hundred meters away the train crossed. Hammering across the tracks the sound of it cut through our ears matching the rattle it made on the Tandy receiver. We looked at each other. We both knew we were thinking the same thoughts.

Chapter 6
The Art of Armed Robbery

...The urban male fox stopped in the shadows a moment to gather its senses. In a bust of movement, sleek and nimble it ran hurriedly on the sure ground it knew well in the fixed waning moonlight. Using shadow cover and melting into its surroundings it manipulated with the twisting turns of its body and speed the streaking light it would pass through. Round the side of flats, along the road and into the tree line of the park, it thought of the vixen back in the den, of the hunt and the best places to catch prey.

The three men of the armed robbery team kept back from the open door of the garage. They inspected the firearms, the ammunition, the bugging equipment. The day before a motorbike a Ducati 750cc had already been taken for a good run and revved and blasted and tested. It would soon be time. The four men of the team had split the day before after a last meeting in the changing rooms of a swimming pool. Aware of the possibility of police activity they had met only three times altogether in the last three months. The phones they communicated with were throw-away pay-as-you-go and had been used only to communicate together. They had been destroyed, thrown in an east London canal and had been replaced with new ones. There were four men in the team. They knew well their allocated roles. Roles include monitoring police movements and listening to the radio receiver, placing the bug, driving the vehicles and emptying the Securicor vans, one to monitor police movements, three to kidnap the driver and place the bug, one to drive the bike and one to prepare everything in front as the team pulled the trap together.

The three men in the garage huddled close and whispered in hushed tones, the smell of oil and petrol filling their senses.

One had the bug in the palm of his hand. A two-inch round black box with a tiny aerial, he held it up in the shadowy light.

'Don't forget, 'he said. A cutting clear rasping voice. 'The fear of god in him, then calm him down. Tape it to the lower part of his ankle. Fix it tight with the aerial pointing upwards. Make sure it's covered from the eye by his trousers and socks. We don't want anyone seeing it, especially the crew....and we need to keep nice and close to the van when it's out on the road. When we're back in the traffic, the receiver has a range of two miles.'

They nodded. They knew. Their eyes were steely now as they thought of what was coming. The bike rider put on his black balaclava and blue/black helmet, kickstarted the motorbike, backed it out of the garage into the streaking yellow moonlight darkness. He turned it now and nodded. A sharp figure that held tight to the bike that he manoeuvred with ease and confidence.

...The other two men stood. They watched in the blackness, in the shadows and one noticed briefly the darting fox. It was gone again, out into the darkened roadway, invisible. The Motorbikes' engine roared. The rider kicked it into gear, pulled the throttle back. They followed it with their eyes. One fast bursting movement into the night that settled and found its rhythm. The coldness of the night closed around them. They could see the motorbike no more. It had disappeared.

Detective Inspector Albert Sixsmith was on the top floor of the high carpark and talking on the radio. He looked out over the London skyline into the busy tight street of north London below him.

He listened, '...Yes, Gov we feel sure today is the day. We

are watching three of the targets. We have trackers on the cars of two others. The team was seen to meet. They were at the garage last night in Hoxton…the bike was moved and is mobile…'

His hard features clenched slightly. A look of painful thought and concentration.

He said, sharp, 'OK…don't lose them. Today will be the day we put a stop to this operation. Two years on this.' He lifted his nose to the air, felt the quick wind of the car parks heights on his cheeks and tussling his hair. He could always feel it when the defining moment drew close, he thought.

'Yes. Good work. Be vigilant. Today we put an end to this lot.'

The walkie talkie was at his side. Below him London hummed with activity. He thought of the long nights with no dinner tracking the armed robbers on his patch. The need and demands from his wife and family for time and for normality for a different feeling and worry and stress that was not the job. At fifty-seven his worry was a daughter at university who struggled at graphic design, a son who worked too late at his office and a wife that cold shouldered him. His passion and focus were with the work. It was all consuming the work of thief catching. He had toiled with his team morning noon and night on this one.

They had waited and pushed and set traps and bait to be followed. They had struggled. They had got little breaks. They had come close and they had batted out. This gang were a little different. More sophisticated than usual. Like bats in caves they had an uncanny way of avoiding the attractive traps he had laid out in front of them. Big wide clear ponds with no fish and many hanging fruits, but no horses had strayed from the herd to drink. They were still reaching their prime, he knew that. Not top of the pile in London's division of infamy and expertise but they were well up at the high end of it. They could and had made mistakes. But they were learning quickly, and they learned well. He knew they would keep going and not stop. He felt that if they were not apprehended they might even evade capture. There was a lot at stake.

He felt the vastness of the open blue even sky above him. Behind him he saw at a quick glance was another Detective in his parked unmarked grey Audi. He understood London could have a vastness like the sky above him for people like these with influential friends and money and resources. They were on a roll. Five Armoured Securicor money vans had been hijacked and cleared of the notes they carried. The robbers had taken over a million pounds in cash already, most of it untraceable.

He grunted unhealthily to himself. A guttural sound that was deep inside his chest. He had gone personally to speak to and interview the drivers and crew on the attacked vans. He had witnessed first-hand the terror of the robberies on the guards faces as they recounted how the attacks had been planned and executed. The panic of danger to them. The conflict of interests they had had to negotiate as they took their colleagues out into danger and told them of the trouble they were in. That a bug was amongst them and it listened to every word spoken. That he had carried the fear but could not say anything, could not warn them of the mortal threat, only drive everyone to a robbery team that waited.

The clearness of the air was drawn deep down in his lungs. He stifled the instinct to cough.

DI Sixsmith, had a checklist in his mind.

Methodically and mentally he ticked it. The tracker placed on the cars that they had replaced one night with the same model then returned with listening equipment and long-range trackers. The directional listening equipment that had listened across restaurants and clubs and parks and carparks collecting information... The photographs. Needed for evidence. Taken singly and of suspects together and of meetings and gatherings. From roof-tops, cars and vans and black cabs and parked lorries both stationary and moving. They had used a wide range of specialist equipment.

This gang was very tech-minded and the anti-surveillance incorporated had been of the highest level.

The list in his head was complete. He had split up his team to close the trap. Some watched safe houses, potential van targets and the main entrances of main Securicor sorting offices. Others followed the trackers and spun the web of observation that had been stretched and amended and tweaked and forged in the street below him. A spider, in the middle of the vast intricate web that he spun, he felt the mixed feelings he always felt at this time. The excitement of pulling a rope that was tightening. Of enticing in wolves to eat and be eaten. An anxious fear that was the apprehension of missing a target. It was there. Twisting, burning a wave inside him and forcing more diligence. He glanced again below at the busy streets. He looked at the front of the main Securicor counting house. It opened, another blue van appeared, turned, entered the fast-moving traffic.

Ants, moving he thought. With a direction and a purpose and a location…

But some would be stopped en route on a day that they had not seen coming. The wind blew now, twisting and throwing his hair. He put on his black police baseball cap. It was chequered at the front, the mark of the flying squad.

He had moved back from the ledge, but he still studied the moving traffic. He thought of the Armed Robbery team and what they knew about them. They had done well, he thought. They were at last four nil up. But this would be their undoing. His operational baseball cap had thwarted the changing wind but it still attacked his forehead, the sides of his face and circled his ears. He stared along the London skyline, across the top of buildings. He muttered, quietly only to himself in the flaring wind, 'they need to be lucky all the time…We only have to be lucky once.'

'Come on get yourselves together, and I want the edge of your clothes pack to be squared properly. Those bed-packs up in the dorm are fuckin' horrendous,' the sharp cutting voice of the prison officer barked.

☙

My first time in prison, a slight skinny fourteen and, like the rest of the inmate children in the changing room hurried to my task of folding my kit exactly to the size as one of the blue tiles on the floor. We were in a long slim room; the recess was where the violence was the worst. A long strip of sinks split a room that had open dark grey lockers holding our prison clothing. The voice continued barking orders. I looked around me. A collection of small immature unformed bodies, I thought. In all stages of undress, tall, gangly, short, chubby, long legs, white and black skin colours and arms and out of shape looks on their faces.

The officers were shouting at a kid with black hair. Unperturbed he went back to his task of lacing his boots and buckling the gaiters around his ankles. Their rage quickened. I watched the boy as they pushed, the violence in their voice at him. He was short for his age but had a spark about him. A slim, long grey streak of grey hair travelled at the side of pitch-black hair. I had not slept a wink. Our dorm was thirty beds side by side with thin mattresses which had starched white sheets and one thin wool green blanket. The nights were freezing with inmates tossing, turning. Children with anxiety from being away from their families and what they knew. Others with paralysing fear at their predicament. Some were more adaptable and would play the joker and laugh and snigger and throw buttons at the night man who stood at his box in the dorm all night watching us.

There was a fight somewhere at the back. I saw the white boy with a red face and terror in his eyes. The other boys who were black and who had ganged up on him.

'You lot at the back! Get back in line!' It was the worst one. Tall, ridged like, with hands tightly behind his back and a peaked cap, eyes that glared and the bright disfigurement of a red burn half the way down his face and neck.

'Now you will do what you are told,' his voice was a sergeant major's scream. A noise that reverberated in my ears, travelled hallways and corridors.

'Attention,' we all pulled our bodies in, erect. Then behind me I heard it.

'Having a bloody laugh him. Who said we were to join the army camp and play soldiers anyway'?

I turned to the voice. It was the boy from earlier, a smile splitting his cheeks and with studying eyes that mocked. My eyes were drawn to the grey streak above his right ear that was a clean line to the back of his neck. He saw me and said, 'when god made me they broke the mould. Even my mum says it. I'm Connie Slaney, from Bermondsey south London. Nice to meet you. And you are?'

… 'Stephen Gillen. I'm from east London.' I took the out stretched hand, shook it firmly. It was a strong hand.
He would be the same age as me, I considered. He had steely grey/ blue eyes that mocked and burned right through you.

We smiled. A moment caught together as we felt the common feeling between us. There was an air of the psychopath about him. A voice that shielded but held violence. A grin that showed great fun and laughter and mischief.
The prison officer shouted, 'Quick march!'

The snigger was in our chests and playing on our lips and flickering in our eyes and it was a struggle but imperative that we kept it hidden.

'Look at him old red neck, 'whispered Connie jokingly behind me. We marched. Boy soldiers lead by the pretend sergeant. Out of the recess, through the side doors, into the sunshine of the yard and by the grey, single level education building.'

Connie continued, 'they say he was on a ship that was bombed and he got that burn on the side of his neck. I just call him red neck,' he sniggered. On purpose he was trying to make me laugh and if we were caught we would be for it. There was no messing here, no second chances. Just a swift cutting slap that stung, a loss of all privileges and the solitary cell.

We were going around the field, on the inside of the tall green fence. We marched. The screws with red neck at the front shouted in a melodic rhythm, 'Left, left, left, right, left...Right wheel.'

The sun, a clear yellow disc that promised a clear burning day, glinted high in a cloudless sky. Birds chirped, crickets and the sounds of summer bathed us.

Connie continued, 'I feel such a mug here like this playing the marching boy. It's like following the geezer from the old war movies.'

It hit me the turning laughter inside me. But I was guarded and wondered if he could be trusted. Friend or foe? The giggles forced their way through. We marched. I turned to him. A wide smile was plastered on his face. We marched, arms swinging. Together we giggled.

It had been a usual and average Friday night in Bethnal Green. We had taken the time away from our planning and scheming, to socialise and enjoy the moment. The barrow boys had finished their work, the busy day people who had shopped and visited the shops and pondered the market stalls, mothers out with their kids and people from the area who met and chatted and ate pie and mash, all had ebbed away with the fading daylight as the dark chill of the city evening had closed in. We were upstairs in the White Heart pub. A busy Friday night throng of people rocked the downstairs dance floor. I took the next line of cocaine. A long thick line, snorted with a fifty-pound note. The building beneath me shook with dance music with CeCe Pendison's 'Finally'.

There was Alfie, and Ian and George. I was moving to the music, dancing. A controlled movement that hit the striking beats. The cocaine was filling my head to bursting point. A rushing, rocket ship was flaming through my body making it light and fuelling my mind with an illusion of invincibility.

They were laughing around me but their eyes were glazed and serious as the near pure white powder was gripping their minds tighter. George rubbed his nose. My teeth were grinding. I danced and I felt I flew high in the clouds of the upper part of my mind where there were no limitations. The music thumped. I saw them, sitting and standing and out of it. The room on top of the pub was like an office with the feeling of a lounge. Keith the new publican had tried to add a relaxed ambience with the red leather sofas and chairs and dark stained wooden desks. But the unpainted, tired blue walls still made it look unlived in, I thought.

'Come on then…let's see who's got the minerals,' he was up. Alfie was on his feet by the desk that was covered in good green leather. He opened the see-through bag of white power as he swayed to the music and with his credit card lined up the cocaine. Sure, quick, confident movements, like an artist finishing a painting.

He continued, 'now look at them. Big, long, large ones… we each use fifty-pound notes. A race. First one to the end takes the money. Winner takes all'.

There was madness in his eyes, a disturbed look, a mind that surfed heavy high waves with no shore.

The walls were thumping with music. I took a sip of my vodka and orange. 'I don't think you got it in you, Alfie.' I had said it as a bait and I smiled as he bit.

'What do you fuckin mean. Come on then. Come on you lot are light weights. A fifty each come on then.'

We were at the start of the long fat line of white glistening white powder. Four of us, music vibrating through us, eyes that turned and heads that were away with the fairies. I be damned, I thought, if I'd let them beat me. We eyed each other. Like gun slingers just before the draw.

'Ready,' said Alfie. The tightly rolled bank notes were in place up our nostrils.

'Go'!

I pushed, hammering along the line of cocaine. The back of my sinuses was loading and I forced forward to steal the victory. The white power was everywhere. It was on our faces and it dripped from our noses and on to the floor.

Robert was waving his arms. 'No way...you are the luckiest bastard.'

My head was feeling it now. The price of victory was a head that spun, a room that produced a rush in my body and heart that was worrying. I focused my glazed eyes through the chemicals I was feeling. I laughed. I knew the secret had been to blow my nose before the start.

I sat in the chair. I suddenly felt the over powering chemicals, needed to steady a moment as I recalibrated, calmed myself into a fit state to still be aware and continue. I took another sip of my drink. We had been at it most of the day. What would start as a great and wonderful night would morph and shatter and cloud into paranoia and the knowledge that the comedown would be crashing. The music had changed to Snap 'Rhythm is a Dancer.

I sat, in this state, limbs loose in the chair with the drink at my lips and my head was edging towards the paranoia of my life. I had not returned to prison after my home leave. I had done everything to go back. They had cajoled me, the people of my circle with my need to be with them. That the important stuff coming up was life-changing and my part was important. It would give me the money I needed to start a new life and take care of the baby boy who needed things.

My head soared. Inside my mind a force was racing upwards. My thoughts were circling, twisting, turning, spinning. Like a fierce wind that blew fire through long halls blowing open doorways. My grip on my decisions was strengthening inside me. I was now unlawfully at large. One foot from now on, would always be in prison. A grey mood was somewhere behind the drugs addling my mind, the soaring elation searing through and in my body. Lingering it hung, a picture that could not be removed from a wall, open and in clear sight.

I took another long gulp of the drink in my hand. I scanned them. Ian sat, a dark cloud of strange energy emitting from him. George's eyes were closed as he flaked out. Alfie, swayed to the music, head completely engrossed. In their own world, I supposed. Inside me, the mental fog was demanding more cocaine now, more drink, more artistry and escapist. It had been a problem these thoughts, these compulsions that set me alight in a high wonderful sky and then sent me hurtling groundward and shattered me like a glass. Somewhere downstairs they shouted, voices raised to the beating music.

I felt the mood of the drugs in me change. My feelings had swung. I thought of the baby. A little thing that jumped and smiled and had the innocence of an angel. My body slumped in the chair felt trapped. I watched them. The room was shifting due to darkness. The police were closing I could feel it and sense it and the knowledge of it poked me constantly. The picture of the sweet face of my son was in my mind…I cared so deeply, but was relieved I didn't have to focus on a relationship as I had enough going on with a life that was in turmoil. Instinctively, I knew deep in me I had made a bad mistake not going back to prison.

❧

…The 750cc motorbike weaved in and out of the traffic. Seamlessly, the two riders settled in behind a red hatchback and took a steady easy unnoticed pace. The pillion rider had been picked up in north London in the early hours at the corner of a built-up street under the yellow glare of a street-light that had spoiled the cold darkness. He held on tight to the rider in front. Inside his zipped black leather jacket, deep in an inside pocket was the gun. A fully loaded Smith and Wesson 38. The Motorbike screamed forward. The road was busy and they had a clear line of sight in front of them. The clear dry, brightness of a normal day had aided them. The cars slowed as they approached the traffic lights in front. Tightly, they were tucked in behind the hatchback. Far along the traffic line the two men on the motorbike focused. They saw it. It was far ahead, one vehicle now behind a car at the traffic lights. They watched, eyes fixed as the big, blue armoured Securicor van came to a full stop.

At the designated operation command spot the Flying Squad had watched the events weave and the patterns unfold. The camera, placed high on a tall block of flats had seen the meeting in the early hours at the garage, had witnessed the team congregate and the motorbike be launched. Other officers had seen two separate trackers activated then at two separate London addresses soon after. Thirty officers from the flying squad were mobile. They tracked and trailed and hovered and closed a net towards the targets that were a nest of armed robbers.

They moved quickly and confidently and were backed up by another twenty-five-armed officers from PT17.

... 'They're on the move again. Target one and target five, 'He was in the back of the van one ear phone held tightly to the side of his ear, and he turned to give them the commentary.

There were three main suspects in this car. They had gone to the address where this motor vehicle was usually parked one frosty evening seven months ago and replaced the tracker with a replica. They had hooked in a long-range tracker and wired it for audio. They listened. They heard the team were moving towards their target.

The crew of the Securicor van glared out through the reinforced glass windows at the streets that passed them. There was no escape. The fear was tangible, and panic was forcing the raised voices.

'We have to call it in, Jeff! We have no choice.' He was the driver's mate. It was his job to check the morning schedule and transfer the money boxes from the premises to the van. He continued, 'I mean this is bloody madness. What if?'

Beneath his fresh grey sock, strapped to his right ankle, the driver could feel the stretched black masking tape that held the bug to his shin. He was terrified.

'They're listening, Danny. They can hear every fuckin' word. They kidnapped me as I got into my car this morning at 4.30. It was dark. I didn't expect it. They came from nowhere. They drove me away and put a gun to my head.'

The crew member in the back of the Van listened hard. It was his job to wait for the keys inside the vans armoured interior set on time delay to drop. He would then open every separate safe and transfer the money in and out of the hatch at the back. Intently he had heard what they said in the front. He looked through the little window at them and said, 'People might get hurt. I'm calling it in.'

The drivers voice was abrupt. It raised high and clear with a sure anger, 'We are not calling it in ok! I told you. When they took me this morning, they have Sharon, they know where the children go to school…They had a picture of Sharon at the school gates for pete's sack! Jesus, there was even the new paint on the gate post in the picture. It was taken recently!'

The van turned. Silent fears moved in each of them. The enormity of it had settled them into silent conformity. The road was littered with moving traffic. Panic was gripping them. Silent fear. Warm and tangible and evident and growing. The streets beside them were lined with shops. Flitting by. Quickly. All the colours of the rainbow. A hurried road on a busy normal day the driver though. Nothing normal about today. There was a warning that felt like a sharp pain in his back. It went up his spine then fanned out and turned at his neck.

Then, in the wing mirror he saw it. Screaming and roaring. A terrifying picture of noise. Clear and desperate and timely. It was coming. The motorbike swerved out from the traffic behind. Purposefully, persistent and forceful it accelerated up the traffic line towards the van. There were two of them. A driver in a black helmet who had his head down into the wind and a pillion rider who watched them carefully. Faces aghast. Full of heightened fear. The men in the blue Securicor van could only watch.

At the next traffic lights they stopped and all heard it. Loud and thumping. The heavy banging on the side of the van. The driver could see out of the window to the two people on the bike beside him. He could see through the visor of the driver's black helmet into the sharp steely green eyes that glared back at him. His heart had dropped as he imagined what was coming. Angrily the pillion rider, the one who had knocked the side of the van pointed forward.

He gestured and in a no-nonsense voice said, 'follow us!'

...From his car on top of the carpark roof Detective Inspector Sixsmith listened intently as the report was given.

'We had them all the way through east India dock road, Gov. They went up Limehouse and veered toward the Rotherhithe tunnel. We pulled back and continued by CCTV. They're somewhere over the south, Sir. Doesn't make sense to the other robberies. We've lost them but still have audio. They keep mentioning East London as rendezvous. Will keep you posted. The surveillance team are re-evaluating and restructuring now, Sir. Over'.

DI Sixsmith grunted. He was out of the car and into the wind and back looking below him at the movements of people, places and things. The walkie talkie was by his side. He held it tightly. The blowing gales of uncertainty were circling in his innermost thoughts. What were they up to? he, wondered. The sky was above him. He could feel again its openness. The wind reminded him of it. He looked up, glanced at it, its massive vastness, his head sweeping around. Alone he stood there.

When the day of freedom had come, the sun had remained a high disc that radiated warmth in a clear azure morning. The prison officer opened the little green Judas gate and I was through it. My first time in prison had been hard and frightening and it had been a rite of passage, I thought. I was overwhelmed. It was behind me. The prison staff had waited until the social worker picking me up had arrived and waited outside. He was bounding towards me. A short chubby man in casual jeans and a checked shirt with shoulder length straggly mousey hair, a beard and thick round spectacles.

'Stephen, you're out. How do you feel?' he was one of the better ones, never no trouble out of him. He was fair and considerate and caring but was out ranked and outnumbered by the horrible bastards he worked with.

We were at the car and he gave me a cigarette when we sat inside. I lit it, gratefully and inhaled the light wafting smoke. We drove. Over the pitted and cratered old tarmac up the slim country lane. Continued left, right through the labyrinth of twisting, turning highways that surrounded the prison. I coughed. The social worker laughed.

'So how was it? Your first time away?'

My head was spinning. I was light headed as my first cigarette in weeks settled. Through the windscreen I watched the green trees and shrubbery and black winding road. The country lanes that continued stretching out in front of me. 'So, he repeated. 'How was it, Stephen? Did you learn your lesson?'

It was a question, intrusive and leading that made me pause.

'Yes, I learned my lesson, 'I offered. 'It was very frightening going in there for the first time. It was like joining the army. We marched everywhere. No cigarettes. It seemed like eight years not eight months. '

He listened as he drove, smiled lightly.

I turned the radio on. Turned up the volume of the pop music.

I sat back a moment and took another pull of the cigarette. The lightness in my head persisted, but I was more aware of his question and my reaction. Had I learnt, his question repeated in my mind. A trick question that felt open-ended. It stood a moment in my mind. A pause that hung and dangled and waited. It circled demanded an answer. I hoped so. To go back would be unthinkable. The loss of freedom. The constant hardships. The violence. The crushing discipline and the threatening shouts. The purgatory of not knowing about the outside or what was going on. The bullying and the fear and the shitty tasks to be finished daily.... My answer was to go back would be unthinkable.

My head and body were aligned with this answer. But deep in my mind with the strange pause and a nagging new knowledge of having had a first spell incarcerated, was a deeper feeling of having crossed a long bridge of fear. A wide place where the unknown of not having been to prison or knowing what it would be like ruled with steely terror. It had inhabited my mind for a long time now. This idea of prison as a place that bolted doors, held terrible acts and threw keys away. It had hunted and haunted my thoughts seizing on any notion I had of escaping my fate or getting away. A place only heard about, where the stories were stretched and reminding and scary and cutting. I had travelled my own road inside there. A small scrawny fourteen-year-old. I had faced the lions and tigers of the fears about being locked-up, and I had survived untouched. I thought of what my real birth mother might be doing, what she was like, where she would be, and if I entered her thoughts?

The social worker drove. We were leaving the country roads near the Detention Centre behind us. Entered wider, busier more expansive streets that would lead to the motorway.

The social worker pressed the accelerator. The music was playing. He was talking about the home. How Fieldhill was still the same. It had been a bit calmer from what it had been a few weeks ago. When I had been sent away there had been upset and trouble. Some people had smashed the TV room, others had run away. A girl had self-harmed. It was better now. More stable. All would be happy to see me. I wound down the window.

The fast-flowing morning traffic noise accompanied by the warmth of the morning flowed in. We were taking the slip road towards the motorway. The car shot forward, then left, navigating fast moving traffic. I was thinking of the home. Of the girl who had self-harmed and who I had lost my virginity to months earlier. It would be good to see her and see that she was ok. See the coy smile and hold her hand and go for our walks in the grounds. I had had thoughts of her in the dark nights and the picture of her had eased my struggling pain.

The noises of the Detention Centre were far back now, behind the tree line and the thermals where a flock of birds gathered. The smells and the feeling and the fears were dissipating with it. I looked directly at the sun. I blinked against the glare and deep inside me I realised there was another part to the question of lessons learnt. It was a knowing and mentally it had been perpetrating the fibre of my mind. A flicking, poking and prodding attack that was soft and subtle in its assault. It was hope, I understood just then. The bright notion that prison was a thing of the past and would be averted. That all would be well and the future that beckoned was clear and safe and secure in its happiness. I would not return to prison…Behind this was the strength of the knowing. It was the knowledge that I hoped it would be the last time I would be imprisoned, but if it happened again I would be ready for it and I could cope.

&

…We had taken every anti surveillance precaution we knew. We had taken out the batteries from our throw-away phones in our pockets in case of tracking. We had come from our separate places in London, one from Bermondsey the other from Bethnal green, on the tube with a couple of swift train changes each into the mingling crowds. Meeting at Tower Bridge we had met at the car and then drove to the decaying Bonamy estate in South Bermondsey. Near the paper factory, under the estate, in the desolate underground carpark, we had made our first car change and transferred into a white Volkswagen.

We were travelling through the blue in the centre of Bermondsey. We watched the banks, the jewellery shops, the security vans. In the passenger seat, my eyes scanning the pavements, the people outside the car, I said, 'we need to be double careful today, Connie. If it's not right we pull out of it agreed?'

He was broader, taller, but the grey/white stripe was still streaking his jet-black hair and his manner was still the same. He was watching the road, serious and trained eyes focused like me. He said, steady and soft, 'of course, Steve we don't want to get nicked. I'm feeling what you are. We get caught they'll throw away the key.'

He smiled then. He said, 'you never know maybe someone will do the prison for us.' He looked side wards eyes shining. He hadn't changed a bit, I thought in all these years. It was a trait, that in the madness and blackest of moments he would turn humour on it. Outside the afternoon was threating to rain. It was a busy late December and the falling evening light was soon to transform into a brisk inky darkness.

I still watched. We were turning in the car and heading back to east London, past Connie's mothers house on Southwark Park road, and over to the place where firearms and ammunition were kept.

There was a desperation that had closed around our world these last weeks, I thought. My universe had folded, turning inwards like a burning building. Floor by floor was being destroyed at a frightening rate. Like a general on top of the hill, I saw the

155

landscape below, and with the variables of ground against me was witnessing the shadows of my isolation creeping closer. I would then be destroyed. I gulped the negativity of my feelings deep inside to a place of strength. I had had a snort of cocaine earlier and it was still trapping in the coldness of my mind the brightness I needed to move forward. We went around the roundabout near the Rotherhithe tunnel three times to check for car surveillance.

Connie Slaney put his foot down. The car accelerated. His face was a stone mask. I sat back in the car as we ventured down deep under the river Thames and into the concrete claustrophobia of the tunnel. My mind was madness and fixed and channelled and focused on only the robbery in front of us. I looked behind us in the rear-view mirror. We had switched and checked. All day we had studied and watched and felt and tested. I would turn defeat to victory, I thought. A fate that was loss of liberty would be changed. I could feel and hear the hum of the car below me, the echo of the tunnel. I had returned the steel I needed to inside myself. The car drove. The lights of the tunnel flickered at the side of my eyes. I stared ahead, unfeeling, unaware, inside the cage of my personal thoughts. Mentally I prepared.

Chapter 7
The Beginning of the End

The police helicopter had kept the suspect high-powered blue BMW under a close watch. Like an experienced carrion hawk high in the late evening floating winds it had hovered from high altitude using specialised equipment hugging the thermals at times manipulating the cloud cover as it stayed concealed over the city skyline. The car below was moving and going towards the city of London. The call had come. Its three male occupants were fleeing the scene of an armed robbery and were armed and thought highly dangerous. From the docklands in east London they had observed the car. Tracking, trailing, sometimes in their high-altitude optical lenses a dot that moved and twisted and turned and would intensify.

'Bravo six. Sky bound, will soon execute hard stop. Over.' It was the ground team. They circled and tightened, focused and prepared. A floating group that was a twelve-car team of vehicles, all of them armed.

The echoing hum of the rotors muttered a high noise. In the cockpit the pilot was answering. A clear, precise targeted voice trained and fluent.

'Still have eyes, over. Repeat Charlie One still mobile along Princes street at the back of Bank of England, copy. Still have eyes. Over...'

DI Sixsmith was in a passenger seat of the four-man car. The chequered caps were on their laps and 38 calibre Smith and Wesson handguns were on their laps. They had missed the van attack by a sheer fluke. They had lost a few of the robbery team earlier in the day and having spread their observation because of potential targets had miscalculated the actual raid point. He asked the driver to steady, to slow down. Soon. The car slotted into the moving traffic behind a bread delivery van. They, the suspects were far up ahead around a mile in the built-up city. DI Sixsmith's weathered face focused, his determined eyes tightening with the growing pressure in his head. They had the suspects in a floating box now. No escape. Cars and a van and two motorbikes moved and swung and weaved around them as their car cruised and navigated the heavy city traffic.

The grey, busy pavements now were the foundations of taller buildings as they went deeper into the heart of the city. High above them, in a forecast of fresh sweeping winds and slight showers, was the police helicopter that was swooping now to use their camera equipment for photographs.

'Can't believe we missed them, Gov,' from one of the detectives in the back seat. 'Lucky for them, 'he continued.

In the passenger seat, the Detective Inspector made a deep hum. Close to a grunt but not quite. He was very aware of the blood bath that could have been, and him and his men would have been very able to meet it. Four trained guns were no match for thirty, he thought. Out of the side of his mouth he growled, 'It was another one for the suspects. Let's be thankful on this one. We need to watch the attention at the moment. This lot are very dodgy. I have no doubt if we had caught them cold at the van it would have been a very dangerous situation. This way is a better solution this time.'

Sixsmith had his hand on his gun in the holster at his hip. He was thinking when to call it. The car flew forward in traffic that picked up speed. The radio in the car crackled. It was a Detective Sargent in one of the lead cars tasked with synchronising the armed officers and the hard stop of the suspect vehicle. The suspects' behaviour, he said suggested they were unaware. They had showed no panicky movements or anti surveillance.

He heard the stopping hiss of the bin lorries hydraulics as it braked at the side of them. He saw the monitor and could see images of the suspects blue BMW. The main operational CCTV team had joined them now on request as an arrest was drawing closer. The car came to life again. Either side of him the tall greyness of buildings tightly enclosed them.

In his mind he was returning to the information he had been given of the robbery just committed. They had lost the two main suspects they had watched from the early hours. They had also had to pull back close cover surveillance on the motorbike. They had done this so as not to alert the suspects they were walking into a carefully crafted trap. They had listened on the audio, watched the long-range trackers. The Robbery team had changed their rendezvous at the last minute and gathered at a place in Islington. Clever bastards, Sixsmith thought. There was a feeling deep down inside him. It was frustration he recognised. They had used the weapon of confusion and they had used it well knowing first a crime would have to be committed and for a conspiracy to stick they would need to be woven together.

He spoke sharply into the mike, 'Bravo One, Bravo Two and Bravo Three! This is India Tango. Repeat India Tango. Hard Stop next junction. Execute. Execute…'
His voice hung for a moment in the moving car. The two-year Operation Nemesis was approaching its end.

They came back now. They had understood the call sign from their senior officer. The order to attack, to move with stealth, eagle-like precision and swoop with noise and screeching tyres and smashing glass and firearms drawn. There were three Detective Sergeant's, who in charge of three separate teams tracked the separate getaway cars that were fleeing across London.

Detective Inspector Sixsmith could see the ambush position far out in front of him. A busy three-way cross road with traffic lights wide open spaces and no chance of escape. He was more aware of the heavy black gun now. The other officers had their chequered caps, their firearms ready.

Adrenalin pumped through Albert Sixsmith's body. From a pounding heart it was quickening, speeding through a labyrinth of arteries and veins. His eyes squinted and his temples were pulsing. It would soon be the end for them, he thought. Two years of punishing tactical work. The robbery behind them had left three guards from Securicor in fear of their lives. On the fenced, rock peppered waste ground, where grass grew in tufts through large cracks in the concrete, by the thrown rubbish and plastic bottles and old rolled-up carpets and under the closed quiet shadows of a bricked railway overhead, the robbery team had waited for the motorbike to escort the armoured blue Securicor van in. Together, four of them had ordered the guards out at gun point, opened the individual safes and cleared it of four hundred and fifteen thousand pounds. Sixsmith was determined, the streets would be free of them. These people who waged fear and toted guns in broad daylight.

The radio squawked to life. 'Copy, India Tango. Message Hard Stop Execute understood, Bravo Two. Over.'

He replied, 'India Tango received. Over. Good luck...'

It sounded in his ears. The car changing gears, the light grey of flitting buildings, pedestrians, passing quickly. The weight of the gun, the top was unclipped now, the fabric of the chequered cap resting on his lap, the adrenalin. He felt it all. The thoughts returned to the quickness of his brain. The robbers had fled the scene as soon as they had taken the money in the crisp plastic Securicor wrappers. Their getaway cars had scattered in different directions. The police safeguards had been activated then. The moving arrows of the trackers had tightly warned and followed while an alert had gone wider. He was happy to remove them to prison, put them away for long years behind heavy closed doors.

'Copy, India Tango. Execute Hard stop. It's clear here. Approaching contact point. Will execute when ready understood. Copy...'

Something pulled at him. Two positioned, he considered. Albert Sixsmith, pressed again the receiver, confirmed, 'Received, Bravo One. India Tango, good luck. Over'. Ahead of him he could just see the suspect vehicle. It approached the ambush point at the junction. The hard stop ambush was just about to be sprung. Everyone had their chequered caps ready, one hand on their gun the other ready to exit the vehicle. It still pulled at him and jostled in his mind. A worm that was eating through the hard thoughts of his subconscious. It was the missing suspects. The surveillance logs had thrown up other collaborators. He knew there were other members of the robbery team. They were suspected. Today they would not be arrested.

It was the last team leader Detective Sergeant. His voice came in clear and precise. 'India Tango, Copy. Execute hard stop. Over and understood. Copy.'

In front of them the traffic had stopped at the traffic lights. The busy typical scene of a city of London junction about to erupt. They were out of the car doors, caps raised and to their heads and guns being raised with them. In unison. In a second. Quickly. A fluent, practiced motion.

'Go! Go!' It was belting on the black hard metal radios, in their ears and echoing and shouted in and around them. The blocking cars screeched in front and at each side of the suspect blue BMW. A torrent of mayhem erupted. Shattering glass. Shouts. Screams. There was no chance of escape for the occupants as the Flying Squad Officers smashed the side of the car windows. They screamed and shouted. The police, surrounding the car with their guns trained forward.

'Show us your hands! Shows us your hands now!'

DI Sixsmith was running. His large frame thumped the pavement. He was slightly behind. He watched a superb arrest. Heard his officers' shouts. It was his intention, his way of showing authority that he would be there, but just arrive at the opportune moment. The suspects had been pulled from the car, were being cuffed behind their backs, spread-eagled on the pavement.

'We're securing the scene, Sir'. It was the young DS. He had the elation of the capture in his eyes, a light that was brightening his face and cheeks.

He looked at the three suspects on the floor. They would be having second thoughts about the day ahead of them now. He knew them. Three hard and clever and slippery men. Target criminals who had needed a fortune to be captured. But there would be more. There would be tomorrow and more guns and more witnesses and more robberies on his patch in the east end. He prided himself that he was clearing his manor, like a powerful hoover that shifted and cleaned hard stains. DI Sixsmith smiled inside then grunted, his only self-congratulation. He walked round to the back of the BMW. One of the team had opened it.

There in an open and unzipped black holdall, still in the plastic wrappers from the Securicor sorting room, were the piles of banknotes newly taken. Clouds high above him were gathering to close in on the London skyline. They were coming in hard from the west and seeking strength as they summoned an hour's worth of rain. The winds he had felt on top of the carpark this morning were subsiding. He was happy with this day's work.

The three suspects were being taken in separate cars. Their car had been moved to the roadside. He stood a moment looking at the scene. He knew it had been repeated simultaneously in two other separate ambushes. He listened. The commentary crackled that the other suspects has also been arrested successfully without any casualties. He stood on the roadside a moment, DI Sixsmith, pensive. Today had been a win for Operation Nemesis, but he thought of the other robbers who had not been arrested. The traffic flowed past him quickly. They were out there, he thought. Somewhere they were holed up, still dangerous planning their next robbery.

❧

The children's home had been full of heightened alarm that day. Turbulence that stretched and released uneven emotions that affected the children. A twelve-year-old girl damaged by memories long past and an inability to erase them had self-harmed again. Adding more deep cuts to her damaged forearms the conjured images of an abusive father had again become too strong. One of the boys had thrown a pool ball through the window shattering the glass. The staff heightened with moved vigilantly. I looked for the boy and tried to hold down the fanning anger inside me. Out the front by the swing main doors, through the empty dinning-hall, which was being mopped, upstairs my footfall hammering the carpeted squeaking floor, round the back by the education building, my eyes scanned and searched but I could not see him.

I pushed the doors into the games room. A slamming motion that slapped the wooden door frame against the wall. I knew he was there, had seen his silhouette from outside floating around the floor tiles with a snooker cue in his hand. I thought of the girl. She was small, a tiny wafer of a thing. She still struggled hard. She played with dolls and tried to overcome terrible memories. He had got her by the hair in the hall way and swung her for no reason. He had bullied her before. I had seen her doll, broken with streaming blond hair and the rage had finally got me. 'What do you want,' he was bigger than me, a good foot in height and wide shoulders on him.

A mocking, pinched face with shaven brown hair and growling brown eyes. He had the pool cue in his hand and he smashed the side of the pool table with it.

My smile disarmed him. A soft beaming one accompanied by calm eyes and a head that was dipped submissively. I had the table tennis bat in my hand, small, compact. The confusion was showing in his eyes, the snooker cue lowering in his grasp. Sure, with silky stealth my trainers squeaked as they moved and I was across the shiny grey tiles. The memory of his bullying rose in me. The snooker cue, my turning grin, the curved wooden bat in my hand and the distance between us had been calculated. The table tennis bat was swung with spot on accuracy. It hit him square on the forehead. The cue had been raised, but I was too close and the next swinging hit of the bat had knocked the resistance from him. He had his hands on my shoulders and we were on the floor grappling, curling, clawing, twisting.

He was trying to fight back but I was hitting him with my fists. Lightning blows that left no return. We turned, twisted. In his ear I said, clear, between the grappling exertion. You won't bully me no more. Not me, not Anabella. No one. His finger was pulling at my eye, but he was listening quietly to the words. It was the come back, I thought. For his sneaky kicks and cutting mental and emotional torture. I had him locked with a hand at his throat and another pulling his ears. He was beat now. I could feel it in his subsiding movements, his waning defence. Could see it in the bewildered eyes, the red face and the pimpled rosy and rising fresh cheeks. His hair was in disarray. He said something but I held him. Tight, vice like so he couldn't move. The bat and the snooker cue were scattered on the shiny grey tiles and some of the other children had arrived because of the noise.

I felt the strength of the strong hands that pulled me up. The staff had arrived. Three of them and they pulled us apart in an easy movement. I left the bully. They had my neck and my arms held back and one of them a fist pulling my hair. I was dragged upwards, backwards unable to move. It was Cooper and Brownson and a lackey. I saw their hissing looks, the strain of their anger and the fear in their eyes. The real violence had started. I was down in a crushing headlock and I struggled for breath. They pulled, tussled. Along the hallways and towards the back of the building. Quick pulling, scraping violence that strangled, clawed, crushed and hammered. I had forgotten the bully, his face was gone, the girl and the others too. I fought their pulling vice-like grappling but I was again slipping in and out of conscious.

With the natural light of the morning seeping through the gripping arms, I knew where they were taking me and inside my body revolted. They had been sure to batter the resistance from me and my spirit with it as I heard the keys open the rusty metal door to the boiler room. It was dark in there, only filtered light. The dank smell of copper and cobwebs and creepy crawlies with rats that shuffled and scratched in the darkness. I was thrown in. A small body with grazes that crumpled on to the concrete floor and I yearned for the brightness of the morning I had just left. The cold of the concrete floor slab was beneath me and I could feel the dirt and dust of it on my fingers.

They forced the metal boiler room door shut. A rattling screech from a rarely used door that needed oil. The darkness was final now, broken by filtering half-light streaming from the door. They were grunting outside and one sniggered and happiness was shared as they collected their spent energy. Cooper was at the door. A panting voice trying to catch breath. 'You'll sit there now with the rats until we say. If we hear you pleading later you might get out sooner.'

I had withdrawn to a corner, away from the slit in the door and the line of sunshine and the eyes and shadows that moved and flitted and looked. They were gone, the skirting shadows and pulling violence and mocking anger with them. The jagged fresh atmosphere of the small shadowed boiler room had brought a coolness that gave me goosepimples. There was movement somewhere. A scratching behind the big boiler pipes that were covered with padded foam and surrounded with aged dirt. I moved back, pulled my legs to my chest and hugged them. I had been here many times before. Sometimes for a whole day.

I closed my eyes and retreated away from the worry of what scratched in the corner. I was finding it difficult to breath and my neck could feel the violence of the assault. My shoulder throbbed and my head thumped. I returned to my innermost thoughts. A hunt for impressions and comforting images. There were faces there and a laughing face that roared with joy at riding the bright yellow Tonka Truck down the slope of the road. There were mountain goats that could never be caught. They hung, three of them precariously, cloven hoofs clattering the unclimbable face of the blue grey mountain rock. The girl was also there smiling as it was a better day and her doll had not been shattered or broken and stamped. The bullies had run away and then the voice was there.

It came in above the steaming water that travelled through the boiler pipes, comforting and taking away the pain.

'...It was way back at the time of the first kings, and all the heroes of the land had a special knowledge of the monkey puzzle tree. It was said on cold misty nights they would even act as a beacon to help the travellers who were lost find their way back home. Tall in the worst of weather they would stand and keep the secrets of their magic against the dawn of the morning. Through the ages, standing proud against the events of the day they would keep the secrets of all the conversations they had heard and listened too. Eternally they listened and watched. Through the cold damaging evenings and the soothing morning mist. The fine tall, strong, courageous and immortal Monkey puzzle trees. Solitary, strong and unmoving the grip of the moving seasons would pass them. It was said the monkey puzzle trees were each a miracle with a gift of real treasure inside and that their spikiness was a protection so that it would never be found...'

...The voice had gone, waned into the blackness. Its comfort, in the little garden with a step. Through the garden window was a woman who washed dishes and wore a tied headscarf. I waited for our eyes to meet, for her to look up. But the image had moved before she did, before I could see and remember her face.

The tears were silently running down. They were in streams on my cheeks and flowing freely. It was increasing gripping the pain in me at not being able to remember and see her face. I sat, for comfort and hugged tighter on my legs. The scratching behind the boiler pipes had got louder. I shifted my body along the concrete floor, tighter into my bricked corner. The cool darkness cloaking me.

ॐ

...At the bus stop I scanned the scene in the cold freshness of the dark December early evening as busy shoppers hurried past. The shop lights threw dim light onto the pavements and mixed with the glint of the Christmas street decorations. We had parked the car close by. We were wrapped tight with clothes and gloves and balaclavas rolled high under the peak of our baseball caps. Wedged down the front of my jeans and shielded by my dark green silk bomber jacket was the loaded twelve bore side-by-side shotgun. Moving slightly. Structured movements. Guarded. My pockets were packed with cartridges, and I was aware as I moved at the bus stop of the weight of the firearm so it remained hidden under my jacket.

Connie was beside me. With sharp eyes we studied the scene. Moving shoppers, teenage girls who grouped and laughed, a mother who held tightly to a child's hand, the homeless guy who turned on the pavement, the man who wound back the awning of his shop and prepared to close. All of it, studied, taken apart, pushed and pulled, poked and prodded. The cold evening air was fresh around my head and ears. Our breath painting pictures of mist in front of us as we breathed. It was surreal, I felt. What was wrong with this picture before me, I wondered?

The moving cars on the busy Bethnal Green road in front of us slowed. A red number eight bus pulled into the bus stop. Passengers were lined up and getting onto the bus. Shielded a moment from the glaring road, my mind was cast back. I looked at the people beside me at the bus stop. An old lady with a child, a younger guy listening to a headset, a young woman in school uniform.

A man with dark, grey flecked hair in a worn and square patterned tweed jacket stood close. A straight back on him, and with a solitary air, he seemed to claim his space. He turned, and our eyes met a moment. He had green eyes. Deep, searching and fathomless, a bottomless and troubled sea, I thought. He took his hand from his pocket and rubbed the slight stubble on his skin, and I saw he had only three fingers. A claw like hand with two smooth stumps where once there had been active moving fingers. He looked away from me now and I watched him as he walked up the Bethnal green Road. There was something about him, I felt. In the moment a connection I couldn't translate. The smell of the tweed touched my senses evoking something. His back was to me and he was gone as quickly as he had appeared.

In my head was Lily.

The phone call had come in the late afternoon from Lily. Quick, hurried, worried words that were unsure and panicked. Callum had been arrested by the Flying Squad on a bit of work. They had all been nicked. Everyone. A Securicor van had been taken, hijacked in North London. A team of people had been arrested. The armed police had come for them that night. To her address and others. Smashing down doors and waving guns and producing a crumpled search warrant. People had been taken in for questioning. Callum was in Tottenham Police station. She didn't know what to do. They had trampled her kitchen and upstairs with their heavy shoes and boots. Screaming, she had cursed and flashed her eyes and targeted and spat her words at them. She had paused then, as if to filter the enormity of it while we stayed on the phone. The door was still smashed the way they had left it…Was I OK? Was I safe? I had to stay away. They were still watching, they had said and were looking for other people.

The last passenger was on the bus. Its double doors hissed closed, its engine working harder to turn into the late evening traffic. Lily had sounded desperate on the phone. I had stood listening with the phone to my ear static and rooted, with the chill of an impending doom sliding down me. I had realised how close I was courting danger, that the police would be searching hard. That all would be harder now and a struggle. Like an outlaw I had been frozen out on the outskirts. My network was being dismantled. My protection and the shield of my associations fractured in pieces.

I thought of Callum in the grey cell of a prison and my son, Terry the baby just born. I had punched the wall and threw the glass I was holding and shattered the see-through coffee table in sudden, explosive frustrated rage. My child's face was the image I held fixed in my mind. That had been a week ago and the freedom I was trying to hold onto was slipping. Cornered, without my usual protective frameworks and resources I was suffering. Across the road high above the awnings, coloured lights twinkled from a shop roof. I studied again, with more intensity the busy road and the people positioned around us. The fear of the police, of capture and prison was drawing closer I felt. Connie looked over the moving traffic in front and across the road and over at the doorway. We had watched it a few times and we had been told and knew from internal sources that it was a main counting house for a betting shop chain. It would be cash and it would be gathered in to a lump in a room that could be caught open.

Cold was about us. Air that would freeze later circled. Inside my senses were heightening to exploding point. It was the way of it before the attack. That gripping adrenaline, curled apprehension, fear and excitement that would fuse and turn and juggle and churn. Over near the blurred light of the doorway someone opened the door and looked into the night.

Readying ourselves, we watched…

Chapter 8
The End of an Age of Freedom

It had been late evening around six when they had finally let me out from the tight damp darkness of the boiler room. I had heard the footsteps first outside. Worn shoes scraping the slim pathway towards the outside of the door. Then jingling keys, the squeaking door had been open and the night had streamed in. It was one of the tall men. The one who worked closely with Cooper and who wore corduroys and square glasses. He had said, they hoped I could behave now. That fighting couldn't be allowed. My limbs had been desperate to escape the solitude but I still came out gingerly. Our pace back to the main building was brisk and steady.

I noticed his face had looked strained on the way back around to the front of the building. In the half-shadow, at the corner of the brickwork, before we turned towards the main door he had slowed, stopped. A brief, strange moment. Turning to me, with the fresh evening around us where no one could see, and he had admitted in a quiet voice that he didn't think it was right some of it. That being locked in the boiler room like that was wrong. He didn't agree with it. But there was nothing he could do.

I had not replied. My plan was being constructed in my head. I trailed behind him in silence, let him walk with his guilt, and as we moved through the main doors into the spreading light and round to the left of the building towards the kitchen for a late supper, I was shaping the last conspiracies of the plan I was hatching.

Through the empty dining hall, into the kitchen that was dim fluorescent light, brown floor tiles, industrial kitchen units, and humming fridges.

'It was never always like this you know,' his head was bowed as he spoke, subdued, as he opened the tall silver industrial fridge.

'There used to be good staff here, with good temperaments. They found other ways to discipline the children.' He passed me the clingfilm covered plate. Cold ham, pasta, potato salad, mixed carrots, and sweetcorn. A pack of crisps, an orange drink, a straw. He continued, 'then we had new staff come in.' He looked at me a moment. I had anger and fear that niggled at me. My eyes said he was genuine but my head warned not to trust.

His slightly watery eyes blinked heavily behind the square glasses.

'Sometimes, Stephen. A few bad apples as they say really can ruin a high percentage of a promising barrel. Just stay out of the way of the bad ones. Some do try to help behind closed doors.'

He escorted me to the dining hall, watched me with focused attention as I sat quietly and had my supper. 'I'll have to take you up after this, Stephen to your room. Because of where you've been in the boiler room, Cooper doesn't want you mixing with the children.'

I would be upstairs, he had confirmed. I was wolfing the food down and was again receiving a glow of normality. My sanctuary upstairs far at the end of the second floor was where I wanted to be. The darkness and the feelings and the smells of the copper smelling dampness of the boiler room were fading from my mind.

The trauma of a rat that couldn't be seen but scratched, isolated darkness and insects that hung and travelled unseen. 'I'm sorry, Stephen.

There's nothing I or the other staff can do about it...'

I was chewing and swallowing the twisted pasta. Eyes staring past and over and through him. I could envisage only the plan. When they had put me in my room, when the noise had settled, I would pack a little change of clothes and a few things, shimmy down from my bedroom window into the freedom of the night. There was a ten-pound note hidden in one of my books for emergencies. It would give me the train fare I needed for London. I would not see the morning light here. I could not go back to the constraining claustrophobia of the boiler room. The threats or the unseen. I would go to see my foster mother.

The sure darkness of the evening had folded like a trap around us.

We were making ourselves ready at the bus stop and behind us, somewhere in a shop that was getting ready to close its doors, I heard it stretch out into the coldness of the busy December traffic. Carols. A choir that sung a soft comforting melody that moved forward and spread out fan-like. With creeping emotional fingers, it tried to stir something inside me.

Quick. With a forceful pace.

We moved forward, towards the lights at the door across the road. In my mind, I had passed the point of no return as on the other side of the road I raised the shotgun from under my jacket. I was at the door, glass, and silver metallic. I kicked it. Connie had the firearm behind me.

'   Get on the floor' Shouted with force and splitting a shard of noise into the light of the room.

'   Armed Police, Drop your weapons!' I had heard it. A dreaded fear arrived with it. From the corner of my eye I saw Connie's silhouette as it darted away. I only had a struggle. A plainclothes officer had appeared. From just inside the door the undercover police officers had waited. He pounced and grabbed the gun. Our eyes locked.

He was big, broad-shouldered and taller than me with short black hair.

A first shot went into the air. A final cracking roar that vibrated and sent wadding and zinc into the night and rang in our ears. It seemed like seconds. Up, down. We were twisting and turning. Pulling and grappling, tearing to control the shotgun. Around me, all hell broke loose. Screaming, shouts, people running, hard. Cars screeched, police sirens screamed. The police officer had the gun and he pulled at it. It weaved and jumped too quick as we struggled on the floor. Again, by accident, another shot went off, ricocheted on the pavement.

I ran for my life. I had left the gun, the police officer behind me on the busy lit road. Took a quick left into Barnet Grove and its street lit darkness. Fear soared through me. A terrifying feeling that heightened my senses put my body on overdrive and gripped my thoughts with an icy hand. It was in slow motion. All of it. The policeman behind. The gun. My panting struggling breath. Limbs that ached. My utter terror. The shout of Armed Police. The desperate running from the brightly lit road and the discarded firearm behind me. The darkness of the road, broken only by dim scattered street light.

Fighting for my life I ran, zig-zagging down the slim pavement. I was throwing the cartridges from my front jacket pockets under the parked cars. In my head amongst the terror of my mind, I was sure I would die. I imagined, as I darted left and right to confuse police firing positions and make a target harder, that the shot would hit me in the back. In surging panic, and under the waxing moon and in the cold street, I continued to run for my life. Across the cracking slimmer and tighter pavement. Between parked cars and with the high black iron railings of the Turin Street estate hugging my left side. My mouth was dry. My breathing stuttered. Devoid of moisture the air was harsher to my lungs

I knew the police were behind me but no bullet came. The night was rent with the scream of police sirens. A drilling whirl that overpowered the night. I could hear them close. Like a swarm of bees, they circled and wove together through the darkened streets closing quickly. I took a left through the small opening in the black railings. One of my gloves came loose and dropped. In my haste, it was left. I was into the thin darkened maze of the flats and desperate to escape.

I saw them. At first glance, A group of shadowy figures with weapons trained on me. I heard it above. A police helicopter that had appeared from nowhere as it rose with the targeted blaring beam of a searchlight that carved the evening blackness. 'Show us your hands. Down! Down!'

They had kicked me to the floor. Held me down. Faces that screwed and growled and were pumped. I couldn't breathe on the floor. My face writhed on the gritted stony tarmac while the streaming glare of the helicopter spotlight watched. I was kicked in the face.

'Fuckin' shoot at us'.

My hands were cuffed tightly. People were on their balconies in the flats screaming.

'Leave him alone!'

'Get inside,' the police threatened. I could hear the rotors of the helicopter, feel the vacuumed air disbursed into the darkness. My mouth was bloody. More police had arrived. Blue light danced around us.

It was over.

I heard them say, 'We need to go to a secure location.' We were going to the high-security Police Station on Leman Street. My face was on the cold dirt of the ground. I was numb and my spiked adrenalin and terror were levelling together.

On the floor, cuffed, my body stretched out, I looked across from me and could see as figures struggled on the floor and Connie Draper was being arrested.

The two members of the flying squad had watched the robbers make their approach to the target on Bethnal Green Road and park their car. They had been part of the team that had had them under surveillance at different times and with different armed robbery teams at separate operations that had cross-pollinated over the last two years. They knew very well who Stephen Gillen and Connie Slaney were, who they were associated with and what they were suspected of being involved in. Together they had made their plan.

One of them, a younger Detective named Steadman viewed the moving scene. He had clear hazel eyes and a pinched face with a mole on the side of his lip that rose when he smiled. The helicopter and its spotlight climbed vertically into the darkness. Neighbours were still out on their balconies hurling abuse. Aimed into the night above them and around them, the racket circled and bounced between the lighted doors and windows. A riot of shouts and accusations and twisted voices. He looked at the suspect Gillen who, cuffed, was being escorted to a police car.

…The two flying Squad Detectives had been tasked with making the scene safe after the incident. As they had searched carefully the route the suspect Gillen had taken after the shots had been fired, under parked cars they had found an assortment of shotgun cartridges and one black woollen glove. The matching glove had been found on the pavement by the iron railings at the entrance to the estate.

Detective Steadman shifted back slightly. He had a slight limp and knew that behind closed doors he was the brunt of wisecracks. He looked at the black woollen glove in his hand. Gillen was getting into the back of the police car under heavy guard.

He smiled to himself.

He had made a point of searching Gillen as he lay cuffed on the floor and he had slipped the other glove back into his pocket with a shotgun cartridge. He looked at his other colleague. He was across the tarmac helping the other Detectives with Slaney. The helicopter had gone now, slipped into the night on another operation. Balconies were becoming empty now. Windows and doors closing and drawing curtains. Excitement over people were quietening down.

The black woollen glove was in his hand. Slaney was twisting and pulling in his cuffs as they lifted him to his feet. Across the stained pavement, with the icy late December blackness freezing their ears and noses and faces the two Detectives eyes met. They looked at the woollen glove one of them held and they nodded. The glove would be taken round to where the shots were discharged and photographed on the ground as evidence. A cartridge and the other glove had been planted on Gillen in the search.

In the darkness, with the suspects now contained and arrested, the Flying Squad officer walked back to arrange things and take the necessary photographs. In his mind, it was easy. When Gillen's clothes were removed for forensics he would put a stocking mask into the inside pocket of his jacket. The gloves would link him to the scenes where the shots were fired…

Twenty Years later…

When the tortuous madness had started to infiltrate my mind and thoughts, it had appeared like a slight, sparse and scattered wind blowing through the corridors of my mind announcing its appearance but leaving no trace behind it. Twisting and turning, pushing and pressing it resembled a strangling vine that would position quickly and surely. A scene that would lighten with abject colour and slightly weird strangeness, accompanying thoughts and hinted at voices, eyes that played tricks and non-lucid moments and feelings that spun and poked and prodded in terrifying ways. The first signs of the mental illness that would accelerate quickly towards a living, walking, dreaming hell. I was thirty-eight years old.

The cell was in disarray. A shadowy throwback to the old days of slop-out when I had been a boy and there were no sinks or toilets only a bucket in the corner. Old filthy walls with an arched ceiling, broken by grey and green paint with uneven brickwork showing. Two little shelves screwed into the walls, one cupboard, the blue framed metal bed with the same old green cotton prison blankets.

It had started in the early evening bang-up. As the yellow disc of the sun vanished and darkness approached.

The voices that talked of chopping and butchering and conspiracy and plot and murder. I would be killed, they promised me. They whispered the ways they would do it.
I had climbed up on the two white pipes that went along the bottom of the cell wall. Peered out at the crumbling light into the empty exercise yard. I was alone with my thoughts, fears, and confusion.

They sounded outside. The laughing, taunting, voices. But they echoed inside my head. Loud, then soft. Whispers then raised talking. Conversations that would be between people then weave into one that spoke directly.

There was a slicing, freezing fear inside me. I knew but did not recognize the voices that cut and punched. They were strange and unknown then would take on the accents of people from the past. Terrible content that spoke in a lull. Laughing. Poking. Prodding. Mocking and ridiculing. From the growling voices of people, I had known but who were not here, could not be here.

'We will kill you.' I heard it. As if was whispered in my ear. As it tumbled and circled in my head. I was powerless to act. 'We will get you. It is your time now. No one walks away. Not you no one.'

I was in the corner on my cell. It was in my head, but it was spoken outside. The arched ceiling spun. A trapped spinning, chemical feeling that twisted the shadows of the cell.
Oh god, I thought. My hands covered my ears. My eyes were closed. I could still hear it. It would come and go. Like lurking ghosts in the dark that pivoted and disappeared.

The shadows crept further across the cell floor. It seemed like an hour but it had been all night. I had turned the cell light on but could not stand it, could hear the conspiracy of the voices rise louder.

So, in the corner, in the darkest safest place I sat, waited. They were laughing again. A pursuing mocking that twisted a paralysing fear and scattered my broken thoughts. It returned to a whisper. I strained to hear its words. No words, but it was putting the feeling into me. It was coming from the pipes right through the building.
Whispers.

They said the prison officers were going to kill me. That this was how it was going to happen. They had killed the likes of me before. Come in the quiet hours and strung people to dangle by strangling twisted sheets at the window. Jumbled thoughts sprinkled with terror dropped in my damaged mind. I watched the back of the locked prison door. Studied the spy hole. I thought it moved, but it didn't. I swore I could hear feet outside on the landing. Shoes that crept and moved and conspired to my murder. The voices hissed. There was no escape. I would not see daylight, they spat. They were coming, the screws that would do the job the voices promised. Turned the corner at the bottom of the stairs on the bottom floor. Their sure feet crept on the shiny floor.

They were coming…

I was broken, I knew that. Something was wrong in the strange maze of my mind. I pulled and reached for clarity, at my sanity, but it eluded me. My thought and feelings were contorted. It was like being in a world of psychedelics I realized. Heavily saturated with serotonin and auditory changes. In the corner, ill with pain and a terror that mocked I screamed in my mind. A heart wrenching, deep visitation that languished too far and was lost for too long. My mouth was open but there was no sound.

Twenty Years earlier…

Detective Inspector Sixsmith and DS Truman were on the other side of the cell door. The latch was open and there was a scratching and triumphant look in their eyes. Sixsmith said in a harsh crunched voice, 'you're lucky, Gillen. You had a lot of luck out there tonight. I told you your time would come. The world is run by stories, and be under no doubt, your story tonight could have been very different. The gods were with you. There were a lot of pedestrians. If we could have got a clearer line of fire…?'

In the cell, although a doom had befallen me, feeling weak, desperate and broken, I felt the fight still grew in me. Trapped desperation, that was the seriousness of my predicament, was loading inside me at an alarming rate. My eyes glared back at them. A brave face, but it was built on the deception of a tumbling foundation inside.

'Shooting at police,' Truman waded in. '…Firearms with intent to endanger life, conspiracy to rob. You're going away for a long time… You'll get eighteen for this.'

Sixsmith chipped in, 'tell us about the other robberies. The Security vans. I can make it easier for you. Help us with the names, the jobs. We can put a note to the judge. We'll make sure you get a lenient sentence.'

'You can go and fuck off. I'd rather eat stones on the road!'
I was at the back of the cell. In my white paper-thin forensic suit, sitting on the cold step as far as possible away from them.

DI Sixsmith's eyes were at the opening. Two weathered, icy green, hard, serious oval-shaped balls that glared menace.

'I'm going to put you, and that Slaney, away for a very long time. Remember, Gillen. All your friends are gone. The robbers, the villains, the gunmen they're all-in prison. We'll get around to the ones who are left. They'll be no more robbers in the east end. I told you I would fix you, Gillen. I'm going to see you get double figures.
The face, the glaring eyes, the menace moved from the metal hatch.
Sixsmith said, angrily, 'DS Truman. Read him the extra charges'

'Gillen. I must caution you…' It was Truman.
His lazy eye squinted. He read, 'On top of the other charges, we are going to add another charge of having a firearm without a license. Do you understand? have you anything to say, Gillen?'
I was at the hatch at the metal door. I lingered by the frame and looked into Truman's mocking face, the angry lazy eye that looked down on me.
Softly, confidently, I said, 'I've got one thing, yes'.
'Which is?' The pen was in Truman's fingers. The File and charge sheet in his hand.
'Ok, I'll stick my hands up to that and you drop all the other charges'. I was in pain, but the laugh had swept through me. A moment of relief. From my mind, the words had surged then spinning back through my body, lips, and eyes. Their faces had switched, changed. From mocking to incredulous red anger.

The metal flap was slammed closed. A final sound that heightened the white spartan isolation of the cell around me again.

From the other side of the door, I heard them. Truman saying, very dodgy, Gov, these two. Sixsmith answering, Very dodgy indeed. Their footsteps moved and got fainter.

At the end of the hall, I heard Patrickson shout, 'You're going away for a long time, Gillen. We're going to personally see to it!'

I sighed. The desperation and the claustrophobia tightened around me. A starched, filthy whiteness that was the distant jingle of Keys and shiny floors mixed with the constant hum of a nearby generator. My body ached. My thoughts were jumbled and torn. I sunk to the floor exhausted.

Twenty Years later...

The prison Doctor, an aged thin figure with short grey hair and horn-rimmed spectacles listened intently to the report from the Senior Officer. He was in his prison surgery office. The file with the name Stephen Gillen was in front of him on the MDF table.

'He does show signs of illness, Doctor. His moods are very unstable. You can see he's not right. We thought he might be playing us. This prisoner has quite a history. Ex Cat A, Special Units, years in segregation, done the rounds. Drug abuse. He has a very large security file. Security watches him very closely.'

The doctor looked at the prisoner officer. An aged bald man with pale skin and a dark beard.

'What are the family circumstances?'

'He gets visits. Has a partner called Lisa and has three children. Two boys, Terry thirteen and Antony one. One girl called Sophia aged two. He is due for release next week. We have been watching him closely on the wing. He is showing signs of schizophrenia. The medics have seen him a couple of times.'

The Doctor was writing in the file, 'and drugs?'

'Yes, we believe so. He has a history of class A's and drug abuse. I've talked to the Principal Officer. We feel it would be wise to have him assessed as he's being released back into the community.'

'OK'. He wrote in the file. The Doctor nodded. 'I'll see him now then. Bring him over.'

…The night had been long and unremitting in its lonely confusion and pain. The day before had stretched and weaved and passed in a haze of light and movement that was confusion. In my cell, I was having a calmer moment. I was battling for my sanity I knew that but the nature of my illness was such that its scattering disillusions would bend fact and fiction, reality and illusion. I would feel in control, then its return would be so subtle I would not see it until its grip had me in a confused emotional state. My mind would race as I heard switching voices in the roles of good and bad. I would imagine things. Forget things. Be high with ecstatic feelings then race with breakneck speed to the depths of despair.

The cell door opened. I had been asking for a Doctor, but only the medics had seen me. I had been left, isolated with my emotional pain and my terrifying thoughts.
'Doctors, Gillen.' The screw stood by the opened cell door.

I went out onto the landing. A dark place of metal, wire mesh, a tall ceiling, and four high open floors. The noise of keys, shouting voices, banging, metal hitting metal rang in my ears. Disinfectant, old soap, and floor polish were attacking my senses and somewhere, above the juddering sounds of the prison workshops, was the aura of bland mass cooked cheap food.

Following. Down the two sets of metal stairs to reach the lower landing and the ground floor. I needed treatment, but I didn't know what. I remembered my visit a few days before. My two young beautiful children Sophia and Anthony had been brought up by their mother Lisa. Two little balls of love and activity. One walking, one on my knee. I had felt love envelope me and we had played, smiled, cuddled and ate chocolate and drunk fizzy drink. The instability of my mind had eased and I had kept it together. After leaving the two-hour visit, with my heart and mind stable and filled with the love of my children, the illness had again visited the weakened parts of my psyche and my mind again had deteriorated.

The officer led. Across the worn lined tarmac of the fenced exercise yard, through the double gates, past the works department and the tall chimney, through another set of gates and past another house block. It was a soft sunny day. Birds littered the isolated trees around the prison. High calming winds were coming from the thermals above and gently massaging my face. Inside I still struggled to keep my thoughts in order. Just the day before, an hour before exercise. The illness has started, voices that said they were a gang that waited for me to come outside and that I was going to be cut, stabbed, beaten. Inside my crunching feelings and thoughts had merged in a battle that was my anger and fear. I had tucked magazines inside the waistband of my jeans to shield me from the knives, ran outside to face them and meet the challenge.

No threat had been there. Only the normality of inmates walking, who talked and minded their own business. I had sat by myself away from everyone and I understood clearly that I was losing my mind. That the years of violent trauma had taken their toll and my mind had finally cracked.

The smell of the dentist's room was in my nostrils as we entered the hospital wing. A sweet smell mixed with the ingredients of sterilization equipment, gases, and medicines. The floor was spotless here. Shiny grey and blue tiles that were scrubbed and polished. People sat on iron benches fixed to a blue waiting room wall. A long corridor burnished strict white stretched far to my right side. I was escorted to a brown door. The prison officer knocked.

'Yes,' muffled.

'Gillen, Sir...?'

'Let him in, 'Clearer. A cut-glass voice that indicated sharpness. The door opened. I was an emotional wreck. In a weakened state, frantically trying to hold onto my sanity, I walked in.

☙

...The dream came with the early morning light. It was warm and brought with it rays of coloured light that was the smile on people's faces, soft curling lips and eyes that watched and shone. We were in the woods by the small crater in the earth. The sound of the wood was around us as we swung across the dell on the rope which had been tied high on the over-hanging tree above us. Flickering, as we moved, the sunlight jumped and winked and flitted between the leaves, shrubbery and trees. Swinging, the blond-haired boy whom I could not recognise and I, ventured fast and high, facing each other, legs pushing and kicking for more leverage.

From the high packed dusty-earth she watched.

At the crest of the secluded hollow by the healthy silver bark of a birch tree. A young, slim, attractive girl with dark raven hair that stretched to the floor.

It was in the glow and shape of their face and in the silk of their hair, I thought and felt. The love and the belonging and the togetherness. A yearning to touch and sense and be part of.

I was caught up in the sound and movement of it all. The stretching rope as we twisted and laughed and moved, the sunlight that danced, the feelings of inner warmth that circled and swam. The colours were heightened, more vibrant and prominent, a riot of wonderfulness that turned, spread and merged.

By the birch the girl smiled. A long, wide and soft gesture that showed dazzling white teeth against the rich darkness of her tumbling hair. I was lost to it, pulled in and beguiled and suddenly I was walking through the forest, across the scattered leaves and protruding roots and twigs and branches. The girl was in front of me, her raven hair getting longer and beginning to knot as it dragged behind her on the earth.

My hand was up. My mouth moved to warn her but no sound arrived. She forged forward, hair turning, tumbling over the leaves and undergrowth. The feelings of ecstasy were dropping inside me and no matter how I tried to reach her she remained the same distance in front. I stumbled, over roots, stones, vines. My instinct was to see her face, to shout out so she would again turn and see me…I was abandoned. Again, I could not reach her. It was a desperation now to not be left again. Ghost like she continued to move through the wood. I followed. Suddenly I looked in my hand and saw teeth, I felt they were falling out. Stretching, loosening, wiggling. The whole landscape had changed. The girl was there, the raven hair, but her face remained hidden, and we were falling. An off-white no man's land of open spaces and patchy clouds. I reached out. She said I can take you to your true mother. Quickly we dived, spinning, falling…

❧

'Stephen! Stephen!' I heard it and felt it at the same time. The girl was gone. The wood, the mystery of it and the changing feelings. Snatched and evaporated.

It jumped on the bed. I opened my eyes. It was my two-year-old foster brother, Jimmy he pushed, pulled and tugged me from my sleep. Jimmy, a square tubby body with a wide frame, mocking green eyes, skewwhiff fair hair and a round forming face. Standing only in swinging tee shirt and bare feet.

He was climbing on me now, crawling over me and his giggles were infectious. I played dead. Then, with one eye open suddenly sprung up and tickled him. It was a good game. He had achieved his mission of pulling me from sleep. I could feel the fresh lightness of the love between us. Good, pure joy and fun as we wrestled on the bed. My sides were splitting with the laughter and we tumbled and held on to each other.

The quilt was on the floor.

He came again, wouldn't go and giggled and jumped and ran around the room. A ball of never-ending energy, like a puppy. I was awake now. Standing with pulled sticking out hair, bleary eyes and a red flustered face and skin.

'Out now. That's enough…Out!'

His laughing heightened, a crescendo that matched the bedroom door as I pulled and they pushed to open it.

Tumbling feet rolled across the carpet outside as he found the other room next door. He had moved to the airing cupboard at the end of the hall. I sat on the bed. Outside the window, across the small back garden the expanse of the morning was hinting of a fair autumn day. The home and the care authorities would have discovered my escape now. Another absconder loose in the world of missing people. It would have been written up and filed and discussed and lodged and handed over.

It had gone well for me so far, I accepted.

I had caught a steady train that had transferred me through the late evening, then a bus and walked the last mile to my mother's house.

I crossed the landing and went into the shower. I had arrived late at my fosters mother's house and knocked the door. Alice Doherty had been shocked to see me, but let me in.

Under the shower, with the hot water streaming over me and freshening my senses I wondered how she would be this morning.

Dressed in fresh jeans and a red jumper I entered the room.

Alice smiled when I saw her, a sideways look joined with questioning eyes that framed the attractive fix of her brunet coloured hair as she ironed.

'Well, see you made a run for it again, Stephen. They'll come here for you. You know you can't stay...'

I took a seat on the wooden chair, by the round table that was facing the main kitchen sink. Jimmy thundered down the stairs, five-year-old Dominic with him. They flew in chasing each other, giggling, laughing, then went next door and played in the sitting room.

I said, 'I know, Alice. I couldn't stay there. They do bad stuff there. I'm always fighting'

The room was a comfortable temperature. The sun was filtering in from the garden spreading the walls and floor around us with warmth and soft glinting light. But her mood was shifting. She rested the iron upright on the ironing board.
'Stephen, you're always fighting. That's your problem, you will never listen.'

'Alice, some of us are forced into this hardness.'

She was moving the iron. Its steam was in the middle of our silences.

'Stephen, you don't know hardness. It was hard for me too. I came to this country I had nothing...I met your foster father when I needed to rent one of the rooms he was working on in a house for his boss.'
I continued, 'I have to survive, Alice. They beat the shit out of us there.
Alice returned, 'You put yourself there.'
It was what she done. Deflected and twisted things in the cold light of day into confusing things that were grey and unredeemable and out of reach.

I could feel it.

The frustration rattled around inside me. Sarcastically, I said, 'Mind you things weren't any better here…'

She tuned then. The iron was lifted but still in her hand. Her eyes flashed, a look I knew well combined with her sharp tongue. 'Now, Stephen he might not be a saint, but Liam was good to you. We had to work hard for everything we ever got. No one ever gave us anything.'

I was silent. It was another strategy she used, moving the furniture of her life around in her head to suit the circumstances of her feelings. A patchwork tapestry where things could be hidden, buried, shifted and remodelled to dovetail with the season or the moment.

I had made a coffee and the strength of it was in my mouth. Alice had still stood in as a surrogate mother. I had missed the smell of her, the Palmolive soap that was freshness and a quality face cream and shampooed hair. The rare times when as mother and son we had achieved a special and bankable moment. Fleeting seconds that would arrive and dissipate like unplanned for fog.

Forcefully, she said, 'You'll have to go, Stephen. We can't have you here. You got yourself into this again, you'll have to get yourself out of it.'

'But I can't see them coming here, Alice?'

'I don't care, Stephen. Liam and I have the kids now. We can't be having no more trouble. This is the way you learn'.

She had always taken this role. A person who was there but not there, who would arrive but would always be gone again.

Alice stood there now, a figure that blocked the inviting light behind her. The iron hissed, steam scattered as it was pushed forward. The children were in. A cluster of noise that pushed now and shoved with play fighting. They appeared, then withdrew again, ran out of the kitchen along the hallway and crashed up the stairs towards the bedrooms and new pastures.

'Alice?' a soft, clear measured voice.

'Yes?'

'Did you ever hear anything about my birth mother? She has been in my head a lot lately, as if she is somewhere and thinks of me?'

Her eyes had clouded, I saw it, but the furniture she had positioned for that part of her life would never be allowed to be removed. I knew it hurt her.

'Things were different then in those days. I'm sorry, Stephen. I didn't know her. But we know she is a good woman and always wished the best for you. You're here now. You are with good people. We took you when you needed a home. Your Aunt Margorie and your Uncles gave you the best of care…you were lucky, you could have been without a home.'

The iron was moving faster I saw, fanning movements with more focus and more force.

I said, 'I need to know the past, I want to know what she looks like, what the answers are to my past?'

'Stephen, sometimes it's better to leave the past alone, to let sleeping dogs lie sleeping. You're here now aren't you. Jesus. We do try our best with you.'

I got up, stood from the chair, seeking more of the light and warmth of the morning sun from the window, and an uncomfortable knowledge was niggling and gnawing at my insides.

'But how will I truly know my future if I do not understand and unravel my past…?'

The iron stopped abruptly. Alice Doherty had her head up, eyes boring into me and through me. I had missed the little times we had had alone in the dark cold nights when we had snuggled on the sofa watching an old film.

She said, 'Stephen. People, all of us sometimes have to make choices we do not want to, sometime we want circumstances, sometimes we don't. To survive is the job of most people'.

I turned from her. To my own thoughts of abandonment that were a picture of jumbled pictures and pains. She was my foster mother and I loved her but it was her way to show and give only enough, bits and pieces, tell everyone how she loved me but never show it or speak directly to me. There was a yearning soaring through me which I couldn't identify as it was accompanied by loss and rising anger.

The emotions twisted and reconfigured, a picture that was incorporated into the fabric of me and was always dominated by internal anger.

Alice was back to the ironing. All knowing but keeping the past close to her like a padlocked closed book.

I was at the door to the hallway. My back was to her silence but I turned and articulated, 'Alice, I'm going to go now. In case they come. I agree the kids are here now. But I feel isolated, Alice. Lost. Like I don't know what to do or where to go. All I feel is loneliness, the anger is all over me. I can't go back, Alice…?'

Mrs Doherty stopped, only a moment. Looked up before she returned to pull the shirt on the ironing board. The light was behind her. It created stretching moving shadows on the tiles between us.

She said, 'Stephen, catch yourself on. You will never learn. You've made your bed you'll have to lie on it!'

Chapter 9
Sentencing at the Old Bailey

The courtroom in the Old Bailey was deathly silent again. A strategic pause in the great theatre, as the Queens Council adjusted his white peruke and theatrically lifted the cuff of his black bar jacket.

He looked to the witness stand, across the packed wooden court room, to Detective Steadman, and in a clear-cut voice, 'Detective Steadman you are an experienced officer of the Flying Squad are you not…?'

He flicked theatrically through the papers in front of him, looked around the court, checked he held the courtroom in the palm of his hand and continued, 'Twenty years luminous service I see with commendations. It is right Detective Steadman, for us mere mortals, for the jury and the rest of us to suppose that someone of your experience who reached such a high position in such a coveted and specialised counter Organised Crime division as the Flying Squad would be a very talented officer indeed?'

The Barrister paused. A lengthy silence that stretched the eyes and ears and minds of the enthralled court room.
DC Steadman nodded. In a grey suit, wearing his Flying Squad badge on the front of his lapel, his face was indicating concern and the black hair he had swept to the side was falling.

'A highly experienced officer, decorated and in one of Scotland Yard's most famous and coveted Divisions. A group by the way so named 'the Flying Squad' as it policed all over London without any boundaries.'

He looked at the jury, three aged and four younger stony-faced women and five listening middle-aged men. An engaging invitation of friendship so as to infiltrate their thoughts. The silence was again held a moment...

'   A squad that moved around London at will. With no boundaries, unseen and accountable to no one...'

Pensively, imposing his personal magnetism upon and around the packed wooden panelled courtroom, the Queens Council for effect quickly again scanned the faces in the room. Across the captivated and seated jury, the red and purpled robed figure of Justice Peterson, the stenographer, the press, police witnesses and public, the black robed Prosecution QC Silk and his junior barrister. Finally the defendants Stephen Gillen and Connie Slaney who sat behind him in the dock.

Then, with a high wave of his arm, he said, 'Your honour, I call exhibit 6.5...'

They watched, all in the court, eyes trailing the trotting usher as he brought the small long, brown paper bag to Detective Constable Steadman.

It was in Steadman's hands. He stood in plain view of all in the court, but as he tumbled out the exhibit's contents, a light grey part of a woman's stocking which had two small torn eye sockets in it, he tried to scrunch it tighter into a ball in his hand.

The Defence Queens Council, quickly interjected, 'No, Mr Steadman, open it out. Open it out. Let the court see.'

From the dock, settled behind the wooden panel with a brass holding bar and in my blue suit and smart blue tie, I studied, Steadman intently. He sweated. The stocking mask was stretched over one hand that was held out in front of him for all to see. He was lying. Everyone could see it.

I scanned the courtroom and stopped suddenly. In the public gallery, I noticed him and the realization struck me. A middle-aged man with sharp, pointed hard and memorable features, a thin, strong moulded face with black, grey flecked hair and deep fathomless green eyes. In a simple white shirt open at the neck, he again rubbed the slight stubble on his cheek with a three fingered hand and I knew, I had seen what had struck me. It was the man from the bus stop who had stood close to me on the night of the robbery and disappeared into the night. I studied his face, willed him to turn his face, his eyes to meet mine. He looked a rigid straight line in front of him. Focused and unresponsive, green eyes staring forward.

'Does that look like part of a robbers kit, Detective Constable Steadman, 'the Barrister continued.
'Yes'. Steadman's voice was slipping, lowering.

'Being such an experienced police officer. A commended member of one of Scotland Yards most prized active units we can then suppose that on containing these two highly dangerous armed robbers you would search them thoroughly. As your experience would have prompted you, your training dictated to you...Am I correct?'
'Yes...'

They watched him now, the jury, the press, the police and the prosecution bench. The Defence waited a few seconds longer so that his words could hang and probe and rattle. He said, 'Your honour I would now like to call exhibit 7.1.'
The usher, was at the witness stand. He passed the next exhibit, a black woollen glove.

'Now Detective Constable Steadman. You were tasked with searching and securing the scene after the incident. Is that correct?'
... 'Yes, I was, 'he fumbled. 'Detective Constable Jones was also asked to accompany me. We then...'
'Please Detective.' The QC's hand was in the air his voice mocking. 'We are all aware of your great police record. But I'm afraid I must ask the questions here.'

You could hear a pin drop. Steadman's face was turning cherry red. An amazing sign of nervousness that made him shine like a beacon.

'I ask again, Detective Constable Steadman. Do these two items... the stocking mask and the black glove look like part of a robbers kit?'

'...Yes, they do.'

'And where did you find them?'

'I searched, Gillen at the scene. He was searched again and a glove was found. I then...'

... 'Mr Steadman, you searched him twice?'

'No, once. There were two gloves. I then'

'Two gloves, Detective Steadman. So, you did search him and you found two gloves?'

'No there was three gloves. I had...'

'There were three gloves?'

'No, I...'

The Queens Council looked around the court. His face smiled knowingly. We knew the officer had been part of moving and planting evidence and our strategy was to expose his lies. The suspense was palpable in the old and aged court room. Its dusty smell had been replaced now by the sweat of the prison officers surrounding us as the court rooms energy raised. From the dock I could feel the jury's confusion and incredulity.

My defence QC's pressed home the attack.

'Let me help you, Detective Constable Steadman... They do look like part of a robber's kit. You are a highly experienced officer. Mr Gillen was searched at the scene. He was searched not once but three times. Twice at the scene as he was arrested on the floor and once more when he arrived at Leman Street Police station. I know that as I have the signed custody logs here in front of me... Detective Constable Steadman, I put it to you 'You did indeed search the defendant at the scene and that having been also the officer asked to contain the scene you saw an opportunity to seal your unsafe conviction and put the glove and cartridge in the Defendant's pockets.

'That is not true. I merely...'

'That on planting the incriminating items, Detective Constable Steadman you then moved the other glove to the scene of the crime where a firearm was discharged tightening further your false case against my client. I put it to now you are totally aware and were complicit in fabricating this evidence Mr Steadman, isn't that right?'

Steadman had turned a lighter shade of purple. His hands grabbed tightly the top of the witness stand in front of him and his jumbled word continued to tumble.

'There were three gloves. I had to log them. I then needed.'

'No Mr Steadman, there were not three gloves. There were of course only two. Both you found discarded from the assailant who escaped into the night. Mr Gillen, my client was unlucky enough to cross your path and after other officers had tackled him to the ground you searched him and placed the glove and shotgun cartridge in his pockets?'

'I didn't...It was not'

'I put it to you, you're lying Detective Constable Steadman!'

The court erupted.

Form my seat I saw it. The police and DI Sixsmith shaking their heads and closing their eyes, the jury stiffening, the press writing. The Prosecution QC, a sharped faced, brute of a silent legal assassin had been especially picked. He sat, the other glove turning in his fingers and he watched with a thin contained smile spreading on his knowing lips.

The Judge, a prominent, grey haired fearsome figure with brown burning and drilling eyes, smashed his gravel, said,' Mr

Nathan, that is enough. Temper your language please.'

'Certainly, Your Honour, I merely need to confirm the truth of the witness.'

'I'm watching Mr Nathan…'

It was planned I thought this whole business. I had sat here for two weeks, coming back and forth under heavy police guard from Brixton Special Security Unity to the Category A suite here, and like a gripping football match Defence and Prosecution were both scoring goals. End to end stuff. But just when you thought you were winning, the referee, in this case My Lord Justice Peterson would wade in, give a bad decision and save them.

He resembled your closest friend now, my Defence Barrister, a killing wolf in sheep's clothing opening a kill zone so the prey could be trapped.

'Detective Constable Steadman. We have heard differing accounts from you already. The fact remains that you would have had to have placed and planted the glove and shotgun cartridge at the scene, moved the other glove to where the attempted robbery took place!'

He turned to the jury conspiratorially. Their heads moved to listen to him, to watch the moving stages of his voice and the theatrical movement of his eyes as he spoke.

'Members of the Jury. Detective Constable Steadman had to have searched the defendant thoroughly as his career suggests, because when he searched him at the scene there is no mention of these items on his person. It was only when he arrived at the police station that the items were logged on his custody record. Also, at that point, there was no mention of a stocking mask. This was found and added as evidence three months later after the defendant's jacket came back from forensics. '

He lifted his shoulders, enforcing silence again. A long, hanging suspense that stretched and infiltrated all present and lodged in the middle of the room.

You see this is the one fly in the police and prosecution's case. The one thing I can't explain. We know he was searched very precisely and methodically, and that on three separate, mysterious occasions these items appeared, because here, in front of me typed clearly in his custody search record from his second search when he arrived at the police station is entered 'one tiny black button'.

❧

...The sea gulls followed us hungrily as we entered the central swell of the sea and left Birkenhead ferry port. Using the freshness of the clear morning breaking light, the squawking birds hovered and traversed, holding and cruising the lifting winds as they diligently searched for food. At fourteen and a half it had been hard to leave my mothers house and England behind, but I was still under the Local Authority Care and I could not bear to go back to the children's home.

The great ship cut through the slicing blue and green waves. From the safety of the top white metal deck railings I watched the gulls. The morning light was dominating the morning dawn. A sky streaked and striking, flecked with spidery yellow orange and blue grey stretched far out into the vast expanse of water ahead of me.

My feelings were moving and dipping inside me. My mind was strangely subdued, and hidden in a far corner and coming into the light of my present thoughts were the memories. Vividly they visited me. Margorie on the settee laughing, for once her black wavy hair was free of her head scarf, and with her hands clasped in her lap there was beaming happiness and contentment stamped on her face. She roared with laughter. A contagious moment, gripping. The embers of the fire in the front room crackled. The fire guard was around the hearth and Gerard rushed as soot and smoke dislodged from the chimney and powered the light brown tiles of the clean hearth.

The soft, awakening winds rushed along the contours of the ship, massaged my face and stroked my short black hair. It had been only six years since I had left Belfast but it felt like an age. I watched the large white seagull out across from me. On the open water, effortlessly it aligned with the ship's movement, matched its speed. In my mind I saw the younger me. I saw the vulnerable boy. On a ship, a small suit case clutched tight with a strange land beckoning. The feeling of the moment reared up high and grabbed me as I remembered the pain I had felt and the searing loss that I had carried.

I walked a little to the front of the great ship. The wind and the vastness of the morning was fiercer here, open and stretching out in a wide coloured tapestry. I stared into the beautiful sky. My hands gripped hard the white iron railings against the strength of the blowing wind and as I felt the freedom of being at one with everything around me. The tears took my eyes.

Twenty-Four Years later

...I had left prison but the voices in my head and the sickness had followed me. Back in the East End with my two beautiful young children, Anthony and Sophia for a while my mind had found the relief it had desperately searched for. The love and the light of my responsibility to them had tamed and checked for a couple months the mental episodes that haunted me.

My twenty-one years old son Terry was the one they had called. A late evening, urgent phone call from my family, that said the delusions were dancing before my eyes and around my head. No one could talk to or reason with me as the crippling schizophrenia had again seized and pressed in on my mind. They had phoned him quickly, and with the worry etched in their voices and the tears dropping, that I was a danger to myself. Could he come and take his dad to the hospital, they were worried about the children seeing their father like this and they needed help?

'It's ok dad...' His hand was on my shoulder. It was my son, Terry, saying the words reassuringly as we walked into the Royal London Hospital in Whitechapel.

At the main desk, 'Can I help you?'

Terry looked at the black woman in front of him. He had grown into a fine-looking young man with a solid wiry strength, knowing hazel eyes, a handsome chiselled face and a sharp cleverness. Behind the glass in a blue hospital uniform she tapped the keys on her computer.

'Yes, I phoned up earlier. My dad is not well. He's hearing things in his head and is very unstable. We're very worried about him. Can he be seen quickly?'

The receptionist looked through the glass to the side of the young man who spoke. To the well-dressed man who shifted strangely and hung behind him. Tall, dark black hair, in grey trousers, black shoes and an expensive looking blue coat, but his movements were staggered. He stood there, turning now, eyes wide and staring at everything around him.

'He's not well. We need him to see someone as soon as possible…he's been acting very strangely'

'Has he a history of mental illness, 'she asked?

'No, but he has mentioned things and has been having issues lately. I keep trying to speak to him but he doesn't really understand me. He's there but not there. I know my dad and he's is definitely in a lot of pain and not right.'

'Has he been diagnosed with anything, any schizophrenic incidents?' She was on the phone.

The receptionist, trained in spotting urgency, watched as the well-dressed man mumbled to himself. He poked the invisible air in front of him aggressively.

'I'm phoning someone now please wait.'

'Dad…' he had me, guided me to stand by some doors away from the busy throng of people scattered and moving across the large shiny grey spartan white main hospital foyer floor.

I knew it was my son. But my mind was showing and whispering and telling me things that were not real. My eyes searched for assassins. My mind told me they followed me, had trailed us and looked for the opportunity to strike. Nervously I looked at the people around me. Walking figures. Tall, fat, slim, black, white, nurses and doctors, orderlies and patients, beds that were pushed to the lifts, I watched them all. Suspicious. A moving mass of danger. It could be any of them, my swirling thoughts dictated.

I closed my eyes a moment and pushed back down the screaming anguish that was circling in me. My emotion was racing unsteadily. Like an overdose it rushed through me, my anger flew then nosedived and jumped to rage then paranoia and fear. They lurked, I waited, watched and prepared. I would be ready when they made their move.

'You, Mr Stephen Gillen?' The two doctors were late fifties. They were in starched white coats. One white, average height and weighty, with hard eyes and a chubby red face, the other Asian with greying dark hair and a stethoscope hanging around his neck.

My son stepped forward, 'No, I'm, Terry I'm his son. My father's here…Dad?'

He had me by the elbow. A comforting feeling as I continued to watch and wait for them. They were here, the assassins, picking their moment to pounce. I could see the men in the white coats leading us though the corridors. Sharp shiny halls of spartan squareness with bright lights and wandering figures where everything was suspect and the lights would suddenly dim.

He had me still by the elbow. As if he knew I needed it. It was my beautiful baby boy but I clung to him as a sailor to a piece of debris in raging seas. We were in a side room. A place of disinfectant smells and doors that were closed and locked and more people wearing white coats had arrived and closed around me. I felt it now. The searing paranoia of the trap as its key turned and bolted and locked.

The doctor with the stethoscope was in front of me, shining the beam of a light into my eyes.

'Stephen? Stephen? How are you feeling? Can you hear my voice?'

Rage was rising in me. Like a boxer about to throw a punch, it came up from the floor through my slightly raised calf and up along my body to my hips…'

'Stephen? How are you feeling?' the doctor tried again.

Fear joined my rage at my middle body as the sensation continued upwards moving across the contours on my back…

The other doctor confirmed, 'He shows signs of an episode. Stephen, can you hear us. Were going to help you, take you somewhere where we can help…'

I saw his face, but the words were inaudible. My mind saw the trap, the guns that were hidden behind their white coats. The movement of the rage was still gathering its momentum, imprinted with fear and gathering pace. It was now at my shoulder as I pivoted my hips and snapped the punch into the doctor's face. He had moved slightly at the last moment. It was a tussle, but I had connected. His face had moved with the impact but the closing bodies had grabbed me from behind and pulled me until I dropped to the floor.

I twisted. In my mind I had to escape certain death but they had me pinned violently to the floor. Knees, elbows, legs, the heavy bodies had sedated me with their weight to the floor. I tried to kick my legs. Move my locked arms to swing again. My right cheek was pinned to cold lino floor and between gasping breath I shouted obscenities, spat curses. They had an injection in my leg.

A fast, swift exercise and done with fluency.

…I saw my son. The worry that settled in his eyes. He was close. I felt his comfort near me. I heard his soft voice as I began to lose consciousness.

'It's ok dad. I'm here. Calm down I'll make sure you're ok…'

Sixteen years earlier 1992

Brixton Special Security unit was a caged prison within a prison. A year earlier Nessan Quinlivan and Pearse McAuley, two IRA men part of an Active Service Unit on the Main-Land had shot their way out going through ten gates to escape into Brixton Hill. A three-floor self-contained Unit with air lock doors in and out to the main prison and a separate central locking system for the doors once they had been closed and vibration proof sensors, upgraded since the audacious escape by Gangsters Jimmy Moody, Stan Thomson and IRA bomber Gerald Tuite, it was classed as the most secure unit in the United Kingdom.

As I listened, the phone to my ear, I could see the other inmates play on the small pool table sandwiched between the five single cells on each side of the small landing. Our cells were on the very top floor for security purposes, the Category A's on protection were on the middle landing and the hot plate where we got our food was at the bottom of tight metal stairs on the bottom floor.

Lily Draper, on the other side of the phone, in a soft soulful voice, whispered, 'Stephen, I hope your ok...I miss you. I've realised now, in these times that we have been apart and with all this happening that my love has opened to you...'

I listened, a warmth spreading in my wounded and battered heart.

...She continued, 'it stays with me. The missing and wondering of you, in the morning when I wake, and when I do my chores in the day, and when I stop a moment and my thoughts are pulled to the picture of your face, the touch of your hand...'

...I said, 'I have thought of you too. These years I questioned would it be possible, would a time ever come that we could talk like this...'

'Stephen, although you're gone, you are not here, I can see your face. A picture that's real and vivid with clear detail. The colour is on your face and your lips and your eyes are without pain… When I look back, to the years past, I now realise that when I was with you, when you were there the normal rules of life have not applied. Instead I have been left with a yearning that is to wonder what you're doing, to see your face, to feel that you are close so that I can speak with you and reveal my feelings…'

'Lily, but it is dangerous to think of me like this, to love me. You do not know what you ask of me. What this will mean for us both…'

'…Stephen, I knew it from the first time I saw you. I was too shy. I remember following you one day just so I could watch you…'

'But I shall be in this place for ever. I am looking at a long time. I would take those years from you?'

'…I will wait, Stephen.'

'I can't put you through years like this. The pain, the sacrifice…'

'We can do it together, Stephen. Together we are made of good stuff.'

'It is too much to ask, Lily…'

'We won't let them beat us. You will be home one day. We can be together, Stephen. Our love can conquer all…'

The phone was to my ear. Her voice was a comfort that soothed and cut and sent wild emotions in me. I was in a tight cage. A prison that was physical and one of the mind that pressed with the walls of emotion.

I said, softly, like a father to a child, 'I can't ask this from you, Lily. To do this is pain beyond words. One that will stretch along and through the years…'

… 'I am prepared, Stephen. We can do it. It's what I want. I'm not leaving you there.'

'How is, Callum?'

'Callum is ok. He has his wife, his children. I have no one, only you…I need only you…'

'Can you finish now, Gillen, please!'

It was one of the prison officers. They were already closing cell doors, taking the wooden snooker cues and packing up the balls on the pool table.

'Lily, you are sure? You know what you are saying, what you commit to?'

'I do. I give myself to us freely…'

The screws watched me. Annoyed eyes that were restless with hands that swung key chains.

'Lily, I'm sorry. I have to go. My god, you've given me a lot to think about. All these years I didn't know…I have to go. Give my best to Callum. Take care…you're in my mind now. I can see you too, through the pain and the bars and the keys and the uncertain future. I can see you and feel you now as if you were here with me…'

I could tell she smiled. She laughed, said, 'remember, Stephen I'm with you take care of yourself. Two peas in a pod ok…'

The phone was against my ear. The doors on either side of the small high security block were being slammed and pulled tight around me.

'Yes, I will. Two peas in a pod…'

John Melton was a confident and sure man. He had forged his career on a fast path of hard work, achievement and being with the right people and doing the right things at the perfect time. He had gone to Cambridge where he had taken a Masters in politics. After a small stint at his fathers printing business he had worked a fast route up the greasy Home Office pole, becoming an attaché to the French Ambassador, and now a senior Executive under the Head of the Prison Service and Chairman of Doc 1 and the Category A committee.

'What level of dangerousness do you think they pose for the prison service? They are target career criminals. Our intelligence paints a very grim picture...'

It was the Superintend Gold Commander, a vibrant young dark-haired man from the Met representing the police chair. Melton looked across the long teak table. There were a selection of experts and area executives who represented different divisions and operational areas that were tasked with containment and security of the country's most dangerous criminal, narcotic and terrorist prison threats.

The Head of the Probation Service, a steely eyed middle-aged woman with a soft voice, said, 'We do have records from Gillen's history. He became known to us regarding the contact to his son, Terry. He's one year old now. Lives in Bow with his grandparent. Gillen was released from HMP Wayland back in August for a home leave and didn't return...'

The Police Commander continued, 'Our intelligence suggests many worrying details about this gang. Very active with firearms, armed robbery, Security, tobacco lorry and Security Van hijacking, Organized Crime. It is a dark and long list I have it here. They are affiliated with other Organized Groups across the country and abroad particularly in Spain, Ireland and South America. They would pose a high escape risk. Her Majesty's Police service would ask they be categorised as High Risk.'

The room become silent, halted.

They looked at the Chair John Melton. An unassuming looking middle-aged man in a grey suit, with focused piercing grey/blue eyes, a round soft manicured face and short brown combed hair.

Melton thought for a moment. His paper shuffling perfectly manicured hands adjusted slightly his blue red striped tie in the collar of his pressed white shirt.

He looked out of the wide bank of windows to his right, out across Millbank and to the River Thames. Saw in the distance the tugboat that slugged through the even waters.

The files were on the table in front of him. This part of the job could be frightening. It was a responsibility not only for the safety of the Public, but necessary to the Police and Security of the State to keep these people contained, transported correctly and kept under the necessary security.

He glanced again at the intelligence files in front of him. The police would always heighten the threat, he thought. But the committee was always agreed and erred on the side of safety and security first. He looked up at them, from the files, and they still gazed and blinked in silence, awaiting his guidance.

He would steer them as always with precision. In a steady soft voice, he said, 'I've heard from you all. Thank you. I have read the background carefully, especially the security and intelligence files. There is, it certainly seems to be a case for a higher nomination of security because of the implications indicated, and because of the seriousness of the offences as well as the further Serious Crime connections. There is also a clear escape risk, and use of violence which is a contributory factor. It is therefore confirmed that Case 360, Stephen Gillen and Case 361 Connie Slaney do pose a substantial security threat and there is sufficient evidence to detain them under High Risk Category A conditions. This measure is taken as it has been proven that they are singularly and by association a threat to the Public, the Police and the security of the State.

The room busted into activity. Chairs moving across the thin grey carpet, shuffling papers, the locks of bags being buttoned, and brief cases being locked. Doc 1 the strategic Security Committee of the Home Office was finished.

John Milton had a measured blank look on his face. The brown file was in his hand. As they left he walked to the window. The Tug was further up the Thames widening the distance from Lambeth Bridge now and the Millbank below him was thick with traffic. He looked next door at the imposing clean white brickwork of the MI5 building. Indeed, he thought, it was a responsibility to do the job he did. He had a job to do, and he meant to do well.

ॐ

…With the birdsong in my ears and the smell of freshly cut grass and freshly turned earth in my nose I studied the shadow of the red kite hover against the glare of the sun. The majestic bird of prey, nearly extinct in Ireland, dipped, turned eastwards and stepped down in the moving winds searching for its prey.

The ferry from Birkenhead had quickly navigated the choppy wave littered Irish sea, and behind it England and the children's home seemed for now a distant and far off thing. I had watched the waves on the crossing and the thoughts that conjured in my mind were of a childhood and times less remembered. I had left the ship and took a train straight to Milltown Cemetery in the Falls Road. Amongst the stone angels and Gaelic crosses and headstones of paramilitary volunteers, I had walked in the gathering sunshine on the wide curving paths and paid my respect to old and far removed relatives.

I had then taken the bus and came here. On the way I had dreamed about my birth mother and what she might be doing. If she washed dishes and prepared food for an evening meal.

I looked at the two small graves in front of me. Side by side with simple marble headstones and grass a little overgrown, with withered flowers leaning and drooping to the black marble ledge they were placed on. Unremarkable for two of the most important, most remarkable people I had known. I fixed the graves, removing the stones and old offerings that spoiled the grass. I stood and looked around. Greencastle Cemetery was a small place. Quiet, private, restful in a good street and far back with a little stone wall and black iron gates. A place of queens and princes. I looked for the Red Kite but it had moved to search the high fields on the other side of the far flats.

I read the *epitaph* with a lump in my throat. 'Gone, but never forgotten. A beloved Sister, mother and friend to all. An Angel taken to her place in heaven most high...'

I put the flowers I had brought, white chrysanthemums, on my aunt Margret's grave. I could feel the movement of the slight wind slide across my face and with it the pushed and hidden emotions were bubbling and rippling deep inside me. I stood, my Uncle Jacks grave was beside me now, and tears were welling in my eyes, the pain strapped across my chest as the warmth of the sun filtered across my skin.

I had stayed for hours with the images in my mind and the unfinished words on my lips. I had asked questions of the graves where they lay and said prayers of comfort and peace and, with the heaviness and emptiness enfolding my body, with the setting sun merging with the coming darkness over the mountains had felt my past lift a little.

At the gate, with the rows of headstone behind me, a last look to the tidied graves and the white fresh flowers that had been newly laid and arranged. The far clouds were moving and spreading with more surety now above the Mourne mountains and there was no sigh of the Red Kite. Down the hill and round the road by the small houses, up the side lane and onto the busy main road. I passed the mirrored and heavily wired, steel and corrugated tin fortified RUC barracks on the corner of Whitewell Road. Up the steep slope of the hill and quickening my pace with the motorway down the deep and fenced dip in the grass verge to my right, and the thinking was to reach my Uncle Gerard and the old house in Serpenton Parade before the darkness was fully in. The houses were small, stacked tightly together and double storey as the road veered left into the back streets towards Antrim Road.

The first thing I saw was their anger and the scowls that creased and lined their faces. Three of them, as I crossed the road to take the winding street up the back way I remembered by the concrete and fenced Secondary school playground at Stella Maris, wearing old jeans, jackets and black doc Martians. A little older than me and they jumped on the boy.
'Fuckin' think you can out run us wee man.' He had long brown hair, a sandy completion and fire in his eyes.
They crowded around the boy they had on the uneven pavement.
'What you got to say now…wee fucker!' They kicked the boy on the floor. He rolled and tried to cover his head, the black hair and the vulnerability of his open face with his arms and hands.
My body baulked. I passed them head down and their eyes flashed a warning as I passed. I head the pleading of the boy as they rained the kicks upon him. Then, spat behind me, 'Hey you? Wee man.'
I wanted to leave but, in my heart, I was constrained to help the boy and I stopped and turned.
'Yeah you. Where you from wee man? I don't remember you from round here? What's your name?

212

'Why don't you leave him alone. Why you hitting him?'

They stopped. The strangeness of my voice throwing them. They moved closer, a tight ring, where a boy moaned in pain on the dirty pavement between us. They made a crescent moon shape, faced me with confused and accusatory faces.

'Wee English man, eh?' One of them said.

'Yeah, did you look at us funny as you just passed wee English man.' He had pushed me back into the green of the hedge as the words were executed. As I swung with my fist hard, hoping to catch him off guard, the anger on his face was coming closer and just at the right distance. We were locked, grappling in and along the hedge. The other two joined in and the blows were coming from places I couldn't see. I kneed the body in front of me and when I felt more space threw out punches as quick as I could.

'Get away from the house! The RUC are coming now to fix ye!' It was the old man from the house behind us who owned the now broken and ripped hedgerow. The boy who was on the floor had risen and swung a stick at our assailants, but all I could do was grapple, my back bouncing and breaking the hedge behind me as I was pinned down and tried to switch round my body weight. Crackling twigs filled my ears as the fine interior of the hedgerow fractured further.

'The police are on their way ye wee fuckers!'

I had the better of them now. The older, bigger boy clung to me. Our arms were locked on each other's shoulders as we circled and stumbled. I elbowed him hard a quick crack flush on the jaw. He yelped, and I swung him to the ground ready to give him a kick.

He moaned as I knocked the wind from him.

They arrived.

I saw them too late and was too tired to run as their grey armoured jeeps accelerated around the corner. They appeared in a second, big black uniforms that swamped the pavement. Peaked caps and bulging bullet proof vests, imposing side arms and shiny buttons on black uniforms.

… 'They fecked my beautiful hedge they did. A bloody state it is look at it.' The redness travelled his features and his finger pointed.

'Bloody, ruffians!'

I heard it as they handcuffed me and the other boy. I questioned the three who had started it and let them go. In the back of the jeep I looked up the road. At the crest of the hill, just at the top of the road was the street I grew up in. Gerard would be there, and I imagined him smoking an Embassy Red and using the poker to stoke the fire. He would be oblivious to the fact that I was on my way to the police station not two minutes down the road.

The court room was silent. A strange, frozen moment in time, where it seemed everything had halted. In our nostrils was the dusty smell of the old chestnut stained panelled wood that surrounded us mixed with shuffled paper and the slight stench of sweat from the packed people present. We stared at the judge.

The trial at the Central Criminal Court of the Old Bailey had been going on now for four weeks. As the accusations to the police witnesses had sliced deep into the integrity of their investigation and had cut sharply on the character of their conduct, Lord Justice Peterson's rulings had become tougher and harder. His mood blacker and darker, and his hawk-like piercing eyes sterner and colder.

He pulled back in his chair now. It was his moment. One he had been waiting for with relish.

His voice was sure and piercing. A commanding solo that sliced clean the air through the courtroom.

'Can the two Defendants stand up.'

You could hear a shoe squeak. Our hands grabbed the brass at the top of the dock to steady ourselves. A little wizened and lined all powerful face under a curled white wig sat high on top of his red, black and purple robes of power and ceremony. His piercing hawk-eyes drilled into us.

'...This has been a long and expensive case. It has been about a highly organized gang of armed robbers who have lived and associated, it seems by the evidence, in a fraternity of other such highly polished criminals and who would let nothing stand in their way in the execution of their crimes...'

The jury and the police who had packed the court for sentencing looked on, shifted in anticipation and waited with bated breath.

'...You have both been found guilty on all counts by a jury of your peers. You have both been defended by highly skilled advocates throughout these proceedings...'

Detective Inspector Sixsmith was smiling with DS Truman. Their Superintendent in full uniform had joined them to gloat and hear the closure of the case.

'...The attempted robbery was vicious in its planning and execution only being foiled by the diligent police work of a highly sophisticated unit from Scotland Yard...'

The jury were spellbound. They had debated long and hard coming back with a ten to two majority verdict. They hung on the judge's words.

'...It was a cold and calculated robbery where two shots were discharged from a firearm in a busy London street full of the public...'

I looked at DI Sixsmith, his cold lips formed a cutting smile loaded with sarcasm. DS Truman turned to him, joined him and his lazy eye brightened and laughed.

'...Two shots, with a pause in between them, discharged by the Defendant Gillen. Thankfully no one was injured and there were no casualties...'

Connie was to my left. He looked ahead, into the face and the words that were aimed at us. Just for a moment, one of the arms that steadied him trembled slightly. There was an emptiness in me. As if I was present, but the words the judge spoke were to someone else.

'...We have heard in your defence that evidence was moved in this case at the scene, and that members of the Flying Squad fabricated evidence, corrupted the due process of their arrest, falsified times, dates and records and perjured themselves to the complicity of these actions...'

Stephen Gillen's and Connie Slaney's eyes looked at each other. A silent language that was a knowing without words. They gulped, swallowed.

'...Therefore, you have aggravated this court with these accusations and have not admitted any guilt on your part for any wrong doing...Stephen Gillen and Connie Slaney I don't think I have come across two more dangerous young men. I have no doubt that you were willing to do whatever was needed in the execution of your crime or to procure your escape from custody...'

...He paused and looked at us with hard eyes a moment. A lengthy moment that positioned his intended impact.

It was coming to the end. It was over.

'...I have no hesitation in sentencing you both to the following. Gillen I will start with you. For Attempted Robbery fourteen years and eleven respectively...For Conspiracy to rob fourteen and eleven years...For firearms with intent to endanger life...'

Stephen Gillen and Connie Slaney stood, brave faces, looking at the judge. They felt the gasp of the jury and inside their emotions had evaporated, dropped. Numb inside the judge's voice, echoing over a hushed and enthralled courtroom, continued with the next sentences that would add up to sixty-nine years.

Chapter 10
Category A & High-Security Prison

T he man with three fingers felt the cool burning flow of the whiskey rush down his throat. In the cheap but clean bedsit chosen for invisibility in Islington. He burped and rolled to his side on the bed covers and pushed his square green, checked tweed cap to the floor. The morning light was fighting to infiltrate the cracks of the blinds he had closed tight at the window and the deep well of his depression and loneliness had returned to take him again.

He blinked his eyes, gulped. It was the hell that was a double life. The two faces to the world that he kept in place for privacy and protection. The guilt and powerlessness were seeping through him again. Like an aggressive cancer it attacked him when he was at his most vulnerable, at his weakest moments. He groaned and got to his stockinged feet, walked to the little sink and looked at his face in the mirror above it. His green eyes were less angry and bitter today. Like moving winds, they had been replaced by pain, anger, loss and guilt.

He moved, as he tended to, his three fingered hand over the stubble on his cheeks and chin. Bare chested, curled hair covering his upper torso and, in his jeans and stockinged feet he walked to the bottle, it was his fourth bottle of whiskey and he slugged at it hard. The day before he had been at the sentencing of the boy at the Old Bailey. He had missed his chance. He pulled the old, torn, black and white photo from his back pocket. He still called him the boy, although he was the man because that's what the Gardner did and was known for. Taking boys, the broken and unique and hard and lost and troublesome. The strays. Like the twisted and different and slightly broken flowers in the pretty and beautiful bunch. That's what he was instructed and driven to do and because of it they reckoned him an important nuisance and called him the Gardener.

He looked again at the old dogeared photo and the pain like a lifting jet pierced through him and his lungs filled with a rattling cry. He smashed the empty bottle of whiskey against the wall with force. He had slipped on his knees to the wooden floor and with his disfigured hand clasped the photo. Dizziness had risen within his aching body and heart and the riveting anger was growing again with every present bitterness. The boy, Stephen Gillen who was now a man might be away and out of his reach for a long time but he would be released one day, and when he was he would be waiting. Next time, at the first opportunity, he would make his decisive move and level the playing field.

…They sat in the front seats of the parked car with the rain lashing against the windscreen on the, slim, side back double road near the main supermarket close to the Old Kent Road.
'It's all there', the driver said as he passed across the small shoe box.
Sitting in the passenger seat the man, who was a serving prison officer, opened the green box. He saw the 22-calibre handgun and ammunition rounds beside it that were black taped, the two small mobile phones that were tidily placed.
'Ok. Now no one's going to get hurt? This was my one request…As long as no one gets hurt…'

The serving prison officer put the top back on the box. He had ten years' service put down and his pension would not be long in coming. Before that, he had been a Royal Marine commando serving in the Falklands. He had even been at the battle of Goose Green, in the interlocking fields as the great ship burned and the heavy and suppressive fire filled the sky with lead and tracer rounds like rain. He knew what guns were used for and what damage they could do.

The driver turned just a brief moment, said, 'no one will get hurt. We just want him out. We need him out. Here's your money'.
The brown envelope was passed.
'Ok, I'll get it into his hands. But it will be in my time. Security is always tight. I won't promise when I can get it through'.

His business was finished. With a last look at the driver, the serving prisoner officer who liked to gamble and who had problems with paying his rent pulled high the collar of his coat against the rain. He closed the car door and disappeared at the corner of the street.

The nights in high security prison close around inmates like the lull before the deafening morning storm. Rows of compartmentalised souls and minds categorised and pigeonholed for control, security, maintenance and smooth running. But no matter what the crime, the circumstance or the person, the deep well of feelings inside them that would constantly tear, rip, shudder and vault would be a struggle to manage, to control and to deal with. Of the many realities and scripts that would play in the inmate's heads, some like re-runs of old and tired B movies, the longing would always be close to the surface of everything. The longing for freedom, and sun on your face joined with the wind and grass beneath your unrestricted feet. To revisit times past so that different plans could be made, and other directions taken. To reclaim your life where you had left it and continue forward experiencing again the reward of full freedom.

In the small white-walled prison cell with the morning light filtering through the round aged bars at the high window the letter was written with a tender heart.

'...I received your last letter, Lily. It was well received with the darkness of my present time in this place of rattling keys and loud shouts. It is surreal, an otherworldly feeling to be sat here apart from you, for all I know with no future. No understanding of what that would be like and the years stretched out ahead of me...They say it can take years for a sentence like this to hit a man. My only thoughts are, after twelve years of this madness what I will be like as a person, what would I look like, what will I become...?

...My eyes can see like never before. My ears hear at an amazing volume. The sounds and feeling are echoed here and all seems to be compounded. They moved me late in the evening yesterday from Brixton Unit. I am now in Wormwood Scrubs, West London. That's the thing with Category A inmates. We never know when we're moving or where we're going. The escort arrives, the dog handlers. You're strip-searched, they take your sterile clothing separately and you'er off. There is a saying the best kept secret in the Home Office is when a Cat A is going to move.

...I watched the streets of London as the police escort moved me yesterday. They look more vivid now, more vibrant and colourful...If only, I had thought a moment. I had envisaged myself walking around the corner at the end of our road in Bethnal Green, a smile beaming on my face. I know now that the most beautiful things in this world cannot be touched, that they must be felt by the heart. My worry is what the years will do to me, Lily. How they will erode me. I worry that even my memories will disappear, that prison for me will not only be physical, but separate me from myself...
It's OK here, I have friends.

I think of you constantly. In the morning, as I eat and walk round the yard. The last thing as my eyes close for sleep. It is the picture and feeling of you. I replay what it is to kiss you, to feel the touch of your hand, move the silky hair from your beautiful face, hear your sweet voice and look into your tender eyes.

…We will get through this together, both of us as I would rather die than buckle or break. The years will turn, and our love will flourish and grow with them…'

The pen was put down on the green top of the bench. Stephen Gillen walked to the window and let the fresh air fill his lungs, the broken sun light rays cover his face. He would not sit idly and let his life be broken and slip away. There was a plan, and the plan was with others outside. A soft sure smile suddenly spilt across his lips, the pain in his heart lessened and his eyes softened. Fortune favoured the brave. A man's destiny was in his own hands. He would get his life back, like a swift hawk he would reclaim his freedom soon.

Fifteen years later…

In the closed psychiatric ward at the London Hospital Whitechapel, a place that was self-contained and treated various forms of mental heath especially forms of schizophrenia, the doctor and senior male nurse walked through the shiny burnished white and soft cream corridor.

'His son Terry's with him now, visiting. It's an interesting case. The patient has a history of long-term imprisonment, violence, other traumas. There is drug abuse. His mind has really been stretched by his lifestyle. He had to be restrained on admittance, was having lucid periods where he believed people were coming to take his life. Then, over the next couple of days, he seemed to retreat more and more from being present. There are currently no signs of engagement or response stimuli. The lights are on Doctor, but no one seems to be home I'm afraid. We're trying antipsychotics…'

The Doctor, a youthful man with black hair and a moustache nodded, said, 'It's a very interesting case. I wonder what the catalyst of his withdrawal from reality has been?'

They moved down the ward, opened the door to the simple room where the patient sat silently in a wheelchair, hands laying on his lap staring out of the wide curtained window.

From beside him, his son rose. 'Hi.'
The doctor shook his hand. 'You're, Terry, Stephen Gillen's son?'
'Yes...'

The doctor looked around the room. A quick scan. The metal bed with pristine blankets and a white sheet, the bed side locker with its jug of water, a locker for the patients' possessions. All clean, sanitised and minimalistic they way he liked it. On the far wall, a wide and large mural of many bursting colours, in the style of a Picasso reached and shouted its brightness.
The doctor smiled, it was a perfect tool to engage the patient and lessen his retreat.
He said, 'So how has he been with you, Terry any response?'
'No...'

The doctor could hear the pain and worry in his voice as it had emerged. He was by the patient, Stephen Gillen.
'Is he going to be alright, Doctor?'

The doctor looked into the patients open, staring, fixed non blinking hazel eyes. As he shone a light into the pupils, he said,' Stephen, how are you today? Your son's visiting. He's here and happy to see you. Isn't that wonderful. What do you think of that?'
Silence.

The patient looked forward, through the light of the wide window with no response, a shadow that lingered unmoving, trapped.

The Doctor pinched the patients forearm slightly looking

for signs of response.

Nothing.

'...Is he going to be OK, Doctor. I mean will he get better, come back to us?' Terry stood by the curtained window, the falling light fanning out across the side of his face highlighting etched and worn worry.

The Doctor continued, 'Stephen, your son, Terry has some wonderful stories. He's wonderful. I bet you remember the day he was born? Do you remember the day your son was born, Stephen? What did you feel that day?'

They were huddled together the three of them in the tiny room and the silence was in front of them unmoving. Stephen Gillen looked pale the Doctor thought. There was a waxy look, a pallor to his unresponsive face muscles. His eyes, blank and withdrawn, had a hollow look that was troubling. Silent, unmoving, and having made a full retreat internally to a deep place of unreachable rooms the patient, it seemed was completely absent.

Twenty-Three earlier...

As the fresh mist of the morning fell from the Mourne mountains, Belfast tried to heal from the violent activity and civil unrest of the night before. I had been transported by RUC to St Patrick's approved training school. Home for troubled and disruptive children as the streets were being cleared of debris and the British Army were raiding properties and forming new checkpoints.

I followed the long black robes of the tall Christian brother in front as he escorted me along the quiet echoing corridor. In my little room, in the juvenile section I had slept badly the night before as the soft blackness had turned into lonely darkness. I had felt deep longing inside me. A juddering set of igniting, worrying emotions that filled my mind with remembered fears. Sat on my small chair, in a spartan single white room with no colour for comfort, I had endured the early hours as they passed, looking out of the third-floor window of the old Victorian workhouse looking building.

'In here, 'he said. A stern face with a hook-like nose hiding behind round glasses.

I went into the office. They were bastards for sure, some of the De La Salle Order. Walking around with faces that wouldn't melt that hid real abuse and harsh ways. Three weeks I had been here. I had felt the sting of it.

St Patrick's training school, which moved in 1957 to purpose-built premises on a 100 acres site on the Glen Road, West Belfast had become an approved school. One of the institutions introduced to replace the existing system of Reformatories and Industrial Schools seven years before.

The door closed behind me. It was a wide study-like office with long, short filled bookshelves. A wooden, teak table covered with green leather with the aged damp of incense filling it. Its sweetness hit my nostrils.

'Stephen…'

I had seen him, slight like he was a broken bird with an aching wing and sitting quiet in a corner chair.

He stood up, 'Stephen.'

My Uncle Gerard. He had me in his embrace. A strong, loving grip and I was melting with the love I had missed.

'How are you', he said. 'How have you been, Stephen. Are you OK here?'

It was in his soft eyes. The past hurt that lingered and the days and nights of worry that were wearing him down.

'I'm ok, Uncle Gerard. God I'm glad to see you…'

'Sit please', It was the Christian Brother from behind the desk, and he feigned a smile. Behind it, I thought was a much darker man.

He continued, 'So, Stephen was taken here a few weeks ago. He's going to go the Crumlin Road court tomorrow. They should release him to your care. They may let him go back to England, or they may not.'

Gerard, was beside me. And I noticed he had still the rolled-up newspaper in his hand.

He said,' It would be good to get him out of here. The worry you know. He hasn't lived here in years. He has the strong English accent now.'

The Christian Brothers eyes narrowed. 'Ah, now, the wee man is fine. We have juniors and Seniors here. He's getting on grand with the other boys. He's being watched like the rest of them...'

I was looking at the rolled-up paper. It triggered the feeling, the image. A child again, and not a care about me and playing cowboys and Indians up in the forest near Cave Hill. The feelings were swirling deep down inside me. A boy walking the roads, and up to church and the myths and stories being put into my head.

'You're OK wee man aren't ye?'

'Yes, no bother...' I answered. It was a half lie. The other children were a mixed but great bunch. It had been hard at first, but they were my people, and when they had prodded and pulled, they had seen and discovered the strange boy with an English accent was one of their own. But I hated the place.

It was time to go and everyone was standing. A group in the middle of the room. The long black robes of the Christian Brother, a weird looking sight, twirled and shifted by the open door.

'Stephen, take care now...' Gerard, said. His loving arms were around me, pulling me in. I could feel the yearning, the lost years of wondering and time past.

'I'll be fine...' I did not want him to go. The force rising inside me was to let him take me by the hand as he had when I was a child and take me out from here.

We were walking down the corridor.

'Consider your past indiscretions now, Stephen. Think of the sum of all the parts that got you here? Pray to God he is merciful tomorrow. Ask for forgiveness and he may let you out of the Crumlin Road Courts...'

His back was to us, floating as we moved down the slim corridor. A slim bank of moving long black cloth. Gerard was looking at me, he held tightly to the rolled-up paper.

'Stephen, take care now. I'm going to get you out of here...'

The Christian Brother was opening the main doors with his keys.

Gerard pulled close to me. I listened as he spoke in my ear. Soft words, whispered, that I was to remember...

I watched him go. The words he had said hung in my head. Straight and clear and true. In my head as the door was locked behind him and the coldness of the place again closed around me, I repeated the words in my mind, 'Stephen, remember son. Sometimes you have to walk with the Devil till you cross the bridge. You keep that close to you if times get hard...'

1993, 5am

The prison officers, a specialist squad trained in control and restraint and riot management, had been briefed by the Security Governor the night before. In a wide room on the first floor of Wormwood Scrubs, on the white board, and with the Principal and Senior Officers present, they had been debriefed about the intelligence they had received about a gun being smuggled into the prison to aid a Category A prisoner in an escape plot.

In full mufti gear, with helmets and shields the ten strong team of Officers had been mindful of the noise as they entered the quietness of the bottom landing on A wing.

Silent.

The sound of their boots moved across the gleaming floor tiles, up the metal of the stairs towards the second floor. At the door, they positioned themselves, pulled the see-through visors on their black helmets down. The shields were held tight and high. The officer had keys in the cell door.

The team were ready. They looked at the Senior Officer awaiting the command. Saw the nod.

Flicked the spy hole on the door and looked in to see the Inmate, LR 3246, Gillen still in bed.

One movement. In, and deafening noise and shouts. A rush, like the strong gale of a fierce wind, the officers were through the cell door with the element of surprise and pinned the inmate to the bed. Gillen woke quickly and turned trying to flip and slide from the shields. Pushing, pulling, pressing against the dominating aggression, he was quickly pinned into a corner and kicked to the floor where he was restrained, put in wrist and head locks and transferred, trussed-up like a Christmas turkey to the segregation block.

Eighteen years later... 4am

I had held the project in my mind for a year now. The fascinating and inspirational journeys, the twists and turns of the worlds Billionaires as they had built their empires. Like a coder building binary code I saw and unravelled their business frameworks, stories, achievements, characters and innovations. I pressed the keys of my computer seeking more research.

Marco was beside me editing our last documentary on Walmart, a fast and riveting thirty-minute piece on the life of Sam and Bud Walton and their incredible rise from nickel and dime back water sales men in Arkansas to the worlds biggest retail giant.

...In the back-sitting room, in our little house in Stepney, East London with the silky grey curtains drawn at the back window shielding us from the early coming dawn, we persevered. Tiredness was upon us, and the fractured interactions were surfacing as the great mental, physical and emotional fatigue we controlled was nearing breaking point.

We were mad, everyone said. Silly, that it would never work and that to do all this slaving was a waste of time. It was our second day and night of work together. One of our usual needed marathons.

I looked at the scattered papers on the table in front of me. A scrawled and categorised collection of companies, dates, pivotal moments, wins, losses and tragedies. It was what made a life, and I would unravel these wonderful stories of the world's greatest empires, I would dive deep with skill into the person at their inception with diligent wonder. Uncovering their tragedies, loves and losses I would find the real person, what truly made them unique and from that set of rooms, uncover their success and travel the amazing journey these unique human beings had taken.

The midnight oil was burning.

We worked in our own separate spaces. Together on the desk, we pushed ourselves beyond human endurance to meet our deadline.

'...And you're listening to the Station that changes the way we see the world. That gives you the worlds most interesting game-changers.... Yes folks, Its Christopher Denning, on the show that will stretch the grey matter to the limit. Channel One FM...Now we are back, with the worlds most unique story of overcoming adversity and, the man in the centre of that story, Stephen Gillen...'

…We sat there. Two people bathed in the dim lights of the studio.

It was time to let the truth be known. It was the show that was live and was raw enough, that didn't play with and edit the truth. A private place of safety where deep questions could be answered for and a soul made lighter with the truth being told…

'…So, sixth question. That's really fascinating. After this life of crime and going into transformation you were becoming and making documentaries on the world most successful people and Billionaires. For the listeners, at this point then. What role models did you have that helped you on this amazing journey. Who did you look up to, Stephen?'

I sipped the water in front of me. In the warm lights of the studio, with the collage of framed faces, caricatures with many masks caught in frozen moments, I said, '…I have had many role models. The trick I have learnt is always be open to learn. To know you have greatness deep inside you and that anything is possible. To surround yourself only with the best of quality people. Study them and take from them only the best virtues, ways of doing things, understandings and ways at progressing quickly forward. You need also to have a picture of the person you want to be constantly in your mind. Attach this to one or maybe a few really successful or famous people who you admire. This is simply a guide to what you admire most about these people, what they do and the lifestyles they have. In the middle is the central core of consistent work, actions, sacrifice and unwavering certainty of getting there. It is the journey that shapes us and the problem solving that forges us, until one day we are amazed to look at our lives and what we have become. We realise that we are that person, that we in some way have even surpassed what we thought we saw…'

The studio fell silent a moment. The radio presenter, said, 'amazing, truly, Stephen. That has such a resonance. I'm sure the listeners will identify with parts of what you've explained there… So, this was the actual start of your rise to prominence, your true transformation. The Eureka moment…?'

I paused. In the warm studio lights that bathed my face in half shadow, thinking a moment, I said, no…Actually…' My voice had trailed off then and the mike again fell silent. '…The true start of my transformation was much more painful than that, much more terrifying…?'

∂

…It was a deep dark dungeon and I knew it well. In the strip cell, sat naked on the floor in the corner of the cell with a small heavy blanket draped around my shoulders, I focussed on the terrible bruising I felt on my arms, shoulders, legs and my genitals. They had dragged me from my bed and down the stairs, and when outside in the corridor away from the sight or hearing of other inmates had really hammered me. Unable to move because of the wrist locks they had kicked, punched and pulled my hair. One of them had grabbed my balls and twisted and squeezed them hard. The pain had nearly made me pass out.

The banging of a truncheon hard on the outside of my locked cell door invaded my thoughts and interrupted the silence. They were back.

Every ten minutes they would bang the door to give me no rest.

Outside, the spy hole moved, and an eye looked in at me and disappeared. It was another one of their tactics. It awakened something Inside me. Deep in the depths of my soul, in place of unmitigated pain was a factory that turned suffering into anger and loneliness to rebellion. It was working now, a smooth and fast process that converted my pride and the physical, mental and emotional torture I felt, into rage and stubbornness.

I moved. I could not stand as the fresh wounds would not allow it. I remembered what had been said in my ear, spittle flecking the side of my face as they held my head down dragging me to the strip cell, cutting my clothes from me, holding me down as they ran vacating the room in a burst of movement and closing the door.

'Getting a gun are you!' Their angry voices were in my head. 'You fuckin see where you'll end up. Think you're a wide boy do you. You'll rot behind the door for a long time. See what you get. Like our little visit this morning, want more? We can give you that every hour on the hour...'

The spyhole outside the door moved again.

The voice was soft, kept low and aimed at me and into the cell through the side of the cell door.

It said, in broken rushed tones. 'Look, I'm sorry for what they done to you. I had no part in it. I'll know you'll get the gun in eventually. I've read your record. But I'm just a family man...I had no part in it...I must go they're coming...I'll do what I can for you.'

...The voice was gone. I heard the movement of keys on the landing, heavy boots, an exodus of movement, coming towards my cell like a herd of travelling elephants.

My instinct told me they were coming. My body braced, readied my mind and hands so I could defend myself. The door flew open. They stood there, a sea of dark blue uniforms and white shirts that blocked completely the entrance to the cell.

'Gillen..."

It was the Governor. A bald man in a grey suit whose head and shoulders strained to see me through the mass of prison officers.

'You were removed from the wing this morning for the security and smooth running of the prison.' He stopped a minute and looked. A burning glance that faltered at the end of our locking eyes.

'We know, Gillen. We've had intelligence of a proposed escape attempt. You will be held down here while an investigation is carried out.'

'I want to speak to my brief?'

'…You will not be speaking to that brief or anyone else for a long time as far as I'm concerned, Gillen…'

The screws glared. They blocked and protected him at the door. A gaggle of attack dogs primed and ready to be unleashed.

The Governor peered at me one last time.

He said, 'Let me tell you, Gillen. When you try stuff like this you see what will happen. You will see where you will end up. Shut the door!'

He had indicated to them. I sat silent, back hard against the cold wall. I stared as the door to the strip cell slammed shut.

Fifteen Years Later...

... 'Dad, Dad...Dad, are you there. Can you hear me Dad, it's, Terry? I'm here. I miss you Dad. I so wish you would come back. Be here with me so that I may not be alone and things can be as they were. I forgive you Dad. I understand how it was. I know that in this life sometimes we do what we have to and we can think of no way back...'

Terry Gillen kissed his father softly on the forehead. He had busied himself with making the room more comfortable. There was a vase of fresh Lilies, a blue bathrobe from home, new toothbrush, toiletries and oranges, grapes, apples and blackcurrant juice. The curtains were open and his father, a solitary, vacant figure who resembled an unmoving block, a carved statue with no recognition, stared unflinchingly out through the sunlight into the little yard with wooden benches and a circular pond which held Koi carp.

He washed a flannel, squeezed it and dabbed his father's brow.

'...Is it good where you are, Dad. Are there great birds and flowing rivers and high mountains? Or is it city streets...Am I there, and your grandson, and little Anthony and Sophia. Is it nice weather? Speak to me, Dad...I have been coming most days after work. Every day, wind, sleet or rain...You would laugh, Dad. You would say don't worry son, you can't keep a good man down. Old soldiers don't die they just fade away...'

...In the hospital foyer the man wearing a tweed jacket and cap, who had travelled through the night as crushing winds had hit the north of Ireland, moved silently through the crowd at reception. He kept his three fingered hand tight in his trouser pocket so as to not leave a trace of his passing and walked head down and stealthily, unremarkable down the corridor toward the psychiatric unit. His mind was focused. A laser beam that saw one mission, one cause, an ending. People passed him on the long white hospital walkway. He did not make eye contact, did not put out the energy of presence. Diligently, so as to become invisible and unnoticed he navigated forwards. His training, learned long ago and deeply embedded inside him, was to be able to move without a trace of his passing and walk through thunder without leaving footsteps.

He was turning, following the sign for the ward he wanted, nearly at the place where an ending could be found. From the corner of his piercing green eyes he saw the door beside the entrance to the ward open and the doctors coming out. Before it closed he caught sight of the grey metal lockers inside. He pretended to study a poster on the wall, waited till it was clear. He would need a white coat so that he could blend unseen.

It was the doctor's job to watch from a far. It was important that from a private place of seclusion he could study his patients' movements, responses and impulses from a place that could be unsullied and relied upon.

The sun from the little yard, where the patients would sometimes sit, streamed through the window into the room painting folded and gleaming light on the side of the patient and the wheelchair he sat in. Stephen Gillen was an interesting case. He had read the file and it had kept him enthralled for hours into a long Friday night. He had seen cases like this before. Hard, forged life journeys that wielded the experience of a litany of harrowing trauma. The mind, an amazing machine, was wired for safety at all costs and with so much consistent and latent abuse the chemicals released to combat these traumas alone could be a cause for concern. Add other imbalances and drug abuse and it was a recipe for the finite threads that set the boundaries for the conscious mind to unbalance.

The other doctor beside him, said, 'What do you think…?'

He watched the patient's son. He tried to administer a sip of water to his father lips.

'Oh…If you had a beautiful violin, how would you play it?'

'I'd play it to the best of my ability.'

'Yes, but 'how' would you play it. How would you get the best out of it?'

'By leaning from a good teacher, practicing…'

'The answer is to play it sweetly…'

The doctor, silent a moment as he watched the unresponsive patient and his son, nodded. He looked at the patient, he was only forty.

'If you had this beautiful violin. Would you hide it from the world or should it be played?'

'…It should be played to audiences, yes.'

'I disagree. I think it should be played to the world. Shared as god intended and played sweetly so it was enriched and respected and elevated…Somewhere in Mr Gillen is the locked sweetness that can return him to the world so his soul may play again…'

'…Dad…Dad, I must go. People to see and planes to catch.' Terry Gillen smiled, but inside him he could cry. It was a hard task, and troubling, for him to see his father vulnerable and distant like this.

'…Bye, Dad. Don't let the bed bugs bite. I'll be back tomorrow, probably after six.'

Terry lingered, by the solitary figure of his father. A man in a distant place that no one knew. He looked at the wide print on the wall. An abstract, and painted in sections, it resembled moving clouds that pulled you in to unravel hidden figures. He could make out a chin, lips a face. With your mind you could see also a bird that soared, the shape of a fish that dived. All in brilliant bright and vibrant colours. Crimson red, blue, yellow, sharp whites and blues and oranges, browns and greens.

His father was behind him now and he nodded to the two doctors who had been standing outside. He was comforted his father was alive. This alone was a miracle. But he would be back and persist as he just knew if he kept on the father he knew would one day return. He pressed the button to leave the ward, waited for clearance to leave. At the open door he saw the orderly who nodded with his head down. He carried a bucket and mop for the shiny floors. Terry's mind winced as he noticed the orderly in the white jacket carried the bucket with a hand that had only three fingers.

At Prison Service Headquarters, John Milton sat at his desk in a blue pin striped suit and studied the report in front of him. Marked 'Urgent' it had come by the fastest, encrypted Security Intelligence channel as he had eaten his salad lunch and had thought of getting back to the squash court and how his daughter Isabella was enjoying her new show jumping lessons.

He read with narrowing eyes.

As the fawning grey clouds, threatening to darken and overtake the surging light covering Lambeth Bridge, fanned out in a selection of pieces, he saw the name and his eyes with concern digested the text.

Inmate 360, Gillen Stephen.

Prison, Wormwood Scrubs
Rank, Governor 2 (Security)

Intelligence Report.
Threat, Level 1

Details.
    An Officer being targeted by internal Security for suspected contraband smuggling into the prison was arrested on the 21st, May. On a search of his car outside, three oz of cannabis resin were found together with two phones and sim cards which were taped together. The Officer, suspected to have been taking contraband into the prison for at least eighteen months to two years, on police questioning then confessed to a plot by the above inmate to procure a firearm into the Prison and escape on one of the bin lorries coming into the facility.
Inmate is a High/Risk Category A Prisoner. Daily Observation logs, prison audio listening devices and monitored phone conversations are being collated.
Actions. Inmate was taken by control and restraint to the segregation unit where he is compliant but continues to be a constant high concern, high security risk and a drain on resources.

Please Advise.
End. Quote.

    Milton felt a tightness suddenly in his chest. The IRA escape from Brixton Special Cecurity Unit was still fresh and the controversy in the newspaper hinting of British Intelligence interference in the incident had seen his division take some serious flack.

…He looked out the window. Out across at the MI5 building. Alright for them he thought, our cousins. They could pretty well come and go and do as they bloody well wanted. He felt sweat appear on his neck under his collar. He recognised it as a final worry that could threaten his position and all he had worked for.

A bloody nightmare. The stuff of lingering indigestion, late nights reading and crushing headaches that thumped. Thankfully, the threat had been neutralised. The window was open, and he was glad of the fresh air that was coming in from the sky above the Thames.

It was a chess game they played with Category A Inmates, each one with their own unique set of posed problems that took constant monitoring and suppression. They were clever, he would give them that. The war had been waged now for years and the way to win it was pragmatic and uncompromising control, an incentive scheme to separate their cohesive groups and clear, current intelligence.

The pen was in his hand. John Milton looked at the report. Under further action, he wrote, signed and dated.

Further Action. Inmate 360, Gillen Stephen. To remain in closed and segregated conditions under Rule 34 (Continuous Assessment) until otherwise directed.

End. Quote

…Milton put the pen down, loosened his blue tie and collar slightly. The threat, Gillen would be put on Continuous Assessment. It was their tool that controlled, broke down, contained, confused, taught and shared a problem among many resources.

Inmate Gillen, a very big threat indeed would stay in twenty-three hour a day solitary, being moved from prison segregation unit to segregation unit up and down the country.

He would become a nomad, a number lost in the system and he would never know when he was moving or where he was going.

Milton, sat back. He envisaged Gillen would be on the 'ghost Train' at least two years. It annoyed him that his security and that of the many prisons he was in charge of could be threatened in this way. His thoughts went back to what day would be best to book for squash and if he got some extra time away from work and go to watch Isabella horse jump more maybe they could rekindle their close relationship and become friends once more.

Ten Years Earlier...

The Irish Sea crossing had been kind with soft waves and a cool breeze. The Judge at the Crumlin Road Court had been kinder, releasing me into my Uncle Gerard's care and letting me go back across the water back home to England.

At Birkenhead Central I sat for a moment, with my bags beside me on the floor and a coffee at my lips, I watched the busy commuters pass. My mind returned to the Judge at the Crumlin Road, a scary figure with a white curled wig and hard eyes. It had been a frightening experience. A large, imposing wooden panelled room with high ceilings, heavy security, stuffy and claustrophobic air and the fear that closed me inside.

'He's a hard-wee man.' The judge had said after looking through spectacles with a long stare. A strange thing for a judge to say to a young boy who could just about see over the dock, I thought.

The public in the train station moved and weaved busily. Busy bees that flitted and flew, turned and hovered.

It had turned out well for me. At last in my life I was beginning to imagine. I was away from Ireland, the depressing and fear laced St Patrick's and being over sixteen now I was out of the reach of the Local care Authority. I was free for the first time in my life.

I sipped my coffee, savoured the hot liquid. I was going to go back to London and my close friend who had his flat in Bethnal Green. We were close and committed and had made a pact together. We had plans and wanted to reach for our big future. I moved across the concourse. The train was due to leave in ten minutes and my mind was on the happiness of being back in the east end. I went through the turn styles and though of my friend whom I would live with. Callum Slaney was a character, and a laugh and a nutter and I was looking forward to meeting his sister Lily.

Chapter 11
The Monkey Puzzle Tree

He had sat still for a while and looked at the still figure before him. The days has turned into weeks and the weeks had turned into years. Short kicking and twisting bouts of pain had found their way to a lingering hurt which had shrunk into a dull ache that was a ball of longing and led to periods of depression.

The soft light covered them both and under its slight warmth and brightness he was overtaken by the quietness of the moment.

His unsure voice, crackling at first, balanced into a soft meaningful easy flow.

'…And the great Monkey Puzzle Tree held judgement on the passing years. There had been times when it had fought, when it had smiled against the light of the morning, and there were times when it had cried. Tall and always proud it stood against the harshness of the weather and although it was planted deep in the ground with strong roots that clung tightly to the earth the bad weather tried to move it, uproot it from its place. In the passing years, as history came and went, The Monkey Puzzle Tree learned to hold its sadness from the world and pack it deep down inside with its great magic…. The winds howled on the mountain side and in the dark city streets. Driving rain fell bursting and swelling the lakes and rivers, and magnificent thunder guided flashing lightning like ghostly threads that lit the landscape. There were people on the mountainside. With axes and swords and knives.

They searched for the magical trees as they were a threat and the great magic, they held deep down in the sap of their bark was not understood. The leader of the men was a harsh man. Driven with hatred and with burnished golden hair that shone under his helmet. The gale kicked, the rain lashed, the lightning crackled, and the men led by the man with burnished golden hair searched and tracked the poor Monkey Puzzle Tree. Many times, they had come close. Some say within a hair's breath with their sharp axes...'

He stopped a moment to catch his breath. It was the emotion and longing, the remembering of a face long past.

'But there was a woman on the mountain who knew the forest and the bogs and the twisting stone streets better than anyone. An ancient soul with sleek hair like the main of a lion and bottomless unforgettable turquoise eyes. She had come into the struggle that was the world and the Monkey Puzzle Tree with a purpose and it was said she was one with the nature spirits and was as old as the wind itself. The bad men with their swords and sharpened axes pushed through the face of the mountain and the cobbles of the near city, but the woman watched them. If they got too close, she would send mist to confuse them, darkness to misdirect them...One day there was a young man on the mountain who had come from the city. An innocent, a child, he had been born into a world of shifting shadows. In the stretching fog that had been directed to hide and make the bad men lose their way, he became lost and unsure as night began to claim the mountain.'

There were tears in his eyes as he recounted the story now. They slid down his cheeks and fell onto the whiteness of his hospital jacket. He kept his voice sure and steady.

...'On the fine smooth and jagged stones and boulders on the rock face of the mountain, and in the dark fog the innocent young man stumbled forwards. He was a step from his death from falling from the cliffside when the Monkey Puzzle Tree spoke. He

242

had strayed close to it and it had heard his thoughts, sensed his panic and fear and knew of the danger. Gratefully the boy stretched out his hand in the gathering fog in thanks, but The Monkey Puzzle Tree used its magic to become invisible and became the rock itself. It said there was danger on the mountain and he must find his way home. The men were twisted of heart and were driven to hunt the magical creatures of the land. The boy gasped. Back, behind the fog bank and clinging darkness he could hear the talk of men, voices that were harsh and metal swords and sharpened tools for cutting and hacking. Stumbling, his bare feet slipping on the wet earth and churned mud and grass, he ventured deeper into the mountainside seeking safety and a way home…The man with burnished golden hair became angry. As if he had sensed the innocent boy and knew he knew where the Monkey Puzzle Tree hid. Long, hard and as the carrion hawks brought the awakening dawn to the land the men chased the boy down the mountain as he ran for home…'

The Gardener had waited a long time. As the seasons had disappeared and the years had become one. He stretched out his three fingered hand and placed it on top Stephen Gillen's. It was lifeless but warm to the touch. He continued. He had been to talk to an Uncle in Belfast, had seen a small back garden where a Monkey Puzzle Tree stood proud.
The tears we clouding his eyes.

'…And the innocent boy in his haste to save himself, to find his way home from the cold mountain had become lost in the maze of the high rocks and dark ravines. The men closed in. Suddenly, he saw a light. Like a flickering moth the light like a beacon guided him forward. It was a natural spirit and it had been sent by the ancient women in charge of all things magical. In the half-light, with the men hot on their heels, as the sky cracked with splitting dawn and the morning dew clustered, they forged forward...'

The Gardener was aware of it. A slight twitch, a movement of the hand beneath his.

'...It was said the woman of the mountain herself told trees to lay down and play dead so the men's way would be barred. But the harsh man with burnished golden hair had been on the mountain many times and knew his way well...'

The Gardener wiped the tears from his eyes. He felt it again. With more strength, more knowing and vibrant. Like a tiny flower once more opening to the day, Stephen Gillen's hand moved, fingers clenched.

The Gardener stood. He picked up the bucket and mop he had placed beside him just as Stephen Gillen's head moved and his eyes looked at him, he had made it to the door. Without a second look, another glance he walked to the corridor and didn't look back.

Twenty-Four years Earlier, 10am

We all slept in the second floor two bedroom flat just off Whitecross Street Market near Old Street roundabout. A drab place of tired wallpaper, worn carpets in need of a clean and a sink that filled too often with un-scraped dishes.

I struggled from bed, sixteen years old, grabbing the morning and feeling, for the first time, free. The night before had been the usual late night of chatter with the four of us who shared the house drinking, talking and smoking cannabis. It had been a good night, funny and passably hilarious and nearly turning violent not productive as we looked at ways to get money.

Callum appeared at the door in blue boxer shorts. 'Have I got news for you, son. We got a pukka bit of work; Stevie I'm telling you...'

'Callum, the shorts bruv. You're hanging.' I smiled.

'Don't fuckin worry about it, son. You wait till you hear what I've got for us.' He sat on one of the worn armchairs that needed a good clean, crossed his bare legs and continued, 'Had a great meet with this guy this morning...'

I said, 'what in them fuckin' shorts!'

'No, for fucks sake. Stop fuckin about. Down the market earlier I went to get a bit of breakfast. There he was. He's a guy from the old days. Good stuff. Old School...'

He talked. As I finished getting dressed and brushed my teeth and threw water on my face and hair. Bent my ears about the guy and the building that was close, and the bit of work and the safes full of jewellery just up by Farringdon.

I listened. While I passed old John the alcoholic we lived with flaked out on the sofa, and young Peter who was a good kid, younger than us and a run-around for the gang eating a bacon sandwich in the messy kitchen.

'Stevie, this is the one, 'Said Callum. He danced quickly. A spoof on a bit of Irish dancing that looked Cossack.

'We'll get a right few quid. I've got us the way in. Nice and easy. We need to have a chat about this, Stevie…I feel good about this one I'm telling you!'

He turned to an innocent Peter whose mouth was full of sandwich. 'What you fuckin' looking at? You looking at me mate? You like these shorts is that it…Question is son, would you like to give me a long length in these shorts. Dirty bastard. I know what you're thinking, Peter you filthy minded so and so!'

Peter, spluttered, choked on his bacon. A smile split his young face. 'Fuck off, Callum. You're not my type mate.'

With a twisted frown, Callum hissed, 'bloody cheek!'

A fit of laughter hit us. We were in bits and turning and holding our stomachs. The toilet window was open and I went over the small hall to the front door seeking light, air and a rest from the giggles.

'…Right wankers, I'm going to get changed and we'll get back to talking about this little earner'.

I opened the door to go outside onto the landing. Peter, and a comatose drunk called, John were back behind me in the flat and I could hear, Cullum's cheerful voice as he washed and sang loudly to himself.

'…Oh, my old man said follow the van and don't dilly dally on the way. Roll out the barrel…'

On the landing outside the flat, the midday afternoon sun rising against the silhouettes of North London, I felt a happiness and a belonging I had never known. It was the camaraderie and fellowship of being all in with likeminded nutters I realised that was appealing. Outlaws without rules and codes of conduct. Free as birds and with the world our oyster. I closed my eyes to feel the sun a moment.

I could picture the great waves of the Ferry crossing the Irish sea a few weeks past and the freedom stretched out now in front of me.

'You ok mate, not disturbing a day dream am I…?

I jumped. It was a short, sweet female cockney accent that pierced and sliced. It continued, 'I mean, penny for them and all that, but any man worth his salt at this time of day would be out grafting and getting the shillings in…I mean, unless of course you're someone who's already had it off. Judging by the clobber you're wearing and the fact you're hanging round this shit hole with my nuisance of a brother I'd say that highly unlikely…You are by the way?'

I starred at her.

A slender well dressed body in a blue matching dress and bag. Knowing, light blue, wide eyes on a finely sculptured face, red lips that were set in a questioning half smile.

I said, 'Well I'm happy to see I get your strong vote of confidence, love.'

Her eyes flashed, smile widened. 'You must be, Stephen?'

She stood taller in her blue heels, eyes looking me up and down and I returned the gesture. In a closed voice, said, 'I may be, depends who's asking, love. Been a few dodgy birds round these parts lately.'

Her hand went to her hip. A mouth that was well formed turned up at the side. 'Joker too are you mate. Listen… I know you're, Stephen. I'm Lily, Callum's sister. There's something you better know. I know my brother Callum's a mental case and a nut-job and a nuisance. But he's my nuisance, and now it seems your nuisance. He's my brother and comes from a good family. What I'm trying to say is he's my brother and we love him dearly so you look after him when you're out and about the pair of you and that kid in there doing whatever'.

Her blue eyes searched my face. A busy sun was climbing, and together with the slight wind that scattered the browning leaves on the ground floor entrance to the flats, it cut shapes of brightness and shadow behind her that illuminated her figure. There was a steeliness to her that together with her slender beauty and cutting sharpness made her attractive.

'I promise I will, Lily. On my life, we stand and fall together.'

We looked at each other a moment. In the back ground, through the slightly open window, in the flat's bathroom amongst the sound of moving water we both heard, 'Oh…my old man said follow the van and don't dilly dally on the way…!'

She turned from me with a stretching smile that moved wider. Walked back the way she had come, hips and bag swinging. I watched the contours of her body move. She shouted behind her as she walked, heels clicking. 'Remember what I said…Ok. I suppose I shall have to take your word for it. I'm late. Got to go. Tell him I turned up, I'll phone him later…'

She pivoted on her heels. I watched her. She was at the end of the landing ready to descend the concrete stairs and turned with a softer smile.

'Only joking about the clothes, Stephen. Don't be a wanker all your life. You've got a good sense of style. Word of advice. Change the red shirt, too loud. Use pastel colours that go with your skin and match your hair. Bye…!'

She was gone. Her words were in my ears. Behind me Callum's voice echoed in the untidy flat and my nose was filled with the compelling scent of the perfume she had left behind.

Ten years later, Wakefield Prison

My repetitive existence was of painful, spartan, concrete cells that trapped my true humanity and twisted my mind and feelings and emotions into jagged caricatures that diminished and shaped my being and soul into hellish shapes that were hard to control. I walked, devoid and stripped of emotion in an unnatural world of inner pain and outer drabness. Days were milestones and the night were broken. As the years had rolled by so to had my human memories of the outside, stolen and overcome instead by a darker part of me that desperately clung to sanity and reality.

I had tried to remain calm for the first ten days when I had arrived here. They had been awaiting my arrival and after the first few days the bullying had started. Dinners that were small and cold, late openings for exercise, staring eyes and growling comments, no showers, it became worse daily. The breaking point had come one morning after I was missed for breakfast. I had ripped a towel, gone to the toilet in a plastic wash bowl and plastered the walls with excrement. It was the stench and the unclean feeling mixed with the potential chance of infection and the disruptive need to run the regime differently and wear protective clothing that was the weapon. Then there was the safety from the beatings and potential violence. They hated it, the screws, dirty protest. A primitive weapon, it pushed them.

In the double-doored grey cell that was specially built and had an inside heavy mesh door that protected a second closed iron cell door, in a clean corner where I sat ate and slept, in a cell covered with faeces smeared walls, I contemplated my options. I had been on dirty protest, in one of three special cells called 'the cages' for two weeks now, protesting against my treatment and continued segregation, and for my own survival against the Prison Officers.

Now, three and half years into my sentence, I had been kept on continuous assessment, 'the ghost train' for over twenty-eight months.

To my right was a clear bulletproof screen which housed behind it a curtain and dormant TV. I felt filthy. My beard was growing, twisted and it itched. I looked up. Outside the window I saw feet pass in the lightness. Someone solitary walked on the two exercise yards outside. I swallowed hard. There was a dryness in my throat, but my sinuses were clear. After a while the terrible stench of my own faeces waned but for the screws it would stay.

I had been to twelve prisons in the last twenty-eight months, mostly on the Northern circuit far away from the south and my home so they could wear me down and break me quicker. Leeds, Winston Green, Leicester, Full Sutton, Frankland, Bristol, Whitemoor, Strangeways, Parkhurst, Cardiff, Walton I had seen them all, some twice and three times. It was a strategic war I realised. One to make a dog that frequently showed teeth and could bite to heel and be battered into submission physically, spiritually, mentally and emotionally. I had tried many times to toe the line but had not been able to settle down to the solitary confinement and only made my bad name worse as a highly disruptive prisoner. My card was marked, the seasons were set. I would give it my best shot to comply but they would not let me on to the normal wings or into general prison population.

Outside, the walking shoes again passed my window. My body was strong from the cell workouts I done daily to keep my strength up but my heart ached. They played with me, the ten officers here who had to be present when my doors were opened, as a cat did a mouse and it brought the lion out in me. A ferocious beast that dug in heels and lived with hatred and was slowly losing all notions of normality, of the outside world and the beautiful emotion I had deep within. An empty vessel. The emotions were being sucked out of me day by day under these conditions. I could hear the movement of the metal dinner trolley being brought over by the kitchen orderly. It was how I timed my days. By noises that were repetitive and food that was rank and eaten so a strength could be kept and a hurting mind be managed in a false tidiness. I opened my mouth to shout, to scream my rage, but no sound would come out.

In the clean corner of the faeces covered cell, in a clinging misery, I searched again in the recesses of my mind for my burning anger. In my life I had met many difficult characters. Narcissists, psychopaths, sociopaths, the violent, the lost and the plain stupid; I had engaged with them all in their better and worse moments and I learned one thing, that there were two types of violent people. One, the majority, who would rather avoid violence but saw it and used it as a tool when needed and their security was threatened. The other, a darker breed stamped with the iron of a twisted insanity, revelled in it and pursued it at times chasing it like a drug that pulled. My feelings of the world had become hollow. My humanity, forced to meet my most primitive and instinctual self was now sheltered in and had clothed its self in stubbornness and anger. It swelled, a soft humming that turned into a gathering thunder.

I could feel it now. They would never beat me. As my freedom had been lost so too had my future been stripped from me, my life, my dreams had been taken and all that I was. My self-respect was all that remained, the core part of me that I held onto and protected...I would rather die than bend. Scolding the renewed life flooded through my weary veins like an elixir, my desperation and anger travelled. Comforted now, I listened to the silent sounds of the cell and the metal dinner trays being unpacked.

Then I heard it. A rush of walking boots and jingling keys. Heavy footsteps hitting shinny buffed floors.

The heavy cell door swung open. They escorted me out and into a cell down the landing.

'...Ok, Sir. There he is. Were just up the landing, let us know if you need anything.'

They left him, a herd of Prison Officers that lurked nearby. From the chair he had indicated, in the fresh clean cell with a lingering smell of fresh paint, across the wide grey table that held his paper and pen, I watched him a moment.

'...Stephen Gillen. May I call you, Stephen? My name is John Milton. I'm from Prison Service Headquarters. I'm part of the Category A committee and I would like to talk to you. Is it alright that we talk here a while, Stephen...?'

A solitary figure, sitting on a chair in a fine blue tailored suit, wearing an elasticated white mask that protected his nose and mouth. Silence stretched. I could see behind the pretence of normality, the falseness of his engaging demeanour, he recoiled and baulked. He shifted his chair back slightly.

'Can we talk, Stephen. I have come a long way to talk to you...?

'...Why have you come here?'

'A matter of necessity I'm afraid. To inform you of a decision we have made.'

I said, 'I am finished with treating you people with reason.'

He moved again, head turned to the side and he tidied his hands in front of him. 'We're in a quandary ourselves at the moment to know what to do with you...'

'Are you going to take me off the 'Book', Cat A?'

'...Sometimes, Stephen. People can be downgraded, yes. But sometimes there are cases where we get intelligence from internal or outside agencies that can determine we take a different view.'

'A different view you call it. You have kept me in segregation all these months...'

'You have been very disruptive, Stephen. Classified as a very high security risk. It is like a chess game the movement of

252

Category A prisoners around the system.'

'Can I go on the wing?'

He paused, and I saw he was struggling with the stench and the picture before him.

'We have decided, Stephen that you are to go to Hull Special Unit. There is a different regime there, very supportive. You'll get much more freedom within the unit, cook your own food and have a chance at education...'

He waited, paused for my response which on purpose didn't come.

He stood. 'It's a new intuitive Hull. We have great hopes for it and it is showing good results. We hope you will do well there...'

He called for the guards. They arrived. The chair was taken. They were at the door.

Quickly, I said, 'When am I going?'

'Soon. I can't tell you when, you know that.'

'Will I have a chance of being taken off the Book?'

They appeared and he met them at the cell door. Like body guards that protected a jewel they surrounded and cloaked him, a throng of white shirts.

Behind his white mask, patting down his now contaminated suit, John Milton looked serious for a moment.

'Gillen, a word of warning, regarding your Category A status. The way you're going you'll be released on it. Close the door.'

The two Detectives tasked to the Nation Crime Squad, an organisation which dealt with national and transnational organised and major crime, had been notified through their specialist channels when the target, Gillen, Stephen had awakened from his hospitalised and comatose state in the psychiatric ward of the London hospital.

Far back, dressed as two tourists in baseball caps and backpacks, sitting amongst a crowd on the side of a grass verge and playing with the cameras hanging around their necks that doubled as long rang directional mikes to record conversations, with smiles as if they talked and non-committal eyes, they watched the target closely as he took the pieces of bread he had in a bag and scattered them to the ducks.

The sun was out and had brought the dense crowds en masse to east London's Victoria Park, making it easy for them to integrate and move easily to the prime positions they needed for their information collection.

Alone, Gillen, who had gone egging on the small island across the lake in front of him as a boy many years earlier, stood at the waterside silently and fed two tall swans which had glided in. Part of a much bigger operation, the Detectives in the main operations room knew that an organised criminal team that stretched to four cities around the UK and covered three continents was mobilising its resources.

The target had been back on the streets for two months.

In the fifth week of his release from hospital, Gillen and another target had been stopped and searched in their car at Dover as they were about to board the ferry to mainland Europe. From there they had been followed on the ferry to Calais then Dunkirk through Ghent, up to Antwerp and Breda crossing the border into Holland at Rotterdam. Another team had then followed them to Utrecht and Amstelveen where they continued to the Centrum of Amsterdam and they were seen to have a series of meetings with known international Criminal figures in the Leidseplein.

Now back in London, tight to the lakeside, Gillen was on the move. He walked further along the waterline and his phone was in his hand.

The Detective pointed the camera. Ducks and wildlife had infiltrated the bank looking for food, and he aimed the directional listening equipment that could record a conversation with clarity at five hundred meters while posing as a camera, as if he was a photographer taking pictures.

The Detective crouched as if he searched for the correct light for the shot. They had been warned on the last debrief that vans had left and returned loaded with contraband at vantage points on the motorways going from London to Manchester. Eagerly, moving as if he waited for the right moment to capture an impression, the Detective from the NCS observed the target, Gillen who held the mobile phone in his hand. The ducks and swans circled and fluttered around the target. If he used his mobile phone he would be ready to listen and record.

Fifteen Years Earlier...

As the slight drizzling rain swept in from Holborn covering the Barbican and Farringdon in a damp haze and the barrow boys divided, stacked and transported the goods for Smithfield meat Market behind us, Callum, Peter and I hugged the shadows of the building near Cowcross street. We were in a side street that went back from the main road. It was 3am, but in the adjacent building some of the higher floor windows still hinted of activity and showed lights.

We looked up. The building, a converted warehouse, was four floors high and littered with wide windows. High, and sticking out from the roof was a red metal hook from the old loading-pulley the warehouse must have used to transfer flour and grain. Above that, and built in to the roof, were the small windows we had been told about.

I pulled, tried the strength of the metal black drainpipe, wet to the touch, that stretched up to the roof, accessed the guttering high on the roof underneath the awnings. Callum was beside me. It would take our weight. The drizzling rain washed our faces and ran rivets of water droplets from the black balaclavas we had rolled high as hats. We listened. Like a night animal who foraged and needed to make sure a way in the darkness was clear, our senses hooked into the sounds of the night around us. Rain had built up in a blocked drain on a building close to us and the overflow dripped annoyingly. Main road traffic could be heard in the distance and somewhere music floated and voices carried in the air.

'Go back to the corner, 'Peter was told. 'Keep a good look out. Keep out of sight. Send a message on the phone if you see anything...'

I climbed first, Callum behind. Up the drainpipe, feet using the wall and casings holding the metal, I shimmied up towards the roof. On the third floor, with a high view with the other buildings around us, I looked in through the window of the building and saw two tall grey, metallic metal safes tight to the wall of the interior.

'Hey, Callum. I see it!'

'What, what can you see?'

'Two safes. Its magnificent. It's all there, and two benches for the jewellery makers and diamond cutters...'

'What else can you see? If you can get down from your high horse and move up a bit'.

'Callum, it's not that you're on a high horse. Its how you sit on top of it, son. It's all there, files, beading pliers, sizing gauges, magnifiers, anvils...I can see a pen for testing the stones. Yeah, your guy was right.'

I climbed, reached the roof and swung my legs round to look in through the stained little top window that was back and covered from the street.

Callum, one flight down, looked into the jewellery workshop. He smiled upwards.
'Come on I said...'

When he joined me at the top my back was to the side of the window and I was aware of the small 22 calibre pistol, cold to the bare skin of my side and stuffed down my waist band. On the ledge, together with the rain sweeping across the broken darkness of the city skyline we looked at each other and grinned. Callum checked the gun he had in his pocket.

'Right, Stevie. We'll smash this glass behind us and wait in the toilet there until they come in the morning, open up and turn the alarms off. This place is like fort Knox's with sensors everywhere. We can't leave this room till they switch everything off in the morning.'

The rain and the climb had soaked our jeans and buttoned jackets. I nodded. In the slight light of the rooftop, with the night rain soaking through us, I saw the excited craziness in Cullum's eyes. Forcefully, he said, 'When they come in the morning, when we hear them, and the bells are off we'll get the combinations, and get them to open the safes and clean them out...'

Twenty-Three years later, 22nd December

I rushed through Mile End park in the early evening cold, and as the snow fall picked up and a bustling wind blew across Mile End stadium scattering the winter leaves, I held my son Anthony and daughter Sophia tighter by the hand. Wrapped in hats, scarfs and gloves we braved the thick falling snow flakes. We passed the tall wired fence of the football field and followed the winding track to the new church on Burdett Road.

We left the park and weaved through the slowing traffic. The tall modern looking new brick church rose in front of us. 'Daddy, is it hard for the homeless people at this time of year? Do they get presents, and can we help them?'

She was nine, and the night before had brought me the gift of an animal bracelet that was forged with love. We had sat on the bed in her room and she had taken me through the colours and animals and I had watched and the love that was sent spread a glowing warmth dancing through me and filled my eyes with water.

'…Yes, Sophia we are going to help them. Good girl, and you, Anthony do you want to help the poor homeless people?'
He smiled, 'Yes Daddy.'

They were my life. Two little ducks, fresh to the world and always vying for my attention.
'Where are their mummies and daddies…?

It was Anthony, brown eyes like two shiny buttons sticking out from a woolly hat pulled down tight around his ears.
His question hit me. A thump that was an oncoming train in the chest. I said, 'they're coming, son. One day they will come…'

I pressed the intercom at the see though glass doors. To the side of me, huddled from the thick confetti-like snow and with their backpacks and worldly belongings on the pavement or on the brick wall or hanging from their backs, were the homeless who would stay at the church tonight. I smiled at them, and in the stirring blizzard, was taken with the pity I felt at the challenges they faced. I went into the church, kids following and down the stairs into the place where twenty makeshift beds were laid out in the church creche.

'Oh, I see you got the little ones', it was, Margret. A sweet, grey haired, Scottish woman with square glasses and a long flowery dress. The senior volunteer, she and her husband had kept the shelter going for the last eight years as they shared with the other churches in the East End a night each in the week over a two-month period at Christmas. The volunteers would join with other organizations to feed the homeless and give them a bed and try to get them into stable education and work.

Wide eyed the children watched me. In the wide room of the creche where the metal beds had been pitched, amongst the cheap decorations and the little Christmas tree that sparkled warm lights, I gave them jobs. Anthony to get the bags of pillow cases and put them on. Sophia to help me stretch out the sheets and shake on the quilts.

Her brown hair was in a band and stretched back. Her little hazel eyes twinkled. 'Daddy, why are the people homeless?'

I pulled the sheets on the bed one at a time and shook the quilts into their covers. She followed me, her little fingers helping the best they could. Anthony, had arrived dragging the white linen sack full of pillow slips.

'Because, Sophia, life is hard. Sometimes unfortunate things can happen. That's why we must always be grateful and think of others. 'But why, Daddy, 'Anthony, said.

'We are not special. We are all equal. You must remember life has a strength. It is like a boomerang. Understand we get back what we put out in this world ...But remember, Anthony, Sophia the darker the night the shinier the star'.

They looked, nodded. We made the beds. Tided the room. Put the spare linen back in storage.

They were coming in now. The homeless, bags on their shoulders, faces happy to be in from the bitter cold outside. We stood by the door to the dinning hall and we smiled as people came and went. In the other room, by the kitchen hatch where people cooked the evening meal, carols were playing. With the children, in the room where a great effort at Christmas decorations had been made and with the calming melody of 'silent night' warming the room, the children and I set the long blue table so that our guests could soon eat.

I sat a moment and watched them. They placed the knives and forks on the long table. In the kitchen the other voluntary workers were nearly ready with the hot food. Some of the best people I had ever met worked in this building. The emotional sounds of Ave Maria starting playing. In the soft corner light, in quiet happiness as I watched my children lay the table and with the heavy snow gathering and twisting in a cold wind outside, I felt the emotion of contentment settle inside me. I had come a long winding road through my personal darkness to get to the light.

Anthony went to the serving hatch and asked for more cups for the table. Sophia turned napkins. It was what I wanted that they would see the world and be creators of goodness within it.

Bravely enough I had walked away from my former self to answer the call of my inner decency. In the chair, with the warmth of the room around me and the glitter of silver and gold tinsel decorations, I listened as the Soprano singing Ave Maria moved into higher notes as the children gathered around me.

ॐ

…We sat there. Two people bathed in the dim lights of the studio.

It was time to let the truth be known. It was the show that was live and was raw enough, that didn't play with and edit the truth. A private place of safety where deep questions could be searched for and a soul made lighter with the truth being told…

Christopher Denning, had a pensive look in his eye. Closing in on the mike in front of him, he said in a concerned voice, 'Seventh question, Stephen. You've said that the real start of your journey of transformation can be pin pointed to a much more painful section of your life, a more terrifying one. I know the listeners are waiting like me. What was it then? Tell us what is the middle bit? How did you really turn everything around to have this amazing life…?'

I paused. Stopped as the reflections of deep, buried wounds and the past again awakened me.

'…I'm going back to a dark period in my life. The real pinnacle where I was at death's door. I know a person's mind can only take so much. I had courted danger, violence and traumatic events for too long and too consistently. The way I was living took a toll on me and I had a breakdown. I was sectioned under the mental health act. I can tell you, to lose control of reality, of your mind is a terrifying thing. It had started when I was in prison and returned when I got released. I was getting hallucinations and started hearing voices. It was a very painful time that saw me retreat into myself. I was in a ward at the London hospital, Whitechapel. They gave me great care in there, I was nursed back to full health. After that incident something changed in me, something intrinsic. Looking back, it was like a switch had been activated, the sharpness of my anger,

261

the force of my craziness had balanced and subsided. It changed me into a slightly different person. This was the very start of a clear and good way forward...'

'...Amazing, 'Said, the radio host. 'You were involved in a lot of charity work around this time, what compelled you then, after all this to keep going?'

'...I think at that point for the first time I had truly come to the crossroads in my development where I had sufficiently worked myself out. I looked at the world differently. With my work and studies going well I looked outside myself to give to the world and help make other people's lives better and creative. It was a real turning point for me to see a way out away from my past. I realised it was possible. The more I gave, the happier, more fulfilled and better my life became. I had unravelled the past and realised that bad programming and instruction had been one of my biggest problems. I nurtured the drive for good in me and took as many clear steps in the right direction everyday as I could...I could see now what I couldn't before. It was like a puzzle I had finally solved. Inside myself, I had resolved to remove the stains from my life...'

మ

Chapter 12
Incarceration & Transformation

In the grubby bedsit he rented in a third floor two bed flat just off the Walworth road, Mr Cooper grunted and swung his tired and aching legs to the side of the bed so he could take a sip of the flask of coffee he always carried. At eighty years old, the small cramped room, painted in a calm lemon with dirty walls, was his latest sanctuary from the world. He pushed out with his wrinkled hand, scattered to the floor the porn magazines stacked on his one piece of bedside furniture. Money was tight. In his mind he cursed them all. The services, the police, the public, his family...

He took the piece of newspaper clipping from his dirty jeans pocket. It said, in bold print: Vile Abuse in The Care Home Nicknamed 'The Prison'.

He was up, and he snorted his disgust. He kept the clipping and looked at it every morning so his anger could be fed, and his old body get the jolt of feeling it needed. The years of service, of controlling delinquents had meant nothing. They were only children that no one wanted. His efforts for society were not thought of as a service. He put on his unwashed blue parka jacket and he felt it. Turning behind his groin, stirring him sexually and sending unwanted pictures and images to his mind. There was still life in the old dog yet.

He closed the door to the bedsit, confined the wafting smell that caused his neighbours problems, and ventured down and along the tight run-down landings and concrete steps.

Back behind him, from the second floor of the mirroring flats across the way, 'Oh...Oh, fuckin nonce. Fuckin die nonce. You wait till we catch you!'

Castleford looked up, peered out from the hood of his parka. It was the teenagers from the estate. He raised his elbow, cowered back behind a car close to him, regrouped. Quickly, Mr Cooper again focused his shattering thoughts and hurried out of the estate.

The prison dog handlers supported the six prison officers as they walked me through the back closed yard of the prison, through four sets of locked gates and into the centre of the prison where the special Unit was. Totally self-contained, a three-floor building enclosed by the green mesh and razor wire of a tall fence, it was a prison in a prison and held some of the country's most dangerous prisoners.

The main doors to the unit's entrance were unlocked. I was escorted in.

It was the smiles of the officers that hit me first. The calm way they introduced themselves and the softness I was treated with.

The escort was told to undo my cuffs.

'   Hi, Stephen. How was your trip? Have you had something to eat? We cook all our own food here. There are two TV rooms. We have our own gym fully equipped. Our own visit rooms. It's totally self-contained. It holds twenty, but we like to keep the numbers down. There's eight here at the moment.'

The officer wore the blue jumper of his uniform. With smiling eyes, in a soft middle-aged face with wavy black hair he continued, 'We have some friends of yours here at the moment, I believe?'

I followed him. Hull Special Unit was a small square. A fish bowl that was an experiment. The main office was on the second floor where you came in. This floor also housed the cells that mirrored each other across the opposite side of the building. Upstairs reflected the second landing with rows of cells that no one used and where the recesses were covered in bird shit left by resting seagulls in from the docks. The ground floor housed the kitchen. Situated in an open corner, it was complete with hobs and fridge-freezers where we would put our food tied in cloth sacks. On the ground floor there was also a perfect gym with free weights, an Olympic bar, a running machine and squatting stack that could be used to bench-press. The door to the visits was around the corner, and to the side of the gym were two TV rooms with soft chairs that were situated on either side of the ground floor landing by the outside gates to the exercise yard.

I had friends here. Good staunch men I had met around the system who had travelled the segregation units and dispersal prison as I had.

'Who is here?' I said. Following him. It was a place of light blue, green and grey. A weird energy hung in the air. Like all was good but great trouble bubbled just under the surface. I could smell the richness of food being cooked downstairs. Spaghetti Bolognese made well with a hint of sugar and good tomatoes.

'Oh, people you know. They knew you were coming today. They've been asking for you. I'll take you to your cell, Stephen. It's different here. Not like anything you've experienced in the system before. Everyone here calls everyone by their first name. I'm, Keith, Stephen and if there's anything you need, anything I can help you with, just give me or one of the other officers a shout…'

He left me. It was May, 1996. I put my bags of belongings on the floor by the small cupboard. It was a normal cell, like any and many I had been through and stayed in. I sat on the bed a moment and looked out of the barred window. The afternoon sun was streaming in to freshen and greet me and the sea gulls were squawking. I felt my life was on a train. It travelled in the night going through echoing tunnels which all looked the same.

Forward it thundered on its route, going I knew not where. Its not the pain, I considered that destroys us. It's what we do to avoid its embrace, the fullness of its march. I started to unpack my belongings. It was a new start for me. I would grasp it with both hands...

...We were all in the old, great hall, a place of high moulded white ceilings and a grand stone fireplace that was used for main meetings and checking-in in the mornings and afternoon. Where the clients of the rehab could build confidence, share a feeling or problem and the councillors could give feedback and pivotal interventions and gauge the progress of the day.

One of two specialist addiction Councillors, a light skinned, highly skilled slight man in his early forties who held in his hands a thick stack of polaroid photographs, told us to spread out around the room. There were twenty-six of us. A real mixture, from young men and women to the old an incontinent. I moved back towards a wide window behind me. Out there was the large rolling grass garden and grounds that belonged to the old main building. It housed, in its well-kept landscape stone statues, quiet places of reflection, paths that led into the forest lands that surrounded the property, and a square paved area with stone columns and benches that were formed in a square to sit on.

By the window, with the morning sun spreading soft light through the burnished glass, I watched the councillor as he walked around the room throwing the polaroid pictures everywhere around us on the rich red carpet.

I liked it here. The Bedfordshire countryside, the quiet and peace and seclusion of the place. I had been here two weeks. Fourteen days, since my foster brother, Dominic by chance having a business meeting near the east end, had met me for a rare coffee and seeing how thin I had become and how bad I looked had broken down, researched, paid and personally driven me here. On the way, having left behind everything I was and owned, a

266

dangerous life of serious villainy that closed-in and a progressive addiction to drugs that raced me towards an untimely death, I had looked out of the window as we left London. At the rolling hills and countryside and I realised I was on deaths door and he had saved my life.

The councillors, two men who themselves had beaten a long life of battering and painful addiction, had a serious look in their eyes, a sober countenance on their faces.

The light skinned one, fifteen years sober who had moved from London full time years back to pursue his crusade to save as many addicts as possible, said,' Right, I want you to look at the photographs on the floor. Walk around and look closely at all the faces in the photographs.

We obeyed. I wandered. My body was starting to shiver, my stomach tightened in a knot of striking cramps. Slight tremors were appearing in the nerve-endings of my feet, legs and hands as withdrawal starting hitting again. My mind, again emotionally shattered, was trying desperately and slowly to repair its self.

The faces in the photographs stared back at me. Pale, thin, with translucent skin, unhealthy, sad and lost faces, framed with the look of desperation and holding a glazed look that projected a kink or flaw of the soul. Old, young, men with hats and coats ruffled and with tussled demeanours, women without makeup and uncombed hair. Vacant eyes that stared and showed a yearning to imbue freshness into their lives.

I walked. Slowly, I looked and pondered over them.

Striding amongst us, for effect and in a no-nonsense voice, one of the councillors said,' Take a good look. All of the people in the photographs, the polaroid's were taken on their arrival here like yours were taken. All these people are now dead!'

The solitary photo of a young twenty-three old man with blond hair was in his hand.

It was held high.

'…This was, James. He was the latest to die. I remember James. He stood here where you are now not nine months ago doing this same exercise. He was extrovert, the life and soul of the party. When he was younger he went to private schools. He had one of the best educations' money could buy. He had dreams of becoming a famous anthropologist, was a talented cricketer and was nearly picked one year to be on the rowing team for Oxford…We got him clean here. He left through that door out the front that you all came in with those dreams. When he got to the train station where his family were due to pick him up he went into the toilet and injected a hit of heroin that was too strong for his recovering body to take. He died right there in the toilet alone and took the dreams of his future with him…'

We stood and the impact of the story tore at us. The room was silent. I had known great adversity and danger but a lump had formed in my throat and the aches and pains of my body were ignored for a moment as a dryness claimed and formed in my mouth. I could see it in the eyes that hung and lingered and gathered and tried to hide. Contemplation, horror, pain, denial, guilt and shame.

We were told to form a circle.

'Right, I want you to look at the person next to you. First to your right, have a good look, and then the person to your left…'

The first week for me had been horrendous here. It was a beautiful place that had been built by a tobacco baron in the early nineteen hundreds. A maze of hidden corners and twisting landings with fine décor, comfortable bedrooms, places to sit and do your written work, and the finest of healthy and attentively cooked foods. But it was structured and succinctly regimented. Everything, the meetings, the timings, the many daily chores and written work given, the attitudes that challenged and poked and prodded were staged and focused towards people's recovery.

'...Take a good look everyone. Within a year, out of the three of you. One will be clean, one will be using and one will be dead... You really are in the fight of your life here...Now if you can follow us into the other meeting room it's time for group therapy...'

I could feel it as we formed a group towards the door. The minds that were deep in thought. Solitary islands that wrestled desperately to remove inner demons and understand their guilt and shame. We walked down the corridor that had white panelled walls, past the fine architraves and into a room with a circle of chairs. The mood was grim, the feeling sullen, the energy dull and stagnant. It was hard not to think of the young man who was a fine rower, who was vibrant, and who had met a finial end alone in a grubby urinal. It hit my nostrils, a nauseating smell that was beautifully cooked vegetables, a choice of meats and hams, mashed potatoes, pastas and a mixture of fresh cakes. Pulling a chair back to sit on I drew back.

It came and went. The waves of sickness that were hot and cold flushes, painful limbs, clenching stomach cramps, fluctuating pains, crushing headaches, emotions that rose and fell. Some were constant, some intermittently fanning out through every cell in my body.

For the first week I had twisted and turned in agony in sweat-soaked sheets and no sleep had found me. I felt the darkness cling to my soul and had fought for it to lift. My mind and emotions were a storm that threw me around like debris in a strong hurricane and through the solitary, quiet darkness I had repeatedly screamed and winced internally. On the deck of that ship my addictions had laughed and flung and tossed me under growling waves whilst I held on refusing treatment. I had fought the good fight night after night as the narcotics slowly left my system, the recuperating nerve-endings in my brain and body healing and reconfiguring as my limbs jolted and jumped uncontrollably.

269

Sitting within the circle of chairs, in the wide room that had soft settees and tables with magazines, rich blue curtains and a library of books, we faced each other uneasily as the main group therapy session of the day was about to open up. People shifted, moved uneasily and fidgeted, as the counsellors took their seats and looked around the group. It was a safe place to share, a sharp, uncomfortable, challenging arena where denial was smashed and unhealthy ways of thinking and feeling were pushed, pulled, opened to the light, destroyed and righted.

The counsellors' experienced eyes searched, stopped at me, and in a calm but pointed tone, 'Stephen, would you open the group today?'

Feeling the flush of my waning physical pains move to my knees and legs, my addled mind found a clearing between the clouds of my gripping and turbulent racing emotions. Steadying myself, and slowly, clearly, I said,' Hi, my name is Stephen and I'm an addict...'

Nine Years Later, 2019

The richness of his life had been hard to translate into meaningful memories with the painful burdens he had carried against the long years. Now, in the later twilight years of his life he had learned that his journey, arranged in his mind and heart as a compartmentalized book of emotive pictures and woven feeling of people, places and times, had become a fine wine that had concentrated and wizened with the growing years.

He had been in England, his mind tinged with nostalgia and a weathered heart that secluded and held wistful feelings, for a week. He had watched them shopping in the West End today, eating at the Ritz at Green Park and walking close together in tender conversation and, as the scattered city daylight had transformed into a shining glitz of gleaming night lights, he had followed them through Leicester Square towards Trafalgar and St Martin-in-the-Fields where they now stood about to go in to listen to Vivaldi's 'Four Seasons' by Candlelight.

Back behind the black railings of the church, with the National Gallery closing its doors behind him, in a new tweed hat and a green Barbour coat, he looked up into and through the milling crowd to where Stephen Gillen and, Daphne Diluce hovered by the door. His face had softened over the passing years, and as he looked at the well-dressed couple who shone with the healthy purpose of a successful life, he was happy he had come. In Ireland, as the landscape had heightened, stuttered and balanced to a lingering peace, he had kept a close watch. In the Autumn of his regrets and the guilt that had transfixed his soul to the Winter of his life had exhibited the gripping hold of pain, depression and alcoholism. He had followed the journey of the boy who had ripened as a man and the brightening sun of later years had directed him to a place which he had bolstered his courage to find Summer and the comforting years of acceptance and understanding. He had one last mission to complete.

They were walking in now, holding tickets and taking good seats in the elaborate and ornate high-ceilinged auditorium where the beautiful music would haunt and beguile an audience.

He felt the slight pain of arthritis in the hand that carried the deformity of three fingers. A wound he had collected as he opened a letter bomb which had been posted through the door of a house where he collected mail long ago. He shuffled forward, he had watched them come here before, a few years back. The Orchestra played. A vibrating and haunting collection of sweet sounds that seduced the senses. From his hidden vantage point, far back behind the packed rows of people as the violins danced and reached a crescendo, he looked at, Stephen Gillen's face far up

271

the hall in the side front row. His eyes were closed, his being lost to the music.

The man, who a long time ago was known as the Gardener, smiled. A tight movement that hid his true intent. He knew that death would soon find him, that the years he had remaining were galloping fast. He would not leave this earth until the mission was finished. He would keep going, as long as there was breath left in his body, to finish, to complete the circle that a little boy who had now matured into a man had activated and propelled many years before.

1997, 2.17am

Huddling under a thin blanket in the darkness of the cell my tortured feelings and the accumulation of my incarceration had evolved into a cutting despair the force of which I had not known before. I listened to the quietness of the segregation unit. Whitemoor, a dispersal prison in Cambridgeshire housed its segregation wing in a separate, isolated part of the prison that faced the high walls of the Special Security Unit. My fifteen months in Hull Special Unit had been uneventful and for the first time in my sentence I had started to make progress. With a well-muscled and chiselled body from intense training, Hull had given me a chance to stabilise my anger, the relaxed regime strengthening for a while my forward-looking mentality to progress quickly through my sentence.

Then the move had come. Not knowing where or why I was going, an escort had appeared one morning and taken me back to segregation.

On the third floor, in the echoing darkness with the floodlights of the yard and the high walls of the special Security Unit lights painting unnatural shadows at the window, my desperation pulled me deeper into the inescapable pit of tearing anguish.

It had crept up, the deep depressive black hole that had swallowed me. Like quicksand, the downward and unrequested depression had started. Tentatively at first, a snowball of grief and longing for freedom that had quickly found the slope of being trapped without a future. The boulder of fear and anxiety had overtaken me then. Hurtling down the recesses of self-pity it tugged and pulled me deeper and deeper. I felt more alone than ever, and dealing with the violence of my circumstances and my mind, my desolation of what my life had become was dragging me, sucking me downwards into the abyss.

I listened again to the stillness. My breathing filled my ears. Short, rushed, shallow and forced movements. My isolation again closed in. In the nightmare that was my tumbling thoughts of how to end it, I heard a voice. Somewhere in the web of sadness that had taken me, it stretched forth in my mind like a pin-prick of light in a darkened room. Once, and in a soft clear, succinct voice it gave the instruction, 'You must go through this...'
'Why,' I answered. 'Why must I go through this living hell?'

It repeated, 'You must go through this'.
I blinked my tear-filled eyes in the dark coldness of the cell, curled my body as a child would in the foetal position seeking warmth and comfort.

I knew I was unwell again, but was too far down the path to care. To end it would be better, easier, kinder to everyone and quicker.

I had heard it, the voice from the centre of my mind, but questioned the sanity of it. The waves of sadness were still alive and prevalent on their onslaught as the turning anguish and anxiety twisted through me.

Like an out of body experience my mind felt like it floated above me in the silence.

It showed me pictures. Violent scenes from my past, mixed with poignant moments engulfed in emotion. My son on my knee, Callum's smiling face, a little girl who held my hand in a children's home long ago, the yellow Tonka truck I had as a child, a tall tree that was spikey and the loving hands of Margret my aunt. Like a moving train, the scenes mixed and morphed in a merging kaleidoscope of stabbing emotions that were bringing more wetness to my eyes. I would kill or be killed in these places, I was sure.

'Oh god, I said. How would I be after twelve years of this.'

Alone, my most terrible moment had arrived.

Then It came…suddenly.

A slow but determined profoundness that originated at the roof of the pitch-black cell celling coming towards me and bringing with it the most wonderful feeling of love and protection. I gasped. Although it had brightened the whole area around me, supressing the darkness I had felt, it's soft light did not startle me. Slowly its power enveloped me, covered and moved through me its love saturating and extinguishing the coldness. My mind and body stopped, transformed and opened with the feelings of pure love, comfort and assurance. My eyes were wide, my heart for an intense moment open to the profoundness of its passing. It lingered, stopped, and then as slowly as it had arrived it again ebbed away.

The darkness had slowly returned. Quietly, I wondered what had just transpired. Under the blanket, still with gaping wounds that cut deep inside me, I felt suddenly renewed. I gulped, brought new saliva to the dryness of my mouth. The experience I had just been through had again awakened my hope and faith.

Chapter 13
Freedom & a New Life

The prison escort this time came to move me to another institution at an unusual hour. Just as I had settled after eating my tea time meal, the cell door burst open. It was the usual drill. Strip search, change into the bright yellow and green jumpsuit used for transport, belongings packed, bagged, logged and cable tied. They double cuffed me. One set of cuffs on both hands, then another set which handcuffed me to an officer. Quickly, with a rush of movement I was escorted down the metal stairs, out the back door of the segregation unit to where the Category A van waited, uncuffed from the officer and locked into a cubicle.

The van moved. The big double gates in front of us leading to the gate house swung open.
Unbeknown to me, this time I was being transported to Full Sutton in York.

❧

We sat there. Two people bathed in the dim lights of the studio.

It was time to let the truth be known. It was the show that was live and was raw enough, that didn't play with and edit the truth. A private place of safety where deep questions could be searched for and a soul made lighter with the truth being told…

The radio host thought it was a fantastic show, the road less travelled. He had been monitoring the questions coming in from the listeners and the engagement was wonderful. Ok, Stephen this is where I take a question from one of the listeners and put it to you. The eighth question, this one is from, Noel in the Angel, North London. He says, 'It's amazing that you have done so well after being in prison for so long. What was it really like to be a high security prisoner, and what were the bits you found the hardest'?

I moved slightly in the comfort of my soft chair. It was the history and images, that pushed down hard and far, were evaded and sidestepped but the feelings that twisted inside me could not be denied.

'…I called it the seventh level of hell. Long term high Security prisons in those days were run by the consent of the inmates. It was very violent. I saw unspeakable acts of cruelty. I saw a few people murdered in front of me in there. There is a hierarchy in prison. Different parts of the country split into their own gangs. At the top of the hierarchy were the top villains, gangsters, importers and terrorists. In my day the London villains were on top. Then you had your guys from Liverpool, Manchester, Leeds and the Geordies. The top people generally behaved because they knew to fall out was very serious indeed. Grudges could last for decades. As we were all Category A's the same people friend or foe would be moved around and around over the years. Sometimes you would arrive somewhere where you had friends, other times you would be unlucky enough to end up at a place full of your enemies. It really was like that and I even saw the prison service move people into serious circumstances on purpose. Over the years I was in there I had to defend myself many times…'

'The hardest times, Stephen,' said Christopher Denning. 'What were the worst things…?'

I paused. As my mind returned to moments I had buried deep in a place never visited, I recoiled. An internal note that struck my brain in remembrance and squeezed tight a hardened heart.

'...It's the loneliness, the loss of freedoms and everything that your life was. As the years blow past you, they are not replenished, they bear no fruit and are dead, gone and buried. You languish in this darkness that is violent, paranoid, crushing and painful. You cling tight to what you think is sanity as every part of your humanity and emotion is being sucked out of you. The years fade, and with them your memories, your understanding of what the world looks like desert you. The worst is, that as you wander forward, feign a resemblance of keeping it together as a human being in this 'walking dead like state' you know you're losing it, and as the long years before you stretch out over the horizon, all your knowledge and understanding of actual freedom, what that looks like and what it actually means to you has deserted you also...'

Vincent Meer thought of himself as the original gangster. At a fair height and with a thick-set and well-muscled physical body he carried with him the strong genes of his father from Tivoli Gardens, Jamaica. Serving twenty-five years for two shootings and importation of cocaine he had a long history of quick violence stretching back to when Dudus's father Lester Coke was running Kingston. In the cell, on D wing in the sprawling prison complex that was high Security Full Sutton with the other three close guys he rolled with, he twisted a moment the short tight, platted braids of his hair and looked out the window across the tall dividing fences towards the main compound of the prison yard.

He fancied himself a stylish man, sophisticated and a long way from his roots running food back in the yard. Like most, the years of his imprisonment cut him deep but like his postured veneer of superiority, he doggedly masked it behind aggression and would never fully show it. It was the rage that kept him going. Even here in the deepest darkest dungeon, he could feel important, someone with a difference who needed to be respected because of what he could do. Stephen Gillen had travelled with him in his mind with the others on his list as he had travelled with his belongings around the prisons of the UK. A name on a list that was long and was to be settled with on sight.

His Breda passed a joint. He waved it away. It was very rarely he would indulge and had to be seen as more aloof, more disciplined and real than the rest. His first meeting with Gillen had been as they both passed through the Special Security Unity in Brixton on remand awaiting trial years back. They had not liked each other at first sight.

Vincent kissed his teeth and laughed to himself. He recognised it. It was a dominance thing. Two alpha males feral and fresh from the hunt and with a driving hunger still rolling in their stomachs. When he and Gillen had fought, two days afterwards the volatile attitude between them had spiked one day by the pool table. It had taken every member of staff on the unit and more when they answered the riot bell to split them.

He had sent the message by word down the gym to be passed to the boy, Gillen on the other wing on hearing of his arrival. Outside, and hidden down the back of a soft chair was a metal, stiletto spike. One of the many weapons he secreted around the movements of his life. The whole prison population were allowed to gather together on exercise at the weekend. The massive area was policed only by watch towers and had a changing room toilet brick building which was hidden from the cameras.

Vincent Meer again kissed his teeth. A long sucking sound that hissed as his breath exhaled. The weekend would soon be here. He and his guys would catch Gillen and whoever else he was with and finish this vendetta forever…

&

The phone call came as the early evening lost its lustre and gave way to a calm late summer encroaching darkness. The two people who communicated in an engaging and positive tone had travelled a long emotive personal internal journey of discovery. A road that had brought them together at this finite point. They had taken different roads in their lives, long winding ones filled with desperate and decisive choices, that dictated for years that they be deadly opposing forces.

Kul Mahay, the ex-high-flying Gold Police Commander and, Stephen Gillen the reformed senior criminal continued their phone conversation.

'...I've looked at your work, Stephen. Great work in transforming your life and helping others. It is a credit to you...'
'Thank you, Kul. You must be thanked for your great service to humanity also. It is amazing we can talk like this.'

They were at opposite ends of the spectrum, in the past sworn enemies. Two people who took different paths, saw different things. Now joined, they shaped a common cause that would change the world and improve hundreds of millions of people's lives for the better.

'...I must admit, Stephen at first, when you told me your story, I thought, do I need to be involved with someone who has a history like this. It was the old programming, but your work is amazing.'

'...Kul, it was the same for me. But I am far along my journey of transformation. What you see with me, the great work behind me of going back into prisons to effect change, my progressive work in the business world is the real thing, a true metamorphosis.'

'People can change, Stephen. I have seen it in the great work I do with my events, in leadership training and emotional intelligence for companies. No matter how far we stray or fall, we can find our way back...'

'…Thank you, Kul, for your kind words. Maybe we can find a way to bring our knowledge to help people…'

'…I would like that, Stephen. Let me think…Well done.' I held the phone, said, feeling the inspirational innovation fall, '…Thank you, really. Let's talk soon…'

Twenty Years Earlier…Full Sutton Prison

I had the two homemade knives stuck down the separate sides of my back so I could reach them quickly. We walked, my friend Shane and I quickly and with a measured pace along the long corridors that joined the main wings of the prison on our way to the football fields where the inmates of the facility gathered for weekend exercise.

We wore the long rough, grey clothed coats given to lifers. Our hearts beat quickly, fiercely. With the midday sun filtering light as we walked past numerous guiding windows, and with the magazines wedged down our waistbands and around the vital organs in our middle bodies for protection against knife attack. We talked to each other from the side of our mouths so the other walking surrounding prisoners couldn't hear us.

'Stephen, we have to watch these. They'll be the four of them he's always with. They'll try to take us slyly.'
'…For sure. Shane, there is no other way. If we don't meet this forcefully they will pick us off singly. We can't have that.'

He walked, nodded. There was a fear in his words, an anxiety and the flush of worry spreading a light redness on his face and neck. He knew, like I did that it was do or die. There was nowhere to run, nowhere to hide. The only way, suicidal and unattractive, was the road travelled by the lesser few. We had to move forward to claim space and time and into certain brutal violence and a possible death.

We looked, watched carefully the other groups of inmates around us for ambush, as we walked into the open spreading sunlit yard. My ears listened intently to the sounds of the day, laughing, talking, the conversation of other prisoners and the rattling keys of the guards behind us as they locked and sealed the exercise gates.

The heat of a burning sun hit our muffled, heavily clothed and protected bodies as we entered the open expanse of the wide rugby field. The tall watch tower loomed behind the back-dividing razor-wired fence and prisoners, soaking the limited light and air littering the green of the far stretching highly protected and walled compound with most gathered in small groups walking clockwise as they talked.

We saw them.

It was an immediate thing. They waited. We looked hard so as not to miss them. Hanging, burning a high-intensity energy and trying to maintain a shadowed autonomy. Three black figures and one white by the front of the outside toilet building with twisted serious faces.

We circled. Walking far up the field, hands deep in the long pockets of our grey jackets, eyes alert, moving at advanced pace as our minds accessed and prepared.

He was definitely there.

I saw him. Vincent Meer, his lips mouthing instructions I could not hear. They pulled back, a tactical withdrawal before the battle. They withdrew into the interior of the changing rooms building awaiting our approach on the next lap.

'They've gone in, Shane...'

'...Yeah, they've seen our padding, our grey jackets. They must know we're tooled up.'

'Absolutely. I don't know how many weapons they have, Shane. Expect many. I didn't see any protection round them.'

'They've put stuff inside the toilets.'

281

We had brought four knives for the protection of our lives, two each. The block of the toilets drew closer. Then it came, fluttering, hard and rising, a mixture of a panic-filled excitement that played havoc as high doses of adrenaline filled my arms and legs. We were near the open door, and although I wanted to turn away, I pushed forward, through the notions of fight or flight and gritted my teeth. Resolve flowed through me.

Slowly, tentatively we entered the dull light smelling of. stale urine. In through the empty changing rooms and left into the toilet area. We moved aware of everything. My heart was beating a drum, sweat was forming a film on my neck, at my temples, converting to beads on my forehead. I felt for the knifes tucked in neatly at the back of my waistband, pulled them out, forward.
'Hey boy. You're dead you know. See, last time you were lucky. Today you pay dearly both of you!'

My hands had the two sharp pieces of metal reworked into deadly weapons in front of me. It was Meer, holding a long thin metal bar in one hand and a sharp piece of metal in the other.
They were around him. Gathered tight, they moved to the flanks, three vicious hyenas who with their innovative craziness searched for a chance to exploit a clear place to strike. They had been in the toilet cubicles and fanned out to create an opening to manoeuvre. The sharpness of their pointed knives in their hands glinted in the soft light.

Shane was beside me. Our eyes glowered, faces screwed up and clenched. With force and clear intent, I stepped forward and shouted it.

'You think we fuckin care! We don't need this, here in this place. But let's do it! We fuckin end it here and die together! Let's do it now here today! Let's kill each other. Come on then, these knives are going to do the talking!'

They paused. Together, on the brink of terrible unmitigated violence everyone stopped. A long moment that finely weaved and stretched in the Mexica-stand off as their eyes pushed and poked and cut at the strength of our intent. Our cliff face, made from desperation and carved with the madness of reckless intent, remained solid. Against their energy, their forceful stance, I felt they were now waning.

Vincent Meer cut his eyes, on a narrowed face a sarcastic thin smile formed.

'You surprised me, Gillen. You got some front to come in here with that talk. You done the best thing…'

We moved back, weapons still held high, Shane and I towards the door back outside and into the light of the sun.

His voice followed us. 'That's, it, Gillen. Not today then, not today… You go back with your little sheepdog. Run back boy. We leave it for now…'

…We moved through the changing room, back out to the field where the air would surround us. We would do a few more laps on the grass field and then go back to the wing.

Vincent Meer's voice still came from the toilets behind us.

'Not today, Gillen…But one day, remember now, one day…!'

Ten Years Earlier, 1989

We stood in the small kitchen at the back of the house that had wooden beams in the celling. I was eighteen, young fit and lithe. I cooked eggs on the cooker for breakfast, bare chested in jeans, and in my head, I was thinking of the night before. It was the age of hip-hop, drum and base and house and the night before, after being taken on a clandestine trek and following the instructions, we had arrived at the Illegal rave Sundance late into the evening. The eggs crackled and spat oil. The music, the field where people danced, the seducing beat of the music, the smiles and the half-naked women who grooved in gilded cages. The kicking ecstasy that peaked in my mind, the fast drive back as we navigated country lanes at breakneck speeds, dominated my thoughts.

He had slid in, come from the shadow of the half-lit stairs with a slinking walk that was unsure and jaded.

It was my foster father, Liam, just up from sleep. Caught and surprised at finding me here with strange eyes that were uncommonly wide.

His naturally wide shoulders rippled, arms bulged. He leaned his face towards me.

'...Go on then do it!'

I turned my head. I had not been to the house much over the last years. Going my own way, and having a life change when Callum and I had secured four hundred thousand pounds worth of gold, watches and diamonds two years earlier, I turned into a strong and independent fine young man with a twinkle in my eye and the world at my feet. We had not looked back. There was an unquenchable fire in my belly, a confident nature in all I did, and a secure glint in my eyes.

'...All them years, Stephen. If you want to do it, do it now!'

His bare cheek and the side of his face was shown. He had been a good man but a bully who had bashed and terrified us through uneven years.

'Get it over with, Stephen...' He repeated.

My eyes narrowed. The picture of it threw me completely. I saw in front of me something I though I never would. Big as a house, with shoulders that were sculptured like granite. A cowering figure, accountable, sorry and pathetic.

I looked at him. He willed the punch, waited for it.

I watched him, he was sincere and with the spatula in my hand I didn't want to move.

Disgust and a renewed anger surfaced and ebbed through me. The moment had gone. In the kitchen, at the back of the house that was shining clean and which had a corner cupboard full of fine china and glass vases and figures, we gauged each other in a new light as the soft light of the morning filtered between us.

As the moment of retaliation had passed so too had the deep feelings of revenge ebbed away. I had never spoken the words. Through the years he had never heard me call him by this name, had never heard me utter the words.

I said, 'Dad, leave it. Its OK, don't worry about it...'

෨

John Milton had been in back to back meetings all day. As the scratching winds had plunged the morning temperatures shaking the buildings windows, and afternoon had elevated the directorates workload to breaking-point, he had taken an aspirin to help his blood flow and headache and had sat in the toilet cubical alone to rebalance his stress levels and regain his composure.

The new Close Supervision Centre in Woodhill Prison, a prison within a prison built at great cost to manage, contain and correct the behaviour of the country's most challenging, disruptive and dangerous inmates was now operational and the systems' worst inmates were being transferred. Modelled on a High Security prison control Unit in America, the CRC was structured on an incentive scheme tier system. Comply, you would get more privileges and your life would be easier. Be uncompliant, and you would lose everything and your life would become highly uncomfortable. With four self-contained units that would hold around ten prisoners, they were aiming at six where most would start in the middle and standard level of the system.

Back at his desk, high in the lofty heights of Clelland House, with the wind still blowing a gale across the rippling waters of the Thames and annoyingly rattling the closed windows, he looked at the list of the seven prisoners already selected and present in the CRC. He winced internally. The HM Inspectorate of Prisons was already trying to reach him to visit the facility. They were not ready.

He wrote quickly, a flowing creative movement, and signed the directive order for the next inmate selected to be moved to the CRC with immediate effect. On his list, a sheet that had the names of the selected inmates in bold, under the name of Charlie Bronson he added the next prisoner to go there. His name was, Stephen Gillen.

❧

The fast-moving waters of the River Thames had stabilised as the deep currents, whirlpools and tides of the late evening slightly evened and subsided.

The phone call alerting about something suspicious had been transferred through as London woke and the busy road arteries of the city started to awaken with activity and accumulate congestion. The woman, an investment specialist who ran the 2.3 miles from Putney Bridge to Battersea every morning before work with her dog, had called it in with the concern drenching her voice.

In his chest, Police Constable Newman had frustration hold his heart in a fist of regret. He had been in the Marine Policing Unit of the Metropolitan Police, formerly know as the Thames Division for seven years. As their fast response Targa 31 cut through the early morning freshness and murky green water of a rapidly stirring Thames, he steered the boat slightly left as he peered through the now lifting smog of the day. His head was filled with the slamming door, and the girlfriend he had argued with, the frustration of words unsaid, but he could see it now. Far back across the choppy and dirty waters, just along from Battersea Bridge and moving back and forth against the water shoreline where the break in the embankment had a tiny stony pebbled beach.

His colleague stood at the front of the boat with binoculars at his eyes, shouted, 'I see it, Harry. Just along from where we expected. The current has pulled it a little further down river. It's a body, Harry. Looks bloated.'

PC Newman pushed forward the boat throttle. The boat rose and arched in the water, turned water spray foaming white as it raced forward. Close to the shore a metal coffee flask bounced off the hull. It bobbed behind them as two officers entered the water and the nautical patrol approached the clothed, bloated body. With black boots sinking into the moving water shaped stones and pebbles, they turned the clothed body over. The face, neck and hands showed vascular marbling and there was a dark discolouration of the skin and soft tissue, putrefaction had occurred in the water showing the body had been there for a while.

The two officers, although trained against such things, felt nauseas as the stench attacked them violently. One of them, checking for ID unzipped the saturated blue parka jacket the victim wore. Inside, from deep in a torn pocket he retrieved the dead man's wallet and brought it into the light. In one of the compartments, behind a small sodden and waterlogged newspaper article was a card with a name on it. It said Mr Rodney Cooper...

Millennium, New Year's Eve, 2000

On my knees, in the calm darkness of my shadowed cell in the Close Supervision Unit, a spartan place that had taken two years of my life, as I listened to the crackling shower of fireworks sprinkle the late evening sky, I closed my eyes against the stretching years of imprisonment behind me and said the prayer and made the vow.

'...Dear god, the universal power of all things, I ask your forgiveness for falling short, for not doing better and making the right choices. Through pain I have learned the ways of this world and as the falling years of my time in prison have taken all the emotion from me, in the deepest pit of my desperation I have been guided to the great courage of my never ending resolve to change the trajectory of my life for the better...I humbly ask you to help me with this, show me the next steps forward...'

In my head was my deal with God. As the world celebrated and partied, the new millennia dawned and the energy of hope electrified around the world, I thought it fitting with humility and strength, from the quietness of my cell on my knees I plugged into the collective mainframe of humanity and delivered my prayer and solemn vow.

Outside the window, while the fireworks erupted and danced in a moonlit sky, I looked at the yellowed, floodlit bathed concrete of the exercise yard. The enclosed fences and walls beyond it that trapped my freedom. I had been away nearly ten years and still remained a Category A prisoner.

It was apparent to me, the truth, that the bitter years of high security imprisonment had battered and clawed away my emotions, ripped and torn them like a thief in the night. My humanity had been stolen. Anger had been my fuel, rebellion my guide. I had been forged with gritted hardness from the inside out. The vow I had whispered was in my head again. I had less than eighteen months to my release date. Part of the vow, wrapped, internalised and kept secret for my heart alone, was that I would not let the anger or bitterness take me, that if I were supported and given the opportunities to change my life, I would seek to help others and reach hard and highly to become the best that I could be...

Chapter 14
Innovation, and a Journey of Success

'…Oh my God. The shit has hit the fan'. The Detective had just enough time to utter the words before the phone was taken from him, handset placed back on its cradle and he was asked to remain at his desk silent and told not touch anything.

They came, like a closing buzzing, busy, organised swarm of hawking hornets, intent on invading a highly-prized bees' nest. With the office midday rush of activity just about to peak and the grey skies of south London turning back towards the east with a bounty of rain. The most secretive section of the Metropolitan polices' anti-corruption unit nicknamed 'The Ghost Squad' infiltrated in one coordinated sweeping motion the offices of the Scotland Yard S08's Flying Squad, East London branch.

From his back office, from where he could watch the main floor and the squad work, Detective Inspector Sixsmith, in the file cluttered space that held his commendations and some festering memorabilia on the walls, saw the covering, forward moving blanket of the police anti-corruption squad as they streamed in. He looked at the black-chequered baseball cap on his desk and the fear of being uncovered shot through him. It was already too late, that he knew. Forward they came, a mass of plain clothed and uniformed officers that stopped his team working, started the evidence collection process, seized paperwork, files, documents and computers.

He sat back in his chair. Outside his team were being escorted from their stations, lined up against the wall and questioned. They were stone faced, forcefully assertive and methodical, the officers of the good standards division. Sixsmith, grunted. More of a snarl, as the deep trenches had and would always demand shadowy solution. Heads would roll, and the chopping block of withdrawn and stopped pensions seemed closer. He opened the drawer on his desk, took a cigarette from the pack he hid, and lit it inhaling deeply.

He had battled the dreaded nicotine for nine months. It had been another sacrifice to his eminent purpose of thief taking and ridding London of the gangster problem. Like his failing marriage, the long nights and the crippling sciatica that made his muscles tremble. They searched the office now, and as the cigarette smoke circled and twirled a pattern in the air in front of him, he saw that they had found some of the evidence they had been planting on suspects. The 'fit-up kits' as the main players on his squad called them, replica handguns, gloves and masks, were structured clusters of collaborating evidence they produced and planted on a target if a suspect had been shot or arrested and they could find no hard evidence.

Jesus, Mary and Joseph, Sixsmith though. The embarrassment would ruin his reputation, and he had just been accepted into a senior position on the murder squad. He inhaled deeply the nicotine into his lungs, coughed slightly and spluttered. He was fucked, a few of them were. His dream was crumbling. Rome was burning, the fleeing rats already searched to save their skins and the instigators of the new revolution would be ruthless in their execution of their purge.

For one of the first times in a long and illustrious career, Albert Sixsmith felt real polarising fear. They would hang him high for this, and beside him in his pleadings would be the other six officers who had been complicit in the sleight-of-hand.

The other nineteen members of the squad, although guilty by averting their eyes and condoning unsavoury actions, he wagered would fare better.

Cigarette smoke filled the room. As he watched them strip the operational notes, briefs and photographs from the suspects walls outside, herd his sheepish staff into a separate room at the end of the hall and saw the skies over Walthamstow bring the darkened rain clouds of January, Detective Inspector Sixsmith knew the ghost squad were keeping the best for last.

He slowly stood. Through the wide windows of his office he saw them, two senior ranks at the head of a thick group of plain clothed officers.

He turned his head quickly at the unfinished and live cases encased in the brown files that littered his office. Big tomes, with dangerous men in them, recidivists, that told violent stories and needed quick endings.

It was the end of an era.

'...Detective Inspector Albert Sixsmith?' They filled the office, fanned out in the small space.

Sixsmith, nodded, 'Yes, that's me. May I ask who's asking…?'

The one with the grey hair, tall and obviously in charge waved his words away, pushed forward hard and with no comfort. 'DI Sixsmith, while we are well aware of your rank and current operational stature, be under no illusion that this will not stop us in the clear execution of our sworn duty here. My name is, DCI Keith Johnson from the Department of Professional Standards. We are here heading an anti-corruption operation into the past and present activities of you and your squad…'

Sixsmith stiffened. The wind was out of his sails and as they read him his right and stepped forward to handcuff him he stood taller,' I'm not wearing them'.

Beside, DCI Johnson, DI Owen Whitter felt a tinge of sorrow. The faintest touch of a feeling that dropped and disappeared. He stepped forward forcefully. He had made his name rising through the ranks of the Police Complaints Office and had been on enough 'grip and pace' meetings to know that it was a few bad apples that were turning the vastly professional police service into a sour and rotting bunch.

'…I'm afraid, DI Sixsmith you have no influence or jurisdiction here, and will have to do as you're told.'

'It's ok, DI Whitter, said his Senior DCI Johnson. He can walk. For the service he's given we can give him that at least.'

They grouped around him.

Flushed with the redness of embarrassment, and as the officers of his squad watched from behind the glass of the locked door they waited in, Detective Inspector Albert Sixsmith made his journey across the sprawling office of the Flying Squad team he had headed, his last walk, a proud one.

He would never return to position as a serving officer again. They turned at the end of the hall. As he walked down the stairs, to the team who surrounded him, he said, 'I think I would like my solicitor'.

Detective Chief Inspector Johnson, answered, 'That would be very wise, Detective Inspector Sixsmith. Very wise…'

Still a Category A prisoner and with only nine months left to serve, as the category A Van transport escort hit the speed of the motorway towards the south and London, in my cubicle and tightly handcuffed I squinted as heavy rain clouded my visibility and hammered the tarmacked road and surrounding area. The armoured vehicle ate the road. Outside, in the bleakness, the world looked the same. But if the long years of soul destroying and violent years of levelling imprisonment had taught me anything, it was to take nothing for granted. From the blue folder on my knees

I took out the brown envelope that held my latest mail. In the main big brown envelope which had arrived yesterday was the report I searched for. From the CPS it showed a reinvestigation of my court case many years ago. It detailed, how the officers involved in my arrest and headed by, DI Sixsmith and a corrupt ring of officers had been investigated by their internal anti-corruption Division.

The sound of the rain attacked the bodywork and window of the cubical, and with a widening large border of grey gathering clouds that split with the nimbus of a light, glinting silver lining across the afternoon sky as we travelled the road to London and my coming release, I focused on the paperwork in front of me. At the top of the page in heavy bold it said: 'Operation Wasteland'

࿊

We sat there. Two people bathed in the dim lights of the studio.

It was time to let the truth be known. It was the show that was live and was raw enough, that didn't play with and edit the truth. A private place of safety where deep questions could be searched for and a soul made lighter with the truth being told…

'…Stephen, this has been epic. It's been a fascinating show of great content and I've personally been on the end of my seat. What a journey, so extreme and emotional. I know people say, there's always someone worse off. What they really mean is if that person can go through that then I can get over my difficulties. Your story is a real testament which is already helping millions. It's the last question, and I've got to ask it. For the listeners, what are the most valuable things you've learnt? What does the future hold now…?'

'…Thank you, Christopher. Thank you to the people out there listening.

I leaned forward in my chair. I had no doubt, only clarity from my journey. Pain had cleansed me of hesitancy.

'...That we are a collective. That we are part of all living things, and our central purpose is to learn, to be more and become more. That one of the tricks of life is not just to pursue the truth, but to unravel the lies. That there is an order to all good things and nothing is by chance. That the journey is vastly more important than the destination. That anything is truly possible if we apply ourselves correctly. That if we truly want to reach the pinnacle of our development, our greatness, we need to get over ourselves and out of our own way. Small steps turn into great strides. As when we look at those before who have changed things, their journey was not without tragedy. They were ridiculed, isolated, stabbed in the back, treated badly, shunned and humiliated. It is our purpose to elevate and gain enlightenment, but as we do it we should expect this road to be uncomfortable. It is the finest example of humility we can show and we should all process as human beings...'

With the soft lights of the studio covering his face in a warm glow, with the framed faces of the pictures surrounding us and gathered in audience, Christopher Denning nodded and showed the thumbs-up.

ॐ

It was called 'Two Extremes'. A unique and true portrayal of two men who, having lived hard and successfully at their chosen paths and who had been at the opposite ends of the spectrum, had unravelled more truth about their purpose and driven destinations. Two people on a global mission of positive change. In the UK they would travel to a city a month on a national tour. Already gaining great traction and media engagement the events, aimed at empowering and helping to affect positive social change, were already booked for parliament and due to share a stage with the Lord Chancellor and Secretary of Justice, one of the highest Ministers in the UK.

In the wide theatre in Derby, the audience had been spellbound as Kul Mahay and Stephen Gillen, joined now in brotherhood and forcing change for the better, had delivered their talks.

A soft smile was on my face. It was the end of the event, and in the large auditorium with the cameras positioned and the lights angled and the vast projected picture of Kul Mahay and me behind us bathing in the brilliance of its light, I had at last found my way back to myself and was stretching out to become the person I was meant to be.

She stood close in her beauty and elegance and leaned in with the introduction. Daphne, in a stunning red dress with her blond hair framed and positioned perfectly, still had the mike in her hand from guiding the Q & A.

'...Stephen, let me introduce you to Delia and her grandson.'

Delia smiled sweetly, a middle-aged Asian lady and she had close by her fourteen-year-old grandson.

'I just wanted to say thank you. I've been having problems with my grandson here. We were sitting back in the audience, and what you said was amazing. He listened and he said listening to you has really helped him. Thank you...'

I touched her gently on the arm in thanks. Her grandson, a tall thin figure stepped forward shyly. A boy who pushed out against the world to become a man, and in that moment, I wondered of my own mother again and I saw her with caring stamped on her face, a shining figure burnished in glittering white who smiled with the love of proudness.

A soft hesitant voice, he said, 'If you could put your best bit of knowledge in one bit of advice what would it be...?'

I smiled warmly. It was a great question, good and insightful and showing great thought.

I answered, 'That's easy, keep doing the next right thing, no matter how hard that may be and I guarantee you will end up somewhere good...'

Carrying the comforting wind, the burnishing force of the midday sun covered the London skyline in freshness as the black Kite soaring high in the tall air thermals, turned its angled wings and adjusted its forked tail toward the glaring brightness to the west. An acrobatic flyer, it had moved from its European flock on its migratory route after the teaming rainfall. One of the worlds most successful hunters, as the shadowed city below baked in the rising warmth, it dipped against the reflected brightness, flexed its sharp talons and searched for its prey of other birds, bats and mice.

We sat in the National Gallery before the 1565 -1570 masterpiece of 'The Family of Darius before Alexander'. On a low wooden bench in front of the massive description of Stateira, King Darius's wife captured with her mother at the Battle of Issus after the last king of the Achaemenid Empire escaped capture. The two of us studied the beautiful richness of colour and drama layered into the painting.

He had been known as the Gardener and many names in his lifetime. To me he was a shadow of questions who had travelled in my quiet moments with attachments of a history long past.

He pointed to the painting with the forefinger of his deformed hand. He said, in a soft clear tone. 'Alexander, displayed forgiveness in victory. Here the wife of the King Darius pleads for the life of her husband in defeat. Although renowned for her beauty, Alexander, thinking it Kinglier to govern himself than to conquer his enemies, sought no intimacy with any of them...'

I had waited for many years in silence with my questions. 'All these years you have been there. Who are you...?'

On the low wooden bench, together in our isolation, amongst the busy moving tourists and crowd of the gallery, he continued. 'What I love about this painting is she mistakes, Alexander the Great for Hephaestion, his counsellor and most intimate friend since childhood...Wonderful, beautiful. What do you think, Stephen, says so much about the man...?'

He had been there it seemed at the important, pivotal junctions of my life. A mysterious figure who moved with clandestine footsteps along the uncertain progress of my journey.'

'...All these years you have shadowed my life. Why?'

'Because of a boy, Stephen. Bright and brave and full of the exuberance of a life to come.'

'A boy?'

'Yes. A boy who was full of vigour. Whom I begged to stay at home one night while riots raged and a street war was fought, while the night coldness cut and a place that ached for peace mourned'.

I pulled back. In my mind it was surfacing, dots were joining, a picture was forming.

'...The boy was my son, Stephen. My beautiful nineteen-year-old who I had sworn to protect like any parent and couldn't...'

'You mean?' I questioned.

'It was the times. Where were all trapped by the times and the history and pain of our sufferings and sacrifices. When he was young, Stephen I tried to get peace in Belfast, tried to lead an example that would show us to put our differences behind us. That together we could live in peace...'

'I don't understand...'

'The boy, Stephen. The boy who was shot in front of you as you cowered under the hedge many long years ago. The boy was my son. I was known in Belfast for starting a youth club where all people were welcome, catholic and protestant alike. You hadn't been born then, but my son was young when they put the letter bomb through the letter box and I opened it.'

He held up his three fingered hand, turned it to me. 'I paid for my rush towards a better future for us all. In any conflict, any terrible struggle there are hardliners...But I always continued. It made me persevere more.'

'My God. I'm so sorry. I see it'. I looked at the painting and was transported. Moved back to a place of suffering where I gripped at cold earth and seizing fear shook me. I could see the smoke, the guns, smell the earth that was mixed with air carried petrol and cordite. I gulped, and in the throng of the moving shifting crowds in the Gallery as it weaved there was only us, together, isolated and focused on a time in history long ago.

'My son got involved. I did everything, but the constant reminder of my deformity and the hardness of our existence was a daily stick that beat him. He found hard to take that at the beginning as I struggled.'

We looked at each other a moment and the widest smile crept over his face.

He continued, 'You know boys, Stephen. They must be boys, especially at that time in their lives. I was there that night. I followed him into the night as I was prone to. To shadow him, look out you know. I though that when the bad moment would come I would be there and some how avert it, change it, protect him'

'Thank you'.

'What?'

'Thank you for your bravery. But why, all these years. Why have you been there as I have travelled my life journey?'

'Because you were like him, Stephen. My sons name was Sean. Sean, Stephen, and I watched you that night as he lay alone dying with his life leaving him on the pavement.

I saw that as young and as terrified as you were you reached out to him when he needed it and I couldn't.

His words reached deep inside me. A fist that gathered the historic pain I held and opened it to the brightness. My eyes filled with the emotion of the moment, the night where tracer rounds lit a night sky, people ran and scattered, gunfire danced and I cowered hidden. The majesty of the masterpiece was in front of us. It preserved the ambiguity of the painting's historic moment in pictorial intelligence.

'Sean died. We tried everything. I vowed, Stephen that I would follow you till I could repay the debt. I knew your family back home, Stephen. It was easy for me to hear the gossip and make enquires…The long years. You have lived a hard life. You have so much of him in you. The 'devil may care' strength and stubbornness, the talent and love of live, the resilience. In the long years I have thought of and carried you in my heart as my own…'

'I'm sorry I couldn't save him…'

'Declan, Stephen. My name is Declan Brown…'

'If I could have reached out in my terror…if I could have made a difference, Declan…?'

'…I know, Stephen. I know. You did all you could child that you were, brave in that night as you could be. I would like to thank you, from me and in the great memory of, Sean's short life, Stephen… Thank you…'

His hand was on my elbow as he started to move and rise. 'We have remembered your act of kindness, Stephen, through the long and testing years. My vow to Sean's memory to be there in his name when you needed me the most is settled. You've turned into a fine man. Your mother would be very proud. Sean will be smiling up there…Can't say there were times I worried for you'.

Surrounded by the beauty of the old masters and the activity of great movement I could only sit speechless a moment as the enormity of the significance compartmentalized the memories inside me.

The Gardener, a man called Declan Brown who was meeting his twilight years but who had never given up hope, stood before me and looked at the painting once more.

With a half-smile, he said, 'What I love about this picture is the presence of nobility and how it mixes humility with great power. Alexander, one of the world's greatest generals who would conquer a third of the world, is clothed with influence but cloaked by his ambiguity. To be everything but be invisible when the need arises takes great skill. There is one more thing I needed to ask.'
'Yes…Anything?'

'…As my son lay dying, I saw he said something. All the years, Stephen. What were his dying words…?'

He looked at me. Striking green eyes, sad and full with memories less aired, with an unspeakable depth, wrought and worn with the deep experience of a life lived with extremes and adversity.

'He said how he loved you. How he loved his mother. He called for you. He had the love of you around him'.

It was a moment. Like a terrible punch to the solar plexus, as he stood and stiffened. He turned, surrounded by the historic masterpieces and in the bustling crowd, a figure that melted easily and without notice into the bleakest of days.
The slip of white paper was in his hand. He said, 'Oh, one last thing, Stephen. My parting gift to you'.
'…What is it'.
'…It's your real mothers name and address, Stephen. Make a better go of it than I did…'

He was gone, and he took a history with him.

Into the ambiguity of the further beguiling halls, and as fast and as silent as he arrived. In the painting, Alexander, had his arms stretched out. As I stood there, with the emotion of a new life change beckoning and looking at the name on the paper ready to embrace the glory of my future, I was aware of the symbolism of the greatness that surrounded me. I was armed with a great experience which, forged by adversity and tempered by the unravelling of measured years, would keep me in good stead for the future. Silently, and with one last look at the painting I disappeared into many moving figures that shrouded the room.

৵

Epilogue

Snapshots from the journey

It had been a usual week. The office had been a hive of activity. There had been more strategy sessions on the white board with senior staff than usual. We were on a roll and the successful momentum of our business initiatives were causing the usual progress in certain areas. Our media machine was gaining traction. Our constant work on global Social platforms was positioning our marketing and advertising adequately. We were in many markets. Film-making, events, PR, pharmaceuticals, Tec, design, and bespoke business creation. There was the usual push to keep on top of things. I was a million miles away.

'Are you ready to have a catch-up?', Daphne, my business and life partner had had an illustrious career in her own right. An international designer and brand expert, she had amongst other things achieved great work in media, being at one time even Tom Jones PA.

'Two minutes, let me just deal with this'. I glanced out the window into the fair medium light of an average afternoon.

I had no premonition of what was about to happen.

I checked the phone, suddenly realizing that I should answer the persistent text messages from, Caroline Heward the Harley Street stress expert as it must be something important. Then Caroline told me. Her words fired out quickly and confidently.

'Stephen. Stephen, can you hear me?'

Caroline said I was to be nominated for the Sunhak

International Peace Prize, which was based in South Korea. It was very prestigious. As a UK Peace Ambassador for the Universal Peace Federation, she had nominated me and together with the Secretary-General, Robin Marsh & UK Director Margret Ali – they thought my story, the work I had done and was doing would be perfect as nomination for Britain. They were hopeful the UK could maybe win this year…

Silence. I listened as Caroline continued. It had been discussed I had had a miracle transformation in my life, that I was a beacon to many. That I had been involved in organised crime to a high level and served over a decade in high security prison at Category A, the highest security category and I had been held in prisons within prisons and at times was seen as one of the most dangerous men in the country. Further, my transformation was unique and amazing and that I was touching hundreds of millions of lives around the world. That she could not think of anyone more inspirational…

So, as she sat in Lancaster Gate, the headquarters of the Global UPF, a body closely aligned with the United Nations with its UK leadership she had asked, 'Is this someone who you would consider nominating?'

'…Absolutely,' it was agreed.

'We're running out of time, Stephen,' she said quickly.

'I've been trying to get you for two days. Tomorrow is the final date for nominations to be in!'

I was aware of the usual office clatter. But in my space, a wide open-plan light room with brilliant clean white walls, cream furniture and a well-made wooden floor, I paused with the phone at my ear.

She continued, 'I'm sending over the details now. There's a form that needs to be filled out, Stephen. We sign off the nomination from our side. It must be cleared and signed off by the Secretary-General. There are only a thousand people around the world who can nominate someone for the Sunhak Prize!'.

'I understand, and Caroline, thank you'.

I replaced the phone in. The enormity of what she had said although the internal emotions I would travel through in the next two weeks had not yet arrived.

My mind retraced the journey. I was in the bathroom area when she had first got me thirty minutes ago. She launched into her vision of what had transpired. She informed me that as a peace ambassador for the UK and for the Universal Peace Federation, she had spoken to the Secretary-General and the UK director there, and she had told them about me and my work going back some years, about my transformation from being a high security prisoner, about the great work I had done in prisons. That I was transforming people's lives by the great work I was doing in the media. That I was in different areas and industries of business, about all the work I had done as a keynote motivational speaker spreading the messages of wisdom, strength and hope.

She also spoke of all the great work I was trying to do in the pharmaceutical industry in Africa, in the open wound industry trying to save many lives. She also talked about all the great people who were around me, who were all working towards the same aims and how my own story was unique.

Caroline went on that the Sunhak was like a Nobel Prize and that there was a million dollars in prize money that would be split between the two winners. I was gobsmacked. It didn't really register with me. There were different categories. One of them was conflict resolution.

Daphne appeared from the other office. Always immaculate, she stood there in a white dress. Her blond shoulder length hair sat wonderfully and she looked at me with the softest knowing green eyes. Highly skilled and intuitive beyond words she could read people at a thousand paces. I was strangely quiet. Then in my usual quick and to the point voice disclosed what I had just discussed on the phone.

'Wonderful,' she smiled slightly in that knowing way. 'You really deserve it, Stephen. I am always with you – I see how hard you work. This will change everything'.

I turned and took a look out the window, far over the well-kept trees and park of the private estate. Over the rooftops to my left my eyes fixed on a calm blue sky. I felt Daphne was right.

…I was in a haze of emotional distraction and turmoil for days. It was a surreal feeling akin to an out-of-body experience. I actually felt different somehow, as if I was not myself, as if something inside me pushed and pulled and kicked. I had not been here before. That was evident. It was yet a new level of responsibility, another great elevation for me as a human being. It was fascinating how my emotions churned inside me. It was the opposite of what I would have expected. I was reminded again that the internal improvement for a human being never finishes. But I was exactly where I was meant to be at this moment. I had been out for one of the walks I took sometimes to internalize my thoughts and emotions, so I could find the right forward visual clarity.

Daphne confronted me.

'You're sabotaging yourself again. I can see it. It's written all over you!'

I was back in the office, by the large window where there was a phone and an orchid. I felt strangely haggard. Together on the outside but churning and unsure inside. She was right of course. The guilty signs were in my heightened anxiousness. My hair-trigger thinking. The difference in my scattered actions and my snappy tone.

She continued her targeted pressing. 'This is very interesting. It always happens. Every time you come up a level and something really wonderful happens the nemesis re-appears'.

I rested my hand on the window ledge. A comforting motion. How could this be possible for someone who had travelled such a hard, violent brutal road? I thought of the darkness, I thought of the misery I had caused. I thought of the times that I had been weak. When I should have been strong and courageous I had turned my head. I thought about the times when I had stood back. Bad things had happened to others. I thought that I was undeserving because of these actions. Deep down inside me I felt unworthy.

It was the nemesis. A figure that lurked in the shadow of my syce always bent on trouble.

For years I had had to deal with and convert the great demons inside me. I had created reinforced frameworks that I had engineered to keep the darkness out. The strict boundaries were very focussed also on keeping the darkness in. I had tools to translate these dangers. They were archetypes, sides of me that had to be controlled. The nemesis, the king, the general. The saboteur. I felt the uncontrollable wave of emotion come up my body. From the pit of my stomach it settled in my brain, face and eyes. More revelation was coming. The tears were in my eyes and I now welcomed them. I was stabilising again. I was aware of the massive responsibility that had entered my life. The enormity of what was to come. It became clear, in that moment, that some of the best world stage Peace Keepers are warriors. Big souls that were forged, saw more and pushed unbelievable shadows. I had reached the next level emotionally. I turned to, Daphne from the window.

'Daphne... I suddenly get it. That this makes a life, my life, worth living'.

❧

Behind the large glass windows of Elstree Aerodrome, the two men in over coats watched the sleek white private jet as it accelerated to top speeds on the run way. Followed it as it elevated sharply into an azure sky. They watched. One took a bite from a fresh green apple. The plane climbed. Quickly elevating. They stood close. Together their eyes followed it long before it had disappeared into an invisible sky.

The Lear jet turned slightly in a perfect blue sky. Its left wing dipped to adjust its course more due north. In the luxury interior I watched this movement outside the window fascinated at its engineering. It was a fine afternoon, sun glinted reflectively on my window as the ground became smaller beneath us. The plane, a Lear jet 70/75, named after its founder Bill Lear, had been developed from the 40 /45. With two crew it had a cruise speed of 465kn (535 mph, 861 km/h) it could hold eight passengers.

' A penny for your thoughts?' Daphne in a blue trouser suite with a white blouse sat facing me, on the other side of the low table between us, with a dairy in her hands.

I continued to watch the cloud nimbus. Over further down on the light blue horizon I saw the rare bird. White, with magnificent blue/black tipped feathers. A white Stork. I studied its elegance as it hovered there in the high thermals. It turned, dipped, swooped towards the yellow glare of the sun. It was gone.

I adjusted the gold/silver cuff link of my white shirt, fixed my grey checked cashmere tailored suit jacket. My brown boot pushed my knees higher towards me and a hand rested on the seam of my jeans. I sipped my coffee. 'Do you know I just saw a white Stork. High in the clouds. The elegance of it'.

She smiled. Looked up from where she wrote in the blue dairy with a pencil.' We have a two o'clock with Lawrence, Secretary-General. We should stay a while with him. At 6pm the founder of the global women's movement is in Zurich...She suggested dinner, should we see her?'

'Such a rare bird the White Stork, Daphne'.

'I can name another one of them,' and she laughed. A conspirator soft sound that fractured the cabin.

I looked over at Tony. He sat, short black hair and glasses, still in the hi Vis he had used at the departure gate as he had headered us out and onto the plain. His head was down reading. He looked up from the magazine he studied. A wide grin creased his face.

'Are you saying I'm a rare bird, Miss Diluce?' I teased.

She pulled back a moment. Her face opened up, 'I'm not saying, Mr Gillen. I bloody well know so…Come on now there is only one of you. Broke the mould…one they'd had to cobble together in the first place…'

A thin smile tightened on her red lips.

God forbid, I wondered.

It had taken me a long time to buy into myself, the things everyone and the press said about me. The more the events of my life progressed, I had now had to consider maybe they were right? My eyes rested on the leather cream interior above me. It was a game of realities, this life. It didn't give you what you wanted – but what you become.

'The founder of the global woman's group?' The pencil was in her fingers. The dairy open.

'Women's empowerment? Let's see…? I sat back.

'Maybe we should be empowering the men, 'said Daphne, a questioning look in her eyes, a smile playing on her lips?'

I echoed, 'Absolutely. Let's put it in provisionally and see'.

Daphne, said, 'My main role today is to pull our new product together. The one we worked on. I have conceptualised. In my head I am pulling it together in its purest form, its design, its authentic framework…'

'…Great, I can then position it and we can scale and automate…,

Coffee was stirred, sipped. The high altitude left a hum in the interior. The plane roared forward. Through the light cloud cover, we were levelling.

This trip to Switzerland was to Zurich on business to a media client. We had lately created a global Digital Marketing platform which we had bolted on to our innovative film and music business Shooting Stars Events. Our Client a wealthy property owner had the Germany Ambassador as a partner in an events business. He was personal friends with and could get Madonna, U2, Cool and the Gang and the Jackson Brothers. It would be great for us to spend time with him. We had great initiatives that needed to be discussed. He waited for us at a private airport neat Zurich and dinner was already booked.

The noise of the plane rose slightly as we dipped again, swerved against the glaring sun.

Daphne looked out the window now. I knew she thought of her son. He lived not far outside 'Zurich where we were landing. A cool guy. The successful banker, who was an action man, good at snow-boarding and riding superbikes at breakneck speeds round the alps.

'We'll get time to see him, Daphne,' I confirmed.

'Yes…I know.' And she had a half smile on her mouth.

I was back to the cloud cover below us. The azure sky and the freedom of the open spaces. I watched out the window. My mind excited at the future.

ॐ

The radio presenter massaged his message into the big blue cushioned Yeti Blackout USB with a clear, focused and measured voice.

'And it's great to be back with you here on Channel One FM. The show that goes deeper with its viewers that any other radio station has gone before. The place where we pull back the onion, where we stir the bees and go to the heart of it….'

The studio was a bright place of now dimmed light. State of the art monitors and broadcasting equipment in a letter L spread along the right wall. Pictures of past interviewees lined the soundproofed room. In colour and in black and white, their faces, taken in a host of different collages, many different poses painted the wide spectrum of human emotion. I searched the photographs. Many experiences. Many different stories of length and depth. I hung my blue cashmere overcoat on a clothes hook by the door. Took one of the four mike stations on the curved table by the side of the presenter, draped my grey tailored suit jacket over the chair beside me, and in my light blue shirt, grey trousers and black shoes, settled in to the soft black chair for the interview.

'I'm Christopher Denning…do I have a treat for you today. He's a globally successfully entrepreneur, an Award winning International Public Speaker, A Film-maker, Author. A TV Presenter, A Peace Ambassador. A humanitarian and philanthropist…. But yes, dare I say it – A Reformed Ex High Security Prisoner who was involved in Organised Crime, Stephen Gillen…You heard right. He's here in front of me. He's the ultimate paradox. The story of inspiration everyone is talking about and he's ready to go deeper than he's ever gone before!'

A smile was at his mouth and he winked at me with one of his piercing deep blue/grey eyes. The ear phones were on our heads,

He spoke into the mike, 'that's right. Remember you heard it here first. With me, you and the man himself, Stephen Gillen. The never before heard real, true story of never before revealed content. Nine Big questions? Nine never before spoken answers...'

We sat there. Two people bathed in the dim lights of the studio.

It was time to let the truth be known. It was the show that was live and was raw enough, that didn't play with and edit the truth. No private place of safety where deep questions could be searched for and a soul made lighter with the truth being told...

'First question, Stephen. We'll start at the beginning... You're a humanitarian, an awarded Peace Ambassador. Last year you were nominated for a prestigious International Peace Prize, but you were brought up in a war zone. In Belfast, the civil war of the early 70's... Tell us from then to now what has the journey taught you?'

A pause, a moment, as a whirlwind of emotive images arrived in my mind. In a soft, clear, consistent voice:
    'That war is never beautiful. That there are no winners. Real Peace Keepers and change-makers are warriors, real people with real histories moving great darkness, not shrinking violets. That there are deeper powers and forces in this world, this universe... One must identify the cycles of its movements, its structures clearly apparent also that it is an unfortunate and uncomfortable truth for us to consider that when a great tornado appears and razes everything to the ground, all that is left is a clear, barren and solid landscape. Only the strong survive it, with the weakest removed. A destruction of the old so a cycle could be completed and a firm foundation formed to support the new... That the nature of human beings is such that not only do we all have the blinding light of creative greatness within us, but a penchant for

destruction and darkness. That there is a duality in life. Like night and day, male and female, hot and cold. Structures and cycles…We have our place in it. A place of continual learning and growing and finding the best of ourselves. A collective purpose together, that is pushed and pulled, torn and shredded for the more personal goals of greed, wealth, position and power…That there is a butterfly in each of us waiting to emerge and the job, like the sun rising and setting, is for us to find the corrects ways to balance the darkness in humanity…'

…We sat there. Two people bathed in the dim lights of the studio. It was time to let the truth be known. It was the show that was live and was raw enough, that didn't play with and edit the truth. A private place of safety where deep questions could be searched for and a soul made lighter with the truth being told…

'…Second question, Stephen. Your life has been great extremes. Tell the listeners, do you think people's upbringing and environment direct their destiny and influences their choices? Can we really overcome the demons of our past?'

A soft quiet, steady voice.

'…I believe as human beings we can only rise above some of our demons. That was constructed this way. That if one looks closely there is reason to all this intelligent design. That on having truly understood them, on that pivotal day where confusion has cleared and the weight of the destruction our actions have caused hits, that the awakening, strength and courage of our epiphanies force the staining influence that was there into a heavily guarded vault in the depths of our recesses where even memories can be erased. Are our dark shadows learned? Are they innate? I say they are both. But we are creators, there is greater plan here, a destiny that boundaries us. It is like the Makings of a fine watch. The main cog will never be disturbed, but the many sub-wheels of our lives can be manipulated. This is free choice. Our right and our left. The purpose is to improve, to learn and grow, to have experiences, to be stretched by the adversity that is sent to forge us, and in this way, we can reach, through the pain of our mistakes, our tribulations, our weakness towards the best that we can become as human beings...'

෨

The dignitaries, many international, had been arriving all morning. The Director-General of the Universal Peace Federation, Robin Marsh and The UK Director, Margret Ali were there to meet them. A lawyer close to the Queen and the Duke of Edinburgh, a cousin to the President of Congo, an important Queen's Council and influential MP, a team brokering a cease-fire in Libya, the General-Secretary of the PPP & former Deputy Speaker to the National Assembly for Pakistan, an ex-Director-General of the Global Bank. Other activists arrived to the tall white grade II stuccoed building. In Bayswater, immediately to the north of Kensington, the Headquarters of the UPF in Lancaster Gate was a striking and imposing busy building set close to the square.

We parked the car, after negotiating the bustling mid-afternoon west end traffic, and stepped surely into the brisk greyness of a normal London day. Across the road the large white concrete pillars of the buildings front entrance beckoned. We crossed the road on the square.

'We've made good time, Daphne…That traffic, not good.' I pulled down the cuffs of my pink shirt, my silver/gold cufflinks.

She had stopped us at the other side of the road. We stood on the pavement, near the kerb line. She had a wonderful eye for things being right. I had fixed my top shirt button, pulled high my collars and she was fixing, turning, twisting and setting my burgundy stripped tie.

'There you go…, 'said Daphne. She stood back. A slimline soft, professional, elegant figure in a silk, grey/blue patterned and platted dress. A smile was fixed high on her cheeks. Cultivated blond hair hung perfectly. Striking turquoise eyes drilled through me, over me once more. Up and down, a skilled and easy motion strict and tight and clear. 'Yes, you look better now. Good colours.' She glanced at my blue suit, black shoes, fine pink shirt. The tie that broke it.

I pushed forward. More people were arriving outside the building. I knew there would be many different kinds of people from around the world present. Activists. Involved in a wide range of activities. From Feeding the poor and the homeless, green and climate projects, working with the Red Cross to distribute supplies, and boycotting damaging initiatives and negotiating ceasefires and rehabilitation in war torn countries. All with one purpose, peace and equality for all gods' peoples of the world.

Up the small step at the front of the building, under the tall porch, over the shiny square black and white tilled floor. We pressed the intercom at the large door.

'Hi, Stephen, Daphne.' His hand was out. He stood there in a light suit and red tie. A slight, elegant, unassuming, gentle and engaging man with a soft face, piercing blue eyes, wavy blond hair and an easy manner. '…It's great to see you both today. Please come in…'

'The traffic, Robin…But we got here in good time. Wonderful to see, 'I answered. '…Margret, is she?'

The Secretary-General was a good man a great friend, and had been a peace activist for over twenty years. He guided us into the hustle and bustle of the reception area. His eyes smiled. Softly, in his usual quiet voice he said, 'she's in there somewhere, Stephen. I'll look forward to speaking to you later'.

He had withdrawn back the way he came, back through the crowd to greet people and shake hands and be seen and introduce and smile engagingly.

The busy room moved. A former large, grand room decorated in white and fading light blue with a tall celling, it had been converted into a meeting room with unconventional furniture and props. People sat, and talked and discussed and lingered all around the room. They were standing by the plated food and tea and coffee counter in a corner.

A moving, sitting, standing cluster of small groups and associations that weaved and turned and floated and melted.

We darted for the tea counter. A strategic movement to settle after a busy day, to get refreshed, find space and to prepare. Through smiles, nods, people who stopped to shake my hand and exchange a few words, I saw him. A young rising star of diplomacy and changing the world for the better. Youthful European looks with short black tailored hair, in a blue suit, white shirt and blue tie. He held the coffee cup in his hand and was leaning into the conversation he was involved in. He saw me. His oval face shone with health, a measured look in his eyes and an authentic smile stretching his lips.

'Hi brother, 'he said. 'Great to see you,' we shook hands. Two friends on a global mission to change the world. Our eyes searched, linked each other. Kirk Vanderplas was a busy peace activist. Owner of many companies, his European parents had left him a wonderful foundation. A platform of change that he positioned for innovative peace. He was involved in great work around the world with many global leaders. One was the Global Equality Initiative, a worldwide initiative that worked for peace and harmony among all humans across the world regardless of race, religion or nationality living as one family.

I said, 'brother we need to speak. The pharm company, joining the board. What we talked about on the phone…the Global Equality Initiative, how we can get involved on a more senior level, support you?'

The noise of the chatter in the room was about us. Voices of all tones and denominations, spinning and turning, a myriad of high and low words and discussions that circled and pushed. We leaned closer to hear each other better above the racket.
His hand was lightly on my shoulder. 'Absolutely brother. We must talk. We'll get time.'

She had pushed through the melee. Seen us in the crowd and forged towards us with purpose.

A short, compact lady, full of strong sprit and clear vision in a long blue patterned dress. A person doing many wonderful things that her grandchildren could be proud of.

Her hands held us at the elbows, 'Stephen, Kirk, please, will you come up to the podium later say something about peace. Just something quick. About peace...' Her eyes sparkled behind her pebble shaped glasses. Brown soft tidy hair hugged her ears. A round soft face with a strong welcoming smile.

She stood there, a figure of authority, commanding. A woman you didn't say no to.

We nodded. Wide smiles confirming our consent.

'Of course, Margaret, it would be my pleasure. When?'

'If it's OK, Stephen. After the Doctor speaks. I'll call you'. She had left as quickly as she had arrived, her mouth turned high in a half smile, and back into the moving crowd. A mother hen to all of us and a great force for good.

I tracked Daphne to the back of the room. She was talking with an aged man. Tall and erect with short grey hair and square glasses he had approached us a few months before looking to collaborate. An accountant who knew the Queen and the Duke of Edinburgh and wished to help lower the terrible suicide statics through the arts. I have a written a play, he had said. I would like you to help me get it into the Royal Albert Hall and raise awareness. I moved towards them, swerved right through the shifting feet, side stepping jostling bodies, softly manoeuvring twisting elbows. We would be going upstairs to the main room soon, I considered and I sought the space of outside air.

I opened the front door. I felt the throng behind me. I had come a long way, I thought from my past, my turbulent history.

The air at the front of the building hit me. It was a moment for me, in the light grey spring afternoon alone, and I had a turning ball of emotions inside me. I knew every rain could pass. That a life was made up of many things. That peace was a very real thing like war. I had climbed the high mountain of myself and along the way I had unravelled the lies of my personal reality fortifying my knowledge and experience with achievement. A place of smoke and twisted mirrors it had defeated me in my pain and failure for many battles until my humanity had railed the best of me. Above the skyline of the building I saw above me the stretching grey horizon of moving clouds. The internal mountain had been conquered. A complicated deception hard to uncover had been unravelled.

I paced on the tidy pavement outside. A slow pensive motion like the smooth rolling waves of the sea. I had withdrawn to my thoughts. It was it the core of my body and my thoughts and my mind. That it had not been easy to be dragged through the streets of my accountability as I had transformed my life. A necessary route, with only my humility and gratitude shielding me, the rocks and sticks of shame and judgement had still marred and stung. They had pointed and laughed and mocked and looked with suspicion and ridiculed.

A soft breeze swept across my face, through my hair. Gratitude soared through me. An uplifting feeling that elated in a second and then rested into comfort.

It was my corner stone. Gratitude. Persistence. Humility. Courage and vision and decisiveness. Along with relentless hard work and discipline. They had been my map. I had travelled the seven levels of hell. At times I had galloped through its surreal darkness wishing for an end. On finding I was human and needed I had found the bad weather of myself but had realised it was experience that makes the man not position or past. I looked at the building. Tall, white, a listed place with expansive windows it stretched wide and imposing. I returned to my internal dialogue. In the old days of struggle my emptiness had been complete, I thought. With no direction or clarity or handmaiden I had been left to transform the mighty beast that dwelled inside me…

The breeze switched. Moved along and across and over me. My eyes went upwards, to the inky blue sky and pale grey moving clouds, scanned the whiteness of the buildings around me.

The war inside me was not complete, but a work in process. The reality of this floated in my mind, like another being I looked back on the wreckage of my past. My complication was that I had eradicated all notion of self. I had only purpose. Future. Achievement. Giving. Continuous development.

He was out of the main front doors. His face controlled but a tight smile carved on his face.

'Kirk…Hey.' I spoke.

He joined me. On the pavement, and looking at his phone for a moment, he said, 'Stephen, Hi. So dear brother, please, let's talk. Tell me. What's happening?'

He listened. I told him of the pharmaceutical company and that I was a board member. That Daphne was also. Of the fantastic product that in Africa was being called the magic power. How it had been in research & development for 8 years and had an international patent. How it was pioneering in the open wound industry. The lives it was saving. The investment already in the company. That we were FDA registered. The governments and police forces and private and public sectors people we were at an advanced stage with.

We walked. Up the road and slightly around the corner. He listened.

We were looking for more investment for operational costs. I had already got proof of funds from a potential investor for one million dollars. We were open to collaboration. He was close to heads of state, finance Ministers, knew many ex Director-Generals of the World Bank. We needed to get this life-saving treatment out to the world. We knew there were massive funds allocated for Africa linked to education that could expedite this needed product...Could he help us...we were open to see how we could go forward together'.

We turned back, retracing our steps towards the building. He said of course he would. We would have a meeting. He had just recently created a company and raised many funds to get much needed medical supplies to rural areas in Cambodia. We dipped our heads, smiled, agreed, strolled.

Kirk said, 'Brother, you must get involved. We are doing so many wonderful things now in the world.'
'It is wonderful work. Really. The world needs these initiatives...I saw the video you sent me, well done.' We stopped for a moment. I was aware of the great movement and service Kirk was getting from and giving to humanity. The potential for great meaningful change.

Kirk continued, 'We have gathered 165 Global Leaders, from 65 countries, over six continents. I've just come back from the US and India. I met with Vice President Dick Cheney and in India, Prime Minister Deve Gowda. Our Aim is to promote peace throughout the world through Education, Sports, Arts and Media...'

We stood. Kirk continued, his hands amplifying his words. I listened. We again moved, strolling slowly toward the front entrance.

'...We are changing the world, Stephen, Equality, Education for those in rural and under privileged areas...We believe everyone has a right to a chance, to education.'
I nodded, adding,' trade, investment. These are channels that needed to be used to make things better.'
'   Absolutely, Stephen. I gave a speech just the other day, there were four finance Ministers in the room. People are really taking notice.'

We were nearly at the door. I had him lightly by the arm. 'It is the way of great people to persist, Kirk to rule with decency, make clear and grasp their futures with sure, steady hands.'

I looked at him. It was the people I searched for to populate my life and time with. Capable, innovative beings with a strong life purpose and who had the central beating heart that focused on improving lives. Who were not faint but pure of heart, mind and soul. Visionary and of loyal blood.

He smiled. He was at the main entrance, pressing the intercom. A warm glow was on his face and a clear light in his eyes.

'Stephen, I'm going to New York in December. We have a meeting with the Secretary-General of the United Nations. I would like you to come with me dear brother. Can you come?'

'Of course. That would be wonderful. I will check my dairy. Just let me know, 'I answered.

He was through the door and I watched him. He had left the smile behind him and a view of the great future that we both pursued. It took one to know one. Like-minded people of resolve, on white chargers flying forward with courage, a plan and purpose.

I would go back inside. There would be talks, and I would be invited to speak. I was aware a moment of the internal movements inside me. There was a steely purpose there. It held frameworks and boundaries that were forged with great resilience, a plan and purpose that was imbued with immense vision and clarity. I had climbed my mountain, I thought. I had come a long way back to myself. There was the remembrance of another life, another person, another reality…It was far behind me. Locked and bolted and padlocked under guard.

Deep in the depths of me in bound vaults in rooms that were not entered. In my trouser pocket my fingers could feel the little plastic moulded figures of the animal wrist bracelet my daughter Sophia had made me. I looked at it. I had it always. Made with pure love, by the innocent love of a daughter for a father, it was one of my most prized possessions. Little tiny elephants, whales, giraffes, fish, Little stars and toy butterflies and tortoise. In many colours, purple, greens, blue, red, yellow and pink. I held it tight in my hand. It was my way, especially in times of stress or important decision making to turn it in my fingers.

I stepped forward. I pressed the intercom.

৵

We sat there. Two people bathed in the dim lights of the studio. It was time to let the truth be known. It was the show that was live and was raw enough, that didn't play with and edit the truth. A private place of safety where deep questions could be searched for and a soul made lighter with the truth being told…

… 'Third question, Stephen. Having lived two lives as it were and having met and had many people from polar opposites in your life history. I'm presuming you would have been close to people in both sections of your journey. What were the differences in these characters?'

Painted in the half light, a face that remembered and smiled. Said in a soft voice that held emotion and a hit of nostalgia.

'…You know people are people. I call it the human condition. I can see now that we all want and are heading towards the same things. That our circumstances and upbringings and teachings and lifestyles are different, but many of the internal problems and drivers have the same lead. Leadership skills are transferable for instance. Crime figure or Chief Executive officer, it's a lot about the internal strengths, intuition, vision, aptitude and ability to lead. To do more, be more. Experience ultimately makes a person. The quality of their thoughts and the people around them determines their character. The conditions they are in will reveal the nature of the problem they need to solve. Their heart quality will govern in many ways if they build or destroy. There is a human condition that is like a matrix of boundaries. We are ultimately ruled by this. It decrees that if a human being is put in 'A' a certain set of circumstances, the likely predicted behaviour will be 'B'. This and the nature of people are the winds that drive and contain us. It's profound and divine coding made simple. There are many realities in one life, many masters and many roles. Don't you agree…?'

'Ok…Fourth question, Stephen. With such a life of ups and downs, highs and lows. Some of the characters you would have met would be fascinating. Are there are any memorable ones that stick out? What influence have they had on your life?'

Quiet a moment, I remembered. Images and faces, feelings and pictures.

'…I think we are where we are meant to be as people. That it is important to remember that we are forged by our experiences and troubles from the past. That some of us sink or swim, but ultimately, we are where we are because of where we have been… That human beings are wonderful things that have wretchedness in them. That my answer was to overcome the wickedness and transmute it into something creative, positive and light…Was this, the people and characters involved in these good and bad stages of my life memorable…of course. But the past is a revolving door that remains only useful to us so we can learn and gather strength from it.'

The curling winds had come in from the west clipping the city skyline and jostling the afternoon greyness settling with the carbon dioxide and light smog of the packed streets below. The three of us sat at the delicatessen. At a far table, across the wooden decked floor and the tables stacked with waffles and cokes and ice cream in the place we would sometimes meet.

Tony sipped his water. A grinning round-faced man in a dodgy coloured blue suit with a bald head and broad US accent. 'It's going to be great believe me, Stephen. I have many followers. I teach public speaking. I just need my channel, my media sorted out. I need it to grow organically. You can do that, no? You and Marco…?

I looked at, Marco. Late twenties with short combed sandy hair, he blinked through his thick glasses. Our eyes locked knowingly a moment. We had met nine months previously. Two people by chance, who had great ideas, as he worked in a phone repair shop and I searched for someone to help with the marketing the expanding business.

Tony's cajoling tone continued. A silky, soft but pitched and sometimes annoying sales voice that was heavily loaded with the northern end of America.

'I'm training great people, man. Great people. Multimillionaires. We can be a great team yes? You can come to my events. I get you on the stage, you can do some public speaking. You do things for me and I can do them for you…'

We heard him. A voice that seduced and span webs and soothed and dressed everything up. Above the teenagers who were having a birthday, the trendy chatter at the other tables, the gushing noise and the sweet smell of cooking waffles, I knew Marco was reading my mind.
'What do you think, Marco, 'I said.

He was nodding. 'Sounds good. But it's a lot of work. We've worked hard on our business. We have studied the algorithm and know how they are indexing so what we have is very valuable. This took us a lot of work. Many long stressful nights. We would need to be paid'

Marco looked at, Tony. He had said it for his benefit. Tony shifted in his seat. His budging eyes glazed slightly and darted and moved as his mind calculated.

He returned, 'I understand, Marco. I do. I do, but I'm bringing a lot of benefit. Money's tight at the moment…'

The coffee was in my mouth. The cup was in my fingers. I watched Tony's lips move, was aware of Marco's returns, their debate that lifted in tempo, but I had withdrawn a moment into my thoughts. My body and back still ached from the building work, and my brain was wired and fatigued with the late nights of research, writing and business development.

The aroma of the coffee was in my nose. It was mixed with the sweetness of the other smells around me. My world was my work and the pursuit of achievement so that my past was further and further behind me.

Marco showed Tony our analytics on the computer. Figures and graphs that constantly fought to rise.

He was a good guy, I thought. Honest and true. From eastern Europe. His sister was advanced in political sciences and had been the first secretary to an ex-President and he had grown up hunting with the sons of generals and politicians. A talented, nerdy type who at fourteen would imprison computer viruses, take them apart then once improved send them back to whoever had sent them.

'Tony, we'll come back to you with our proposal, 'I said. They both paused a moment. It was time to strategically stop the negotiations.

We stood. Marco waiting in the wings to the left. Tony was up. A large weighty figure that embraced us and took too much of our personal space. He forced a false smile upon us.

'Great to meet you guys. Phone me. We speak yes!'

We watched him leave. A slimy image that moved silently and waved as he opened the windowed front doors of the shop. 'He's not to be trusted, 'reminded, Marco

We walked to the bustling street outside. We were across from the Turkish restaurant just along from the busy tube station. The Mile End Road hummed with colour, traffic and people.

'We should consider working with him,' Marco was fixing the laptop bag on his shoulder. I could recognise the stress in his voice.

I could feel his pain. For all our hard work, we were still a start-up and I had a separate building business two young children and the bills were crushing.

He continued, 'we need loads of things for the business. New equipment, new staff, someone to do the marketing, a team for filming. We need someone to help with the editing. Others to help you with research while you write the documentaries. We need funds, Stephen or we won't survive. I'm worried…I have rent…'

I stood taller and looked him in the eyes.

'Don't worry, 'the smile was on my face, the light in my eyes. All the forces were against us. It was frustrating, mental, stupid and dangerous in its effect. We were waiting for many people to do tasks that weren't being done to the necessary standard or on time. It was killing us. I suddenly realised why the statistics for business start-ups failing were so astronomically high.

'We're going to do it all ourselves!'

His eyes blinked on the other side of the silver framed glasses. His look was pinched, serious.

'What?' he questioned.

'I'm not relying on these people anymore. It's a slow death. The marketing, the filming, the advertising, learning the IT, the research for the documentaries, the editing and everything else we need - we'll do it all ourselves!'

'That's crazy. We have so much that we need to learn. We don't have the time!'

I walked away from him, down towards the tube station and through the moving crowd of people, but I knew his face was folded and creased with frustration and concern.
I turned, shouted back,' Marco We don't need them. We'll do it ourselves!'

'You're mad. One mad fucker!'
I kept walking. I did not answer. I knew he thought of the times we were working sometimes for two days continuously. Times filled with burning oil, computer screens, research and editing. A place of frayed brains and where the body fatigue would attack from every approach and, without proper rest and food, we would become snappy and argue.

'You're a crazy man, 'I heard him shout again. I knew he smiled.
He was behind me now. My hand was in my in my pocket. I could feel and played with the plastic, bright coloured animal bracelet my daughter had made me. My lips curved. Inside me and behind my eyes lifted and my thoughts had the persistence of certainty. The obstacle of the moving crowds was weaving in front of me. Confidently, with silky smoothness, I navigated my way through them, kept going.

Stephen Gillen and Daphne Diluce in their office

Stephen Gillen and Kul Mahey

Stephen with Oscar winner Tim Cavagin

Stephen and Kul Mahey

Stephen and Sally Bundock BBC

Aunt Margaret

Stephen with Robin Marsh, Secretary-General,
Keith best QC and Caoline Heward